P9-CQD-444

About the Editor

B ill Wheeler has had a lifelong interest in aviation, beginning with his boyhood in Port Arthur, Ontario, when he would cycle to a nearby seaplane base to watch the aircraft taking off and landing. He grew up during the 1930s—the years of air racing and record-setting flight—and the Second World War. Like so many people of his era, he was fascinated by the romance and adventure of flight.

After graduating from the Ontario College of Art in Toronto, he worked in commercial art studios, as a book and magazine illustrator, and finally as a high-school art teacher. His previous publications include *Flying Under Fire: Canadian Fliers Recall the Second World War, Skippers of the Sky: The Early Years of Bush Flying,* and *Images of Flight: A Canadian Aviation Art Portfolio,* as well as numerous historical aviation articles. In 1962, he was one of the founders of the Canadian Aviation Historical Society (CAHS), which researches and records flying history to document the influence of aviation in Canada's development. Bill Wheeler is a former president of the CAHS and has edited its *Journal* for forty years. He lives in Markham, Ontario.

Bill Wheeler with Clark Seaborn's 1933
vintage Waco UIC Standard. *Bill Wheeler*

FLYING
UNDER
FIRE

VOLUME TWO

More Aviation Tales
from the Second World War

Selected and edited by
William J. Wheeler
of the
Canadian Aviation Historical Society

FIFTH
HOUSE

Introduction © 2003 William J. Wheeler
Excerpts © 2003 The Authors
Stories originally published in the Canadian Historical Society *Journal*

All rights reserved. No part of this publication may be reproduced, stored in a retrieval system, or transmitted, in any form or by any means, electronic, mechanical, recording, or otherwise, without the prior written permission of the publisher, except in the case of a reviewer, who may quote brief passages in a review to print in a magazine or newspaper, or broadcast on radio or television. In the case of photocopying or other reprographic copying, users must obtain a licence from the Canadian Copyright Licencing Agency.

Cover and interior design by John Luckhurst / GDL
Edited by Roberta Coulter
Proofread by Geri Rowlatt

The publisher gratefully acknowledges the support of The Canada Council for the Arts and the Department of Canadian Heritage. We acknowledge the financial support of the Government of Canada through the Book Publishing Industry Development Program (BPIDP) for our publishing activities.

THE CANADA COUNCIL | LE CONSEIL DES ARTS
FOR THE ARTS | DU CANADA
SINCE 1957 | DEPUIS 1957

Printed in Canada by Friesens

03 04 05 06 07/ 5 4 3 2 1

First published in the United States in 2003

National Library of Canada Cataloguing in Publication Data

Main entry under title:

Flying under fire : Canadian fliers recall the Second World War /
selected and edited by William J. Wheeler.

Vol. 2 has subtitle: More aviation tales from the Second World War.
Complete contents: Vols. 1-2.
ISBN 1-894004-79-5 (v. 1). — ISBN 1-894856-07-4 (v. 2)

1. World War, 1939-1945—Aerial operations, Canadian. 2. World War,
1939-1945—Personal narratives, Canadian. I. Wheeler, William J., 1930-

D792.C2F59 2001   940.54'4971'0922   C2001-911268-8

Editor's note: Rather than interrupt the narrative in these stories, we have chosen to retain the language of the storytellers, which reflects the time in which they were written. Metric conversions have not been added.

FIFTH HOUSE LTD.
A Fitzhenry & Whiteside Company
1511-1800 4 Street SW
Calgary, Alberta, Canada
T2S 2S5

Fitzhenry & Whiteside
121 Harvard Avenue, Suite 2
Allston, MA 02134

1-800-387-9776
www.fitzhenry.ca

Contents

Foreword

Although I have never met Bill Wheeler, I have followed his dedicated efforts, focused on the recording of Canada's flying history, as Editor of the *Journal* of the Canadian Aviation Historical Society. This, his latest book, is the third in a series recounting at first-hand the experiences of Canadian airmen, both civil and military, in stories adapted from the pages of the *Journal*.

The nine accounts in this book emphasize not only gallantry under fire, but also the many and varied roles filled by the RCAF, while leaving to our imagination the spectre of the deadly risks that aircrew faced in times of war. Put more dramatically, of the roughly thirty-five thousand Canadian airmen who engaged in hostile action during the Second World War, more than 50 percent made the supreme sacrifice, while additional thousands spent years as prisoners of war or were maimed for life.

Canada has been tardy in recognizing the importance of their stories and in recording the vital contribution that aviation has made in the growth of this great country. The impressive development of the Canada Aviation Museum in Ottawa and of Canada's Aviation Hall of Fame in Alberta are means of addressing this shortcoming. Success in these ventures requires great individual initiative. Fortunately, people like Bill Wheeler have made a lifetime commitment to researching and recording the significant role that aviation has played in our nation's progress.

But time is our enemy—those of us, now grown old, who lived this chapter of our history, have a special obligation, before it is too late, to put pen to paper. I refer to those individuals whose stories are essential to historians like Bill Wheeler if the record is to grow apace and provide the historical basis for Canadian accomplishments in all aspects of aviation.

"It is indeed a desirable thing to be well descended, but the glory belongs to our ancestors." –Plutarch

Lt. General David R. Adamson CD, LOM (Ret'd)

Acknowledgements

This book owes its existence to many people, and I would like to recognize their contributions. I will begin by thanking those who permitted me to reprint their stories: Air Commodore Len Birchall OBE, DFC; Joan Braithwaite, daughter of the late Bill McKenzie; Lieutenant General Bill Carr DFC; Terry Collier, son of the late Jim Collier DFC; Bob Fowler OC, who not only provided a story but read the glossary; Bill McRae; Chuck McKenzie, son of the late Bill McKenzie; Mrs Helen Ross, wife of the late Martin "Cy" Cybulski/Ross DFC; Art Wahlroth; and Jack Winship DFC.

I am also grateful to Lieutenant General David Adamson, for his very generous foreword; Jack Ritch DFC, the second Canadian to fly a jet and a colleague of Bill McKenzie on 616 Squadron and later in Canada, for the loan of illustrations; Les Waller, for his dramatic cover art; Kerri Button, of Canada's Aviation Hall of Fame, for photographs from the Hall's collection; Norman Malayney, for arranging the initial appearance of Jack Winship's story in the CAHS *Journal*; David Godfrey and Alan Wingate, for assistance with the glossary; and Alan Williams, for scans of photographs from the CAHS *Journal*.

There are also the many people at Fifth House to whom I am indebted: publisher Charlene Dobmeier, who approved the book and made its appearance possible; senior editor Lesley Reynolds, who has very patiently and efficiently dealt with every question and problem; editor Roberta Coulter; proofreader Geri Rowlatt; and Simone Lee, for promoting the book. John Luckhurst provided a crisp design, and Cheryl McDougall at St. Solo Computer Graphics scanned the photographs.

Finally, I would like to thank my wife, Pat, for her support, and for once again suggesting many of the words in the glossary.

William J. (Bill) Wheeler
Markham, Ontario, June 2003

Introduction

These reminiscences by Canadian airmen who flew in the Second World War have been chosen to complement those that appeared in the first volume of *Flying Under Fire*. Their words provide a broader understanding of the often daunting challenges faced by young Canadian airmen in a conflict that ended almost a half-century ago—beyond the memory of many.

Naturally, they represent only a very small part of what occurred in a war that spanned the globe. And again, they have been adapted from articles originally published in the *Journal* of the Canadian Aviation Historical Society.

All of the contributors to this book describe with obvious affection the characteristics of the aeroplane on which they did most of their flying—the Tiger Moth, Fawn, Anson, Stranraer, Wellington, Spitfire, Mosquito, Kittyhawk, Mitchell, or the then-revolutionary new Meteor.

The Curtiss P-40E Kittyhawk IAs flown by Jim Collier, for instance, were designed for defence and outdated even before the war began. And yet they were the sole American fighter available in quantity early in the war—almost

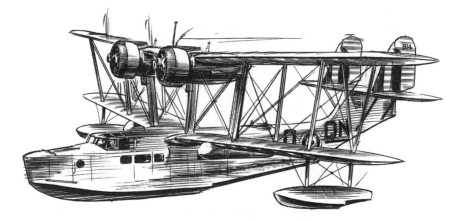

Canadian Vickers/Supermarine Stranraer. *William Wheeler*

fourteen thousand would be built. The Thunderbolt, Mustang, and Lightning were still under development or in only limited production.

Overmatched against the Focke-Wulf Fw 190 and their other Axis counterparts in Europe, P-40s were relegated to secondary theatres such as North Africa and to ground-attack and Army-cooperation roles where their poor climb mattered less and their rugged construction and heavy firepower were decided assets. Their pilots, as Jim Collier explains, evolved defensive tactics that allowed them to fly the Kittyhawk effectively, even when opposed by such superior-performing Axis fighters as the Messerschmitt Bf 109 and the Macchi MC-202. Collier, who later flew the far more nimble Spitfire, always remembered the sturdy Kittyhawk with fondness.

When Bob Fowler joined a Mitchell squadron in England he was immediately impressed with the North American bomber's superiority over the Lockheed Venturas—a military adaptation of a commercial airliner—on which he had trained, and which had been briefly, and disastrously, used by another RAF unit on similar low-level tactical day operations. While the Ventura boasted much larger engines, the Mitchell—designed from the outset as a bomber—outperformed it on every count. Mitchells would be flown post-war by several RCAF Auxiliary Squadrons.

Having trained on the ponderous Armstrong Whitworth Whitley, Art Wahlroth's reaction to the Vickers Wellingtons that equipped his first squadron was much the same as Bob Fowler's. In fact, he writes at some length of the positive characteristics and many virtues of Barnes Wallace's innovative bomber. While the Whitley was actually designed to a later specification than the Wellington, it was the product of earlier and outdated thinking, whereas the "Wimpy" was ahead of its time. Its strength, flexibility, and ability to absorb battle damage was legendary, and its high-aspect wings anticipated those of much later machines. Fitted with larger engines and otherwise upgraded, it served effectively throughout the war.

Only a few types of aircraft—on either side—were remarkable for their versatility. Four of the aircraft featured in the following accounts were among that select group.

The aforementioned Wellington entered RAF service as a medium bomber on daylight operations. The concentration of fire from the turrets of aircraft flying in close formation—unescorted by fighters—would supposedly deter

Lockheed Ventura. *William Wheeler*

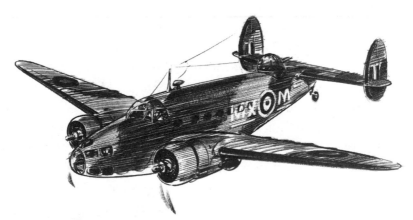

Lockheed Hudson. *William Wheeler*

attackers. This proved a disastrous fallacy. The decimation of formations on early raids led to the Wimpy's immediate reassignment to night bombing ops.

In this role it excelled, bearing the brunt of the bombing offensive against Germany until four-engine Stirlings, Halifaxes, and Lancasters became available. The Wellington was then deployed to secondary theatres and adapted for coastal patrol and even transport duties. Some 14,500 Wellingtons were built.

The Gloster Meteor, which Bill McKenzie introduced to operational flying, would remain in service for a dozen more years. Its twin-engine configuration had been chosen because of the limited power of early jet engines: just 1,700 pounds of thrust from each of the Wellands that powered 616 Squadron's first Meteor Mk Is. But the design possessed the "stretch" needed to accept more powerful engines. Indeed one of the Meteor's significant uses was as a test bed for new engines. The Meteor Mk IVs, which Bill flew in Canada, had double the power of the Mk Is. RAF Meteors would eventually serve not only as interceptors, but for training, ground attack, and reconnaissance.

The de Havilland D.H. 98 Mosquito was undoubtedly the most adaptable aeroplane the Allies possessed. Conceived as a private-venture light bomber fast enough to negate the need for defensive armament, the Mosquito could carry a bomb load comparable to that of a medium bomber, at much greater speeds, and over longer ranges. In the photo-reconnaissance role it excelled, as Jack Winship will attest. And as a fighter-bomber roving far behind enemy lines, it was unmatched. The Mosquito served into the fifties and was also used civilly for high-altitude photo-mapping.

The Supermarine Spitfire first flew in 1936 and remained on RAF strength into the early fifties. The only Allied fighter in production throughout the war, the Spitfire progressed through successively heavier and more powerful marks, culminating in a Rolls-Royce Griffin-powered variant with twice the power of the prototype and a 30 percent higher top speed. It was used in all theatres and by every Allied Air Force. Spitfires performed multiple roles, from high-altitude interception and photo-reconnaissance to dive bombing and ground attack. The Seafire, a beefed-up development fitted with a tail-hook and folding wings, flew from aircraft carriers.

The Spitfire was even tested experimentally as a glider tug. To improve mobility, 401 Squadron experimented with a Hotspur glider towed off the ground by one of their Spitfire Vs. Theoretically, a six-place Hotspur towed by each Spitfire could carry the support personnel for that machine. Although proven feasible, the practice was never adopted—probably to the great relief of 401's ground crew. The pilot who carried out the successful towing experiments was Bill McRae.

Bill Carr and Bill McRae both flew Spitfires; their experiences differed greatly, but both derived obvious satisfaction from flying this superlative aeroplane. Bill Carr flew alone and as unobtrusively as possible, whereas if Bill McRae ever found himself isolated, as occasionally happened, his situation could be dire. In combat he flew with a wingman, each covering the other's blind spots. And they in turn were usually teamed with another pair of Spitfires in the standard finger-four formation. When they weren't flying bomber escort, Bill McRae and the members of his squadron actively sought out the enemy, whether in the form of bombers, fighters, or ground targets.

On the other hand, Bill Carr, flying a Spitfire armed only with cameras, assiduously avoided contact, not only with hostile aircraft but with friendly—and possibly trigger-happy—Allied fighters.

Mosquito pilots Cy Cybulski and Jack Winship were also involved in quite different activities. Cy harassed the enemy at every opportunity, while Jack was intent only on obtaining his photographs—and returning safely to base.

Invariably flying alone, photo-reconnaissance (PR) pilots became highly self-reliant. There was little opportunity to develop the camaraderie of a fighter or bomber squadron where airmen functioned as a team.

Unless they were members of Canada's miniscule prewar Air Force, all airmen were obliged to pass through the successive stages of the highly successful British Commonwealth Air Training Plan (BCATP).

Of the contributors, only Len Birchall was not a product of the BCATP. Having learned to fly while a cadet at the Royal Military College (RMC) in Kingston, he was already an officer in the RCAF when war broke out. He was one of the important cadre of permanent RCAF officers who would assume positions of leadership in Canada's rapidly expanding Air Force.

An aircraft's crew was in many ways like a team. This is even reflected in the manner by which crews came together, not unlike the choosing of a pick-up team. Customarily, the gunners would link up first, and then pilots with navigators; operational training unit (OTU) trainees were usually given three days to crew up. If they could not link up on their own, they were told, it would be done for them.

It was important that they trust and like one another. Art Wahlroth and Bob Fowler, flying semi-heavy and medium bombers, respectively, recall instances where the quick, intuitive reaction of crew members—a product of training and practice—got them through difficult situations. Wahlroth also cites at least one occasion where the opposite was very nearly true. A crew member who, in the eyes of his fellows, came up short would soon be gone, usually of his own volition.

The captain and crew of a Halifax flew an aircraft that had required seventy thousand man-hours to build. Only in time of war would such a youthful group, after relatively brief training, be given this daunting responsibility.

While time spent at an OTU absorbing the teachings and wisdom of airmen fresh from an operational tour was important, the first weeks of actual flying against the enemy provided the real test. How well had they absorbed the lessons taught at their OTU? The answer was critical to a crew's survival. During this period, attrition was at its highest. A good crew became a cohesive unit and, as Art Wahlroth and Bob Fowler point out, the small but vital things that could not be taught were learned. Experience, often harsh and unforgiving, was invariably the most effective teacher. Crews that survived those hazardous initial few weeks had a better chance, statistically, of completing their tour.

The extreme youth of the participants is noteworthy. Bill McRae was twenty when he enlisted, Bob Fowler and Bill McKenzie nineteen, and Art Wahlroth a venerable twenty-four. On a squadron a crew member in his mid twenties would often be nicknamed "Uncle" or "Pops." Their ages are typical of young RCAF volunteers in the Second World War (no one was drafted into the Air Force)—usually fresh out of high school.

They matured rapidly, handling the stress of combat flying and learning to cope with the loss of squadron mates who had become friends. Living with the almost daily risk of death made extreme demands on youthful confidence and stamina. As has so often been said, boys became men almost overnight.

Enough cannot be said about the courage of these men—boys—who fought and died a half-century ago. Succeeding generations have, very fortunately, not been called upon to make sacrifices in such numbers. The memory of their gallantry must be kept fresh, their stories told and retold.

The history of Canadian aviation is rich in adventure and accomplishment. If it holds a special appeal for you and you would like to learn more or meet others who share your enthusiasm, contact the Canadian Aviation Historical Society, P.O. Box 224, Stn "A," Willowdale, ON, M2N 5S8, or visit the Society's web site at www.cahs.com.

Trenton to Dartmouth

Flying in the RCAF 1937–1940

LEONARD J. (LEN) BIRCHALL CM, OBE, DFC
AIR COMMODORE RCAF (RET'D)

While the expression "a legend in his own time" may be overworked, it can be applied very aptly to Len Birchall. Flying a 413 Squadron Catalina on patrol out of Lake Koggala in what is now Sri Lanka in April 1942, he and his crew spotted an approaching Japanese force. Before they were shot down by carrier-based fighters, they managed to radio back a warning alerting the island's defences. The element of surprise lost, the Japanese abandoned their attack. Dubbed "The Saviour of Ceylon" by Winston Churchill, Birchall was awarded a Distinguished Flying Cross.

He and his five surviving crew members spent the remainder of the war—forty months—in the grim confines of Japanese prison camps. As senior officer and spokesman for his fellow POWs, his courage in standing up on their behalf to protest unnecessarily harsh treatment and demand medical aid was recognized by the award of the Order of the British Empire for Gallantry.

Birchall took flying lessons as a teenager in his native St. Catharines. In the early years of the war he flew Supermarine Stranraer flying boats with No. 5 Bomber Reconnaissance (BR) Squadron out of Dartmouth, Nova Scotia. Late in 1942 he moved to Ferry Command and then to 413 Squadron RCAF, flying patrols on PBY-5s out of the Shetland Islands. The squadron was transferred to Ceylon.

Following his release from prison camp, Birchall remained in the RCAF. Now a Wing Commander, he returned to Japan as a member of the prosecution in the trials of Japanese war criminals. Subsequently, he was named Assistant Air Attaché, Canadian Joint Staff, Washington, DC; Commanding Officer of RCAF Station Goose Bay, Labrador; Senior Personnel Staff Officer

9

of Air Material Command; member of the Canadian NATO delegation; Commanding Officer of RCAF Station North Bay (where he was checked out on the CF-100); Chief of Operations, AFHQ. Promoted to Air Commodore, he became External Affairs Chief Administrator, NATO; Commandant of Royal Military College (RMC), where he had been a cadet a quarter-century earlier; and Honorary Aide de Campe to their Excellencies, Governors General Vanier and Michener.

In 1968, Birchall retired from the RCAF to become Chief Administrative Officer of the Faculty of Administrative Studies at York University, remaining there for fourteen years. While in Toronto, he served as Honourary Colonel with No. 400, City of Toronto Air Reserve Squadron, where he completed fifty-two years of Canadian Forces service. He was inducted into Canada's Aviation Hall of Fame in 2001.

I started my flying back in 1932, at the St. Catharines airport. It was just an open field with a hangar sitting on it. We had a Reid Rambler and Gipsy or a Cirrus Moth—the federal government gave flying clubs an aeroplane like the Moth if they agreed to buy a Rambler. Unfortunately, in those days there wasn't much flying business. Few people were learning to fly and not many jobs were done by air. So, the revenues were not great and the cost per flying hour was high.

One way around this was to get on your bicycle in the wee hours of the morning, pedal on out to the airfield, wipe down the aeroplane, and refuel it. This meant going over to a 45-gallon drum and wobble-pumping gas into a five-gallon can, which you lugged over to the aircraft. You climbed up on a stepladder and poured the gas through a chamois and a funnel into the fuel tank that formed the centre section of the upper wing. Then you checked the oil and, if you were smart, brewed a cup of coffee for the instructor. By this time the instructor was on his way out to the field. When he got there, depending on his mood, you might be allowed to get into the aeroplane with him while he did his check flight. This could be anything from a quick trip around the field to maybe flying around the city, again depending upon what he had done the night before. And if you were real lucky, you got to do touch-and-go landings!

Shrewdly, I correlated all of this with the taste of the coffee. I took lessons on how to do a good job of making it.

As I recall, all we had in the way of instruments was a tachometer, an oil pressure gauge, and an on-off switch. The air speed indicator was out on the wing, a little spring-loaded plate which the air pressure pushed back to give you a reading in miles per hour. You judged whether you were sliding in or out of your turns by wind on either cheek, and if you wanted to cheat just a little, you tied a piece of wool on one of the flying wires—if it didn't stream straight back you knew that you were slipping in or out. We had no needle and ball, but we did have a compass, one of those with a needle that floated on alcohol. If memory serves, those Ramblers took off, flew, glided, and landed all at the same speed—almost—and that was with the throttle full open. You simply opened her up and away you went. You kept it there until you were just about ready to touch down and then you closed the bloody thing. She immediately dropped like a rock and down you came into the field, which fortunately was just grass.

Toward the end we were given a windsock by Shell Oil. It was the biggest improvement to the field in all the time I was there, and it did help.

The tarpaper shacks built to house the workmen who built the RCAF station at Trenton in the early 1930s later provided quarters for the first group of Provisional Pilot Officers during their flying training. The roadsters were owned by the more affluent among them. *L. J. Birchall*

Somebody told me that the cadets at RMC (Royal Military College, Kingston) not only got flying instruction for nothing at Camp Borden during the summer, but they got paid for it as Provisional Pilot Officers (PPOs).

Well, this sounded too good to be true, and in the final analysis, it was. But it was the reason I went to RMC. Sure enough, that was the year they cancelled the flying!

I did manage to get to Borden with the Royal Canadian School of Signals, and to get close to the aeroplanes. But once they had me hooked into RMC, I couldn't get out. I had to stay there during school term and then work in the summers, which ended all of my efforts to get in some flying until I graduated.

In those days, the Imperial Forces, the Canadian Permanent Forces, offered permanent commissions, and we had to compete for them. In my year there were three commissions offered by the RCAF. I guess my fairy god-mother must have felt guilty about gypping me out of flying for the four years I had been there. She allowed me to win one of them.

General Andy McNaughton, during the Depression years, had used un-employed men to build Army, Navy, and Air Force installations, one of these being Trenton. It was just about finished in 1937, when I graduated. They moved the RCAF Flying Training School from Camp Borden down to Trenton and, in July, that was where I went. "Just about finished," I've said. One of the unfinished buildings was the officers' mess and quarters. So we PPOs were quartered in a tarpaper shack, a temporary building erected to house the unemployed labourers who had worked constructing the station.

We got our meals in the basement of one of the barrack blocks. Believe me, you don't know just how low on the totem pole you can be if you've never been a PPO, in those prewar days. It got so bad that we would go around salut-ing the AC 2s! The chap who was in charge of the school, Alan Hull (I think he was a Squadron Leader, at the time), was soon nicknamed "Alan H. Bligh," for obvious reasons.

Our aircraft were Fleets, mostly. There were some Moths around, but we usually flew the Fleets, which were Civet- and Kinner-powered. They were real modern jobs with needle-and-ball indicators to tell us if we were slipping out of turns, inside airspeed indicators, a tachometer, oil pressure and fuel gauges, and a compass, which of course was still liquid-filled.

In those days, Trenton was just a big grass field, but with an innovation. We

A Fleet Fawn (RCAF 197) of the RCAF Air Navigation and Seaplane School at Trenton in 1937. *L. J. Birchall*

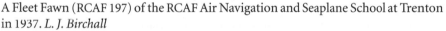

had a round circle painted out in the centre with lime, and in its centre was a smokepot, which would tell us wind direction when we came in to land. With it and the windsocks around the perimeter, we certainly knew the wind was blowing. But invariably I had difficulty trying to compensate for drift, either landing or taking off.

There had been thirteen in my class, but one was killed very shortly after we started. The remaining bunch of crazy goons took off, landed, and did everything else, all in the circuit. An asset, I always thought, would have been a head on a swivel. We had no radios; our only intercommunication between pilot and student was by means of a Gosport tube. If those on the ground wished you to land, all they could do was fire a great big red Very light. It was the only signal we ever received. So there we were, charging all around the ruddy place, slipping in and out on turns, and crossing in front of one another.

Trying to do landings and takeoffs, we would get nicely set up with an eye on the aircraft to one side when, all at once, another one would drift in from the other side. Our feet were going at the same time as we turned our heads, pushing automatically on the rudder bar and causing the aircraft to skid—and the

Len Birchall with one of the Fleet 7 Fawns on which he trained as a Provisional Pilot Officer at Trenton in 1937. *L. J. Birchall via Canada's Aviation Hall of Fame*

instructor to begin yelling. Believe me, it was a wonder that any of us ever learned to fly.

We also did instrument flying, using an old canvas hood that pulled up and over the head of the student. When we flew a circuit, we had to count the turns in seconds before straightening out and waiting for the compass to settle down and show us just how many tens of degrees we were out on the turn. One very hot day when I was not feeling too well, having been out the night before, my instructor, a chap named Bradshaw from RMC, was giving me some instrument flying instruction and I was sitting beneath the bag in the back seat. I was hot and miserable and just could not get anything coordinated, so I undid my straps to relax a little. There I was, flying around with everything loose, and all the while, my instructor was getting increasingly fed up in front.

When an instructor wanted to take over the controls the practice was for him to take the stick and rap it back and forth sharply so that it struck the knees of the student repeatedly. I was trying to hold the stick when suddenly it jumped out of my hands, and bang, bang, bang, bang, both of my knees were bruised. Immediately we went straight up and over onto our backs. I made a desperate grab for the seat and held on grimly. I'm sure my arms were extended about three inches by the time he completed that damned manoeuvre. In the meantime, he was yelling at me through the Gosport tube—with me unable to answer. I couldn't let go of the seat to pick up the mouthpiece. Had I done so, I was gone forever. I didn't want to learn parachuting at that stage of the game. However, I did manage to survive. When we landed I had to tell him what I had done. My foolishness meant three circuits of the field, complete with seat pack, running all the way.

Those old aircraft were remarkable machines. They had no brakes, only a tail skid. On the ground, the only way you could turn the damn things was to blow the tail around, literally. A quick burst of throttle produced a sufficient gust of air hitting the deflected rudder to swing the tail sideways. When you got the aircraft stopped, you applied slight forward pressure on the stick, put on full rudder, and then gave her a real good blast on the engine. Away you would go, praying to God that you could get turned before you went charging into the fence or whatever else was in front of you. In a real strong wind, there was no way to get them turned without having someone running alongside to grab a wingtip and hold it until you spun around.

Trenton had a long line of hangars with the aircraft parked in a line perpendicular to them. Right underneath the old control tower was Alan Hull's office, a sort of bulge in the hangar wall extending out from the front of the building. From there he would watch all of his neophytes doing their circuits. "Knobby" Fee, a classmate of mine from RMC, came in to park his aeroplane; when he turned downwind the damned thing—understandably—began to pick up speed. There was no way he could stop. He came charging down the line of aircraft, knowing he would not be able to turn in among them without writing off at least four machines. He was praying that the thing would stop before it reached the hangar. It didn't, and he went careering through the open doors!

Alan Hull just happened to look up in time to see Fee's aeroplane rushing along behind the line aircraft, about to head into the hangar. He dove underneath his desk, waiting for the whole building to blow up. Fortuitously, a couple of crewmen were standing on the hangar threshold where they could grab a wing of the aeroplane as it went by. They hung on and spun it around, sending Knobby, who gave it a burst of power, back out on the field.

Alan Hull waited and waited, but the big bang never came. He crawled out from under the desk, looked around, and was surprised to see that everything was okay. Barging out into the hangar, he roared at the crewmen standing there.

"Where is that so-and-so aeroplane that was about to crash into this hangar?"

"Aeroplane, sir? What aeroplane? Not here, sir."

He never found out who the pilot was. But we had four extra parades, no explanation given.

One of my mates from the Class of '38, Joe Gatray, became a flying instructor. He recalled a pupil who, much like myself, couldn't detect drift as he neared the ground. Joe decided that he would really give the student a lesson to remember and chose a windy day. He began their approach at 90 degrees to the wind direction on a long drag in with the engine almost off. The poor kid was up front, with Joe demanding, "Do you see that ground? Do you see it moving? Which way is it moving? Which way did you say?" And the kid was trying desperately to give answers.

"Which way should we turn?" asked Joe. The ground was moving faster and faster beneath them. When they were only about five feet up he asked, "Now do you understand what I mean?"

"Yes, sir." Whereupon Joe cranked open the throttle. The engine gave one great cough and died completely with the prop standing uselessly straight up and down. The glide had been too long and the engine had cooled off. That Fleet did the damnedest ground loop, wiping off both the undercarriage and the lower mainplanes. Happily, no one was hurt.

When all the dust and grass had settled, poor old Joe and the student climbed out and walked back to the hangar. Of course, the other students were there watching. When the pair arrived, the kid, with eyes popping, was not short of an audience. "My God in Heaven," he says, "just wait till you get to the sequence on drift. It'll be the damnedest thing you've ever had in your life!"

But back to my own experiences. From Flying Instruction, we went on to Air Navigation and Seaplane School, which was run by "Mawdie" Mawdesley, a fondly remembered character in the Air Force of that era. He operated his school out of the old seaplane hangar at Trenton, where we had Vickers

Vedettes, a Fleet, and some Fairchilds, the two latter types on floats. As a special treat, just before we graduated, we were allowed to fly the float-equipped Noorduyn Norseman, the queen of our fleet.

However, most of our work was done on the Vedette, a fantastic old flying boat with a wooden, canvas-covered hull and a Lynx engine mounted up behind the cockpit just below the uppermost of the two wings. The moment of force from that pusher engine, high up as it was, was straight forward, and substantial, forcing the nose down into the water. To counteract this thrust, we had a large lever in the cockpit, which we called the "cheese cutter." It raised or lowered the whole horizontal tail. On takeoff, if the cheese cutter wasn't well back with the engine at full power it was impossible to get the nose up. Similarly, if the engine ever cut, it was impossible to hold the nose down unless the cheese cutter was fully forward.

The throttles were located on a bar between the pilot and co-pilot, who sat side-by-side in an open cockpit. One crewman sat up forward in a single circular open cockpit; if he wasn't there, we carried a 150-pound sack of sand in his stead. We couldn't fly without that weight up front. Because that cheese cutter was such a vital control, when we took off we opened the throttle and left it open. Then we grabbed the cheese cutter and never let it go. We had to have a hand on it in case the engine quit, which it frequently did.

And there were other peculiarities. For instance, the Vedette had a gravity-flow fuel tank up beneath the upper wing to feed the engine, with a main tank below, in the hull. To fill the gravity tank, there was a little pump which ran at about 110 percent efficiency, passing the gas through a ground-glass indicator on the instrument panel, causing the little ball contained inside to jump around. The 10 percent of fuel that wasn't used came down a tube, back into the main tank. We had to keep an eye on that bouncing ball all the time; should movement stop, we knew that we had a maximum of ten minutes flying time before the gravity tank ran dry!

Still on peculiarities, the space between the wings forward of the engine and aft of the cockpit was filled with a screen of chicken wire. It was there to catch any objects that might accidentally dislodge from the cockpit in rough air, an abrupt manoeuvre, or on landing. It not only protected the propeller, but allowed us to retrieve such objects. Unfortunately if we ever crashed, or even came in too heavily, the weight of the engine sitting high up behind us on its mounting would bring the whole structure down on top of the cockpit. If the engine didn't crush you, the chicken wire trapped you.

To taxi, we had the crewman stand behind us and, when we wanted to turn, we would wave an arm in the desired direction. He would clamber out on the lower wing, just far enough to force the wingtip float on that side down into the water and drag us around. Then we would wave him back to his central position in the cockpit. Obviously he had to be agile.

In those days we were young and rambunctious. We enjoyed playing around with the Vedettes. We found that, as we opened the throttle with the cheese cutter right back and got her on the step, in order to get off, we had to yank back on the stick to overcome the torque of the engine holding the nose down. Instead of doing that, we would close the throttle and open it again, causing the aeroplane to leap, literally, twenty feet into the air. I don't think that it occurred to any of us just what would have happened had that engine not come back on. In that tiny interval it would have been impossible to get the cheese cutter forward again.

We had this little manoeuvre perfected when one day, Frank Miller (who ended up as an Air Chief Marshall), one of our instructors, took me out to check on how I was progressing with the Vedette. We went out and taxied, picked up moorings, went into the dock, and did all of the basic nonsense. Finally, he motioned me forward, and away we went.

I headed into the wind, opened the throttle, and got her up on the step. Things were going beautifully, and just as I got to what I thought was the proper speed, I closed the throttle. As I did so, he undid his straps and started over the side. I opened throttle again and suddenly we were twenty feet up and he was looking straight down at the water. He climbed back into his seat and there was no mistaking his signal. He wanted down! We landed and taxied in to the dock where, believe me, I learned just who my ancestors had been, and a few other things as well. How in the name of God I was allowed to stay in the Air Force after that, I'll never know.

One day Mawdesley asked, "Who wants a free trip to Montreal for the weekend?" We all put our hands up and, of course, we had to draw straws. I "won." Then I found out what the trip was all about. The aircraft in question was a Vedette, which the inspectors had decreed must be pulled from the water, dismantled, and put on a flatcar for the trip back to the Canadian Vickers factory. Mawdesley would not allow one of his aircraft to suffer the indignity of being put on a ruddy flatcar. If the thing could still fly, then it was going to be flown. So I was the lucky one. Blissfully, with my 150 pounds of ballast up front, I set out. After climbing all the way from Trenton to Montreal, I still had to circle around Mount Royale once I got there. I had been on the verge of stalling all the way—it was a great day! I landed on the river by Vickers and taxied in to where a group of employees were yelling, "For Christ sake, sink it! Sink it! Don't bring it in here!"

On our graduation from Navigation School, Mawdesley decided that we would all celebrate by taking a trip. We took all of our Vedettes, including the only metal one—the Mk VI, which was a nicer machine to fly—a couple of Fairchilds, and the Norseman and set out for Kenora by stages. We stayed there for two or three days, outdoors under canvas, and then came back. Mawdie had it worked out. He would phone ahead to each location where we intended to land and alert the press. Making sure that he was the first one down, he corralled the reporters and regaled them with the damnedest stories about our aeroplanes, our training, and such nonsense.

One of the places we came into was a lake near Thunder Bay, where he outdid himself with the press. The Norseman was our only aircraft with a radio, and it had a long antennae that trailed down beneath it for transmission in flight. The wire, which was normally reeled up in the aircraft, was weighted by big lead balls to ensure that it wound out smoothly when the operator wished to transmit. The Norseman was our most impressive aircraft, and its pilot had been instructed to bring it in last and make a spectacular landing close to the shore.

Mawdesley had the press spellbound on the beach when in came the Norseman—trailing the aerial, which someone had forgotten to wind up. We were standing there when there was a shrill whistle and these big balls of lead went right through our midst, hitting the sand just in front of us. Suddenly, there was wire all over the place. "What in hell was that?" they wanted to know.

Mawdesley rose to the occasion. "Gentlemen, I must swear all of you to secrecy, right now! You should never have seen that! It's a secret instrument that we are perfecting in the Air Force for doing glassy-water landings. I don't want any word of this to get out. I must trust you." They all believed him and no word about it was ever printed.

The Forced Landing Competition was a part of the graduation of our class. We went up with our old Fleets and were given numbers dictating the sequence in which we were to land. It was a spectacular occasion with all of the officers in their best bib and tucker and their wives sitting in chairs along the side. When the competition was over, there was to be a grand tea party over at the mess. A great big brush jump, a big artificial hedge, was erected out in the middle of the field, and the judges set up their tables and chairs beside it.

The rules of the competition required that we climb to 3,000 feet and circle round until they fired a green Very light. With each signal the next man in the sequence would chop his engine as he passed over the field and come circling down dead-stick to land just over the hedge. The chap who landed closest to the hedge won.

Well, we weren't very good at this, and some of the guys disappeared 'way off the end of the field. Others undershot so badly that they had to put on power and go around again. But there was one fellow in our class, Wilf Stapley, who was determined that he was going to win this thing. He had worked out just how he was going to do it. When he had glided down to about 1,000 feet he

Securing beaching gear to the hull of a Vickers Supermarine Stranraer was a cold and difficult operation, especially in winter. *L. J. Birchall via Canada's Aviation Hall of Fame*

was going to put his Fleet into a perfect stall, positioned directly above the spot in front of the hedge where he calculated he would come down and land.

This was fine, except that he had forgotten to bring the wind into his calculations. So here he was coming down in a perfect stall when it became increasingly obvious that he wasn't going to make it over the hedge. The judges watched and watched and watched and then it dawned on them too just what was going to happen. Suddenly, there was the biggest scuffle ever, with officers trying to dig their way out or find cover—under another officer if necessary!

Stapley hit the hedge, the desks, everything. Suddenly it was just one great big mess, which ended the Forced Landing Competition for our class. I don't think a winner was ever declared.

The Munich Crisis came up just as we graduated in '38. We went down to Dartmouth, where we were going to form 5 BR (Bomber Reconnaissance) Squadron using Vickers Supermarine Stranraers—big, elderly flying boats which were just then being built by Canadian Vickers. The Stranraer first went into production in 1935. It had two big Bristol Pegasus engines and was a marvellously sturdy old boat.

When we got to Dartmouth, all we actually had were some rather old Fairchilds the RCAF was using to help the RCMP control rum-running around the French-owned islands St. Pierre and Miquelon.

These machines tried to locate the sea-going boats from which booze would be transferred to smaller local boats and smuggled ashore. Anyway, we had our introduction to the east coast of Canada on those aircraft. It is rocky north of Halifax, while to the southwest there are stretches of beach. By recognizing these geographic characteristics, we knew whether to turn right or left for Halifax when we came in over the coast.

I did a mercy mission with Flight Lieutenant Carscallen out to Sable Island, which is little more than a sand bar. It is actually the centre of a series of sand bars extending in two directions, and the only part that is above water. They operated a wireless there, and a lighthouse. The operator's wife had become ill and they radioed in to arrange for her to be taken out. Normally this would have been done by means of rafts floated in from ships anchored in deep water, but using the rafts was too lengthy a process in an emergency such as this.

"Cars" took off in one of our Fairchilds and I went with him as his navigator. It was quite an ambitious venture. We flew up to Sydney, Cape Breton, where he filled our gas tanks to the very top, giving us as much range as possible. We were positioned to fly straight out to sea and hit Sable Island—or some part or other of the chain of sand bars—perpendicularly. We had very carefully calculated just how far we could fly out over the Atlantic before having to turn and come back—there was no fuel out there! Our only additional navigational aid was a sheet of clear plastic set on the floor with lines inscribed on it. To use this device, I gazed through it at the little bits of froth on the wave tops and calculated our drift from our changing relation with them.

Then I had the pilot kick 60 degrees off while I took another drift reading. Then 120 degrees back we came for a third reading, after which we would straighten out to what we thought had been our original track. I had three drift readings and from these I calculated our wind vector, and away we went. When I remember that trip to Sable Island—I would no more try that trip today than . . . Yet, in those days, it was just routine, almost.

Finally we got our brand-new Stranraers, marvellous aeroplanes. I certainly enjoyed flying them. And Mawdesley came with them, a fantastic old guy! He was to be responsible for training 5 BR aircrew. He had been given the job because he had flown Short Singapores in England and also delivered them to the Far East. He was one of the best on flying boats in Canada.

We had a wardroom on the Stranny where the pilots ate, separated from the rest of the crew by a door.

In the way of navigational equipment, we had a loop antennae, a real modern thing in those days, stuck outside the hull up between the two wings. To operate it, there was a big wheel down inside the aircraft which could be turned. When we put on earphones, we in effect became a radio compass. We would swing this thing around until we got the two aural nulls. There was no way of knowing which one of the nulls pointed to the station so we had to follow a procedure such as we used in later years, flying the old A and M (Morse letters) beacons to determine the direction of the station.

Other than the loop, the only navigational equipment we had was a drift reader located in the back turret, which we could turn to obtain readings. By pointing it, we could learn the number of degrees of drift we had. We carried boxes of aluminum dust. When one of these was thrown out, it would create a large spot on the surface of the water. After a couple of minutes we would take a drift reading from it, a back bearing, and then the old 60 degrees off, 120

Supermarine Stranraer "D" (RCAF 914) of 5 (BR) Squadron (code QN) circles a topsail schooner. *DND PL2731*

degrees back bit, with two more boxes of dust. When we returned to our original course thinking we had a fair handle on where we were, the wind would change, pushing us off in the wrong direction. Apart from this "sophisticated" equipment, the Stranny was essentially a very basic aeroplane.

I think we were the last station in the RCAF to have homing pigeons, complete with pigeon loft and a loftsman. Every time we were to go flying, the loftsman would come down carrying a basket with a couple of pigeons in it. To exercise these birds occasionally, we would fly out to a certain spot, at a certain altitude, and release them. There was quite a trick to dropping pigeons out of an aeroplane: we had to hold them with their heads toward us and our hands right around them. Then we held them out in the slipstream and let go. The pigeon had enough sense or instinct to keep its wings, undercarriage, and everything tucked in until it had lost speed to the point where it could safely fly. If you simply threw them out, the poor birds would open their wings immediately. Feathers and everything would go, and dead pigeons would be the result.

I can only remember one instance when we actually used the pigeons. In bad weather we flew back toward where we thought the coast was and then turned at an angle which became shallower the closer we got to shore. Usually we contrived to have the coast come up our port side. We would keep a close watch and, the minute we saw a rock, cliff, or anything definite, we immediately came in closer and eased our way along until we finally spotted a little opening. Then we would duck through, drop into the water, throw out the anchor, and stay there until the weather cleared.

On one particular occasion, amid snow and ice, we landed safely and dropped the anchor. We got the stove going, spread the tablecloth, and began to build ourselves a meal. At this point, we heard a noise and looked outside to see a couple of locals who had rowed over to us. They gave us the name of the harbour that had become our refuge.

"This is fine," we thought. "We'll get word to Halifax and let them know where we are." We couldn't contact them by wireless because our trailing antennae could not be lowered and, while we had an aerial which could be flown from a kite, it was too damn cold to attempt anything so ridiculous. "Why not let the pigeons do a little work?" someone suggested. We wrote out our messages, put them in the little capsules, and attached these to their legs. Then we threw them out. The damned birds made one quick circuit of our aircraft then landed on a wing!

While the wings were fabric-covered, they had a narrow walkway along the spar. Out along these we went, carrying big brooms normally used for sweeping off snow and ice. We shooed the pigeons from their perches and watched them do another circuit before landing on the opposite wing. We crossed over to the other wing and shooed them off again. Guess where they went! After three such performances, both we and the pigeons got fed up with the nonsense. It was recognized as a stalemate. They knew they weren't going to get back in the aeroplane and we knew they weren't going anywhere. "To hell with them," we decided, and left them there to roost for the night. The next morning, we took off, leaving them no choice but to do likewise. We reached Halifax about noon, just in time for lunch. They got in around four o'clock that afternoon.

Around this time, you may recall, the Princess Patricia Mine disaster occurred up in Cape Breton. A car with a party of miners on board broke loose and plunged down a tunnel to rack up at the end, killing quite a few of the men and causing extensive damage. The weather was terrible and they couldn't get anyone in with the emergency supplies. So they asked the Air Force if we could fly in.

Once again, Cars undertook the flight because he had the most experience. I went with him as second pilot and navigator. We had an awful time getting in. We landed on Bras d'Or Lake and it took several cracks at getting over the trees, bridges, and whatnot before we finally reached Sydney, in the north harbour, where we landed off one of the docks. A boat came out to pick up the doctors and the medical supplies.

"You go ashore with them," says Cars, "and see what you can find out about the weather. Phone and see if we can get back into Halifax. Take a couple of crewmen with you. If we can't get back, we'll tie up to the wharf—where you and the crewmen will be a great help." So I went ashore with two crewmen and, after much trying, finally got through to Halifax to be told that they were experiencing the worst storm in some time. I shouldn't really have asked—it was only necessary to look out the window.

We struggled back to the pier to find that Cars had thrown out an anchor. The wind was blowing him straight at us and he was only fifteen feet from hitting the pier with his tail. He began to signal us with an Aldis lamp: "Get out here! We need everybody!" Now how were we going to get out to that ruddy aeroplane? There was a ferry running across Sydney harbour and we contacted the captain. Was he going to make another run? He was. So we decided to find a dory. The three of us would get in and he would tow us out in front of the aeroplane and then ease back until we could climb aboard. He agreed to our plan.

Easier said than done! Out we went in that damned dory. I've never had such a ride in my life! I thought any second we were going over! There we were, the three of us, lying flat in the bottom of the dory, hanging on desperately to a bloody rope. We were out in front of the aeroplane when we began to wonder if we were actually drifting back. One of the crewmen raised himself up on his knees to have a look. Seeing this, the captain thought we had made it and released the rope. We began to pick up speed and were charging down on the aeroplane, but a little to one side, right at a great big piling that was close behind it.

"This is it!" we thought. Just then we bounced by a wing tip float which rose from the water as we passed. I made a flying leap and grabbed for the bloody thing, and caught the strut at the top of the float. The crewman thought I was going overboard and hung on to my ankles. One minute I was stretched straight up in the air and the next I was down and under water! Up I came, gulping air and praying that the Stranny would continue rocking sufficiently to keep bringing me up. We did about ten minutes of this before Cars and the others on board finally got us into the aeroplane.

We stayed there all night, gunning the engines and doing whatever else was necessary to keep us afloat and away from the shore. In the morning, when it cleared up enough for us to taxi out of there, we discovered that we couldn't raise our anchor. We abandoned it and taxied on in, where we learned that the local telephones had just gone dead. We knew what had happened—our anchor had broken the cable where it crossed the harbour bottom—but we sure as hell were not going to tell anybody.

Then the war broke out. The RCAF flew their old Westland Wapitis down to Halifax, taking the wings off them the minute they arrived. Presumably this

Like the Stranraer, the Northrop Delta was built under licence by Canadian Vickers. It was the first low-wing, all-metal, relatively high-performance aircraft operated by the RCAF. On floats it could display a reluctance to leave the water. This aircraft was operated by 120 (BR) Squadron in 1940. *Via D. E. Anderson*

was because, had they used them, we would have been doing nothing but search-and-rescue missions looking for them. The only other aircraft of any significance flown by the Air Force in that part of the world was the Northrop Delta. With no wings on the Wapitis and no bomber force in position in Halifax, they needed aircraft.

And so the Air Force brought down some Deltas, low-wing monoplanes on floats. I don't think there has ever been an aeroplane that was quite as noisy as the Delta, with the possible exception of the Harvard in fine pitch, at full throttle. It was still not a bad aeroplane, except taking off on floats on glassy water. Under such conditions, a vacuum would form just behind the step and hold the float down. Once the pilot got it up on the step, expecting to take off, the wing developed a slight negative lift. When he tried to ease back on the stick to regain positive lift, the suction would take over and slow the aircraft down below flying speed. He would find himself galloping up and down the harbour alternately rushing ahead then falling back.

We all had to take a crack at flying the Delta because every once in a while, they would send us up to Sydney where the Northrops were in use. We would be there for two or three days flying the damn things before we were allowed to escape from purgatory and resume flying our Strannies.

One day, I was up there with Jack Twigg, a very good friend whom I knew from RMC. I tried and tried to get a Delta off the water and I just could not. So I returned to the dock.

"It's all in the fingers," says Jack.

"Be my guest," I responded.

And so we climbed back into the machine and began roaring up and down, with Jack getting hotter and hotter under the collar. He wasn't going to get off either. Finally he turned back up the harbour and I knew that, this time, we were either going to take off or go charging up on the shore. At the very last moment, he gave it the damnedest yank and bounced it right out of the water a couple of times. With each bounce he gained a little more flying speed. Finally we got off. Barely missing the trees on the shore, we roared on up the side of a hill. At the top was a very large convent, which we cleared by zilch feet. I'm sure we broke a few of the windows with our noise! Immediately we realized that we could have a serious problem, beating up a convent. Turning steeply, we landed back in the harbour.

"We had better get the hell up there," says Jack, "and tell them we were on a vital war mission—give 'em some sort of apology." So we jumped into a car and over we went to the convent. We agreed that there was nothing like going straight to the top, so we asked for the Mother Superior. This gracious lady invited us in and we presented our case. One of our aeroplanes, we explained, had just taken off and appeared to have come quite close to the roof of her convent. We hoped that it had not upset anyone—it was on a very urgent war mission. There were submarines out there and our courageous crew was risking life and limb, trying to locate them.

"Don't worry," she told us, "this is really a hospital. Our delivery room is located on the top floor, and you have no idea how much help you gave those poor girls!"

Wellington Pilot

Early Night Bombing Raids over the Continent

ARTHUR B. (ART) WAHLROTH
FLIGHT LIEUTENANT RCAF (RET'D)

B orn and raised in Toronto, Art Wahlroth joined the RCAF on 22 June 1940. From Manning Pool on the Canadian National Exhibition grounds, he was soon sent west to become a member of only the second Initial Training School (ITS) class held at the Regina Normal School, where aircrew trainees temporarily replaced student teachers. Streamed to become a pilot, Art received his training on Tiger Moths from civilian instructors at an Elementary Flying Training School (EFTS) operated by the Moose Jaw Flying Club.

In keeping with the RCAF penchant for moving trainees around the country, Art was returned to Ontario, to the Service Flying Training School at Brantford, for advanced instruction. When his group arrived, they were confronted with an apron crowded with Harvards. Immediately their hopes of becoming fighter pilots rose, only to be dashed when the advanced trainers were replaced with more docile twin-engine Anson Is. They were to become bomber pilots after all.

Proudly wearing his new RCAF pilot's wings, Art sailed for England on the SS *Georgic,* a peacetime liner that, because of its speed, was not required to travel in convoy. His memories of the relatively quick trip are pleasant. The food, he recalls, was the best he would eat for the next several years. In England, he enjoyed train rides through the deceptively peaceful countryside. Shortly, he found himself at an RAF Operational Training Unit (OTU) at Abingdon in Berkshire, where he would learn to handle the unwieldy Armstrong Whitworth Whitley. His subsequent operational posting was to the newly formed 405 Squadron, the first RCAF bomber unit, where Art was the first Canadian Sergeant Pilot. The squadron's Pegasus- and Merlin-powered Wellingtons would rank among his favourite aircraft.

Following his tour with 405 Squadron, Art spent several months instructing on an OTU, and then did a second tour on Wellingtons (Mk Xs) with 37 Squadron, RAF, in the Middle East. He finished the war in Canada with 413 Photographic Survey Squadron, RCAF, flying out of Rockcliffe Air Station in Ottawa. His post-war career—spending summers flying in the bush and winters studying optometry—is described in *Skippers of the Sky*, a Fifth House anthology of first-hand accounts of bush flying, published in 2000.

A good many lifetimes ago, as measured by the span of a Wellington pilot, I spent the summer working at the Toronto Flying Club. One evening after an air pageant, the instructor, J. T. O'Brien Saint, had to return a borrowed Tiger Moth, CF-APL—the first of its kind in Canada—to the factory of de Havilland Aircraft Company of Canada Ltd., which was across the field. He invited me along and saw to it that I was securely strapped into the front cockpit. On the way over, he treated me to a session of aerobatics that motivated me for the next several decades.

I learned to fly in the RCAF in 1940 on Tiger Moths. The aerobatics I had been painstakingly perfecting came to nothing, for the next phase of training was on the gentlemanly Avro Anson. This was followed in England by training on cumbersome Armstrong Whitworth Whitleys and more spritely Vickers Wellingtons.

In June 1941, I was posted to 405 Squadron, the first Royal Canadian Air Force bomber unit, at Driffield, Yorkshire. Though not the first to arrive, I was the first Canadian Sergeant Pilot on strength. The squadron was being formed by Wing Commander P. A. Gilchrist and two Squadron Leaders, Canadians in the RAF. It comprised a polyglot assortment of Brits, Australians, Canadians, New Zealanders, and South Africans; all from the British Commonwealth Air Training Plan and mostly trained in Canada. The squadron was built around a nucleus of experienced RAF pilots who would train green second pilots or sprogs—of which I was one—as aircraft captains while completing their tours.

We were equipped with Wellingtons, a heavy (later a medium) bomber made by Vickers. Wellingtons served in all theatres of war, and in every

Art Wahlroth (left) as a Sergeant Pilot with 405 Squadron RCAF on 11 September 1941. In the middle is Pilot Officer Glen Lochyear (RAF) and Sergeant Al Lomas from Toronto, Art's rear gunner. *A. B. Wahlroth*

Airmen embarking for England on an unidentified liner adapted for carrying troops. Windows below the bridge have been blacked out. *DND PL2759*

command except Fighter Command. It was regarded as the main strike weapon of Bomber Command until the introduction of the four-engine heavy bombers. It embodied many details that were ahead of its time: cockpit heating, retractable tailwheel, constant-speed propellers, propeller and wing de-icing, self-sealing fuel tanks, and balloon wire cutters. Modifications were later made to provide for 4,000-pound Blockbuster bombs, torpedoes, anti-submarine detection radar, glider and fighter towing, mine sweeping, mine laying, and long-range fuel supply.

We were of the generation nurtured on the "Strength through Spinach" philosophy of the popular "Popeye the Sailor" comic strip. Popeye's bosom pal was the hamburger-loving J. Wellington Wimpy, hence the machine's nickname.

Crews approached the Wimpy from the front and climbed in under the nose by means of a ladder, which was then drawn up into the aircraft. The door was padded on the inside, and formed the section on which the bomb-aimer lay when dropping the bombs. Forward of his position was a window through which he viewed the ground and over which was suspended the bomb-sight. Immediately forward was the door to the front turret. On the starboard wall was the electrical panel for the bomb circuits, and on the port side, under the pilot's platform, was stowage for the camera, which shot vertically downward through a small window. Passing the pilot's platform, one climbed a few steps and entered the main cabin. The radio operator was immediately behind the pilot. A quarter-inch of steel armour plate separated him from the navigator to his rear. The fuel gauges were on the starboard wall just inside the door, and the batteries, or accumulators as the British called them, on the floor by the navigator's seat.

It was necessary to climb over the main spar to get to the rear fuselage. Oxygen bottles were stowed on the port wall; fuel cocks and controls for cabin heating were located by the spar at the wing roots. On some Marks, there was a 28-gallon tank of oil with an attached pump, since oil had to be pumped to each engine every hour and, in the tropics, on takeoff.

Aft of the spar was the flare chute and flare stowage on the starboard wall with a folding cot on the port side. In the roof, a plastic bubble, the astro-dome, permitted the taking of star shots or just observing. To the rear of the cot was the Elsan, our chemical convenience. At this point you negotiated a rather large step down into the nearly empty rear fuselage. This step incorporated a couple of windows through which the bomb racks could be viewed to check for hangups. After leaving the target, a crew member always looked to see that the bombs were all gone. Some Wellingtons had large triangular windows in the side walls at this point, with a single Browning machine gun mounted on each side. On each wall, further back, were the ammunition stowage cans for the four Brownings in the tail turret, with tracks running back to the turret.

In this area, one walked on a narrow catwalk laid on the centre of the floor. A misplaced foot could go right through the fabric-skinned underside of the aircraft. About halfway back to the tail, a section of geodetic members in the bottom of the machine had been removed and a wooden push-out escape hatch substituted. If one accidentally stepped on this in the dark, it was goodbye, Charlie!

We practised going through the aircraft wearing gloves and blindfolded so that we could do everything by touch alone. We had to be able to locate and connect intercom plugs and oxygen connectors, regulate gas cocks, remove and drop flares—and we dare not show lights.

The Wellington, by nature of its structure, was extremely flexible. It was a favourite trick of seasoned crew to lure neophytes to stand in the astro-dome while the pilot either pump-handled the stick to make the wings flap, or caused the entire tail structure to swing back and forth by executing a series of

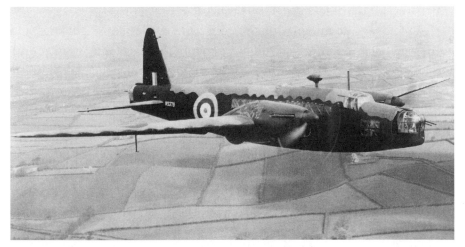

The Vickers Armstrong Wellington Mk II was fitted with Rolls Royce Merlin engines. This factory-fresh aeroplane had not yet been delivered to a squadron. *Vickers*

steep banks. The Wellington had a complete set of external lights, which in wartime were seldom or never turned on. Beside the standard navigation lights there were position-keeping lights on the outer trailing edges of the wings, presumably for night formation flying which, to my knowledge, was never done. There were a couple of other lights, one on the nose and one on the tail; as I never saw them hooked up I haven't the foggiest idea what they were for.

Under the nose, forward of the door, was an amber light controlled with a key or switch, and visible only from the ground. On entering the circuit the pilot would flash his identifying letter in Morse code. If he got a red light from the ground he would answer with one long flash and go around again, repeating his signal when he got back into the proper position. When he received a green light, he would switch the light on and make his landing.

The pilot, sitting up on a platform like a little tin god, had a lot of controls within reach. At his left side, low down, were fuel cocks to each engine as well as a cross-feed valve, and forward of these, a small horizontal wheel that, if turned, was the rudder trim, or if pulled back or pushed forward was the nose trim, with a star-wheel for fine adjustment. Forward on the cockpit wall were controls for boost, revs, mixture, and supercharger. The brakes were not on the pedals, as on American machines, but were activated by a handle on the control wheel. They acted on both wheels if the rudder pedals were equalized, or on whichever side the rudder pedal was pushed.

The compass was mounted on the front panel by the pilot's right knee, and above were two handles, painted different colours, one rectangular, one round, for the wheels and flaps. Down at the pilot's right was the switch for the TR-9 (the short-range radio), a lever for seat adjustment, and, back by the swing-down armrest, a hand pump with which to put the wheels down if the hydraulic system was not working. I had to use it twice.

The panel of flying instruments was the standard British type, so easy to use that I'm still amazed that it isn't in universal use. There were six instruments on it: in the centre the artificial horizon; to the left the airspeed indicator, so arranged that the cruising speed of the aircraft was in the horizontal position; to the right the rate of climb indicator; and below these the turn and bank (British version with two needles), the altimeter, and the directional gyro. Since your further livelihood depended on seeing other aircraft in the sky, you didn't spend too much time with your eyes glued to the panel. Instead, you made a regular sweep of the sky, then back across the panel. As long as everything was in a straight line you would carry on. If the artificial horizon showed the little indicator aircraft below the line, and both the airspeed and the rate of climb indicators were pointing down, you would automatically heave back on the stick to regain straight and level.

Eventually the Squadron Leader said he'd check me out on the Wellington. He flew two or three circuits, then he handed the machine over to me and I flew it around for a similar number of circuits. There being a seat in this particular machine permitting it to be flown with dual controls, I brought another sprog along with me. The other fellow sat with me and, on coming in for our first solo landing, he thought he'd be helpful. Just as we turned in, at about 800 feet, he dropped the flaps. On the Wimpy, if you didn't have the trim control aft of the neutral position, the result of flap application was drastic, to say the least. Never had I seen the ground come up at me so fast. We just about stood on our nose! Believe me, those flaps came off in a hurry! Thereafter we had the trim well back so that the flaps and trim were interconnected and there was no change in attitude. All in all, we found the Wimpy a nice machine to fly.

When I was crewed up, it was with one of the most highly strung skippers in the RAF. We did several cross-country trips as familiarization. Finally, operations! A run to Cologne! I don't remember much about that trip. Perhaps I was too scared. Then Bremen, a couple of days later. And I don't recall much about that one, either. Our third trip, however, was a horse of a different colour. We went out over the North Sea, headed about due east. The northern lights were bright and, from the German side, we were silhouetted against them.

The captain was in a bit of a flap, as usual, and had me stationed in the astro-dome keeping my eyes on the dark side of the sky in case of attack by a night fighter. He had me so scared that when he wanted the cabin heat turned on I wouldn't take my eyes from the sky long enough to bend down and operate the controls. Somebody else had to do it.

After a time, I decided that this was ridiculous. Why should I let this guy scare me? I think we were going to Heligoland before turning south to Wilhelmshaven, our target city, flying at about 12,000 or 13,000 feet, on oxygen. Suddenly the captain disconnected George, the automatic pilot. The right wing dropped and we went into a terrific spiral dive that took the two of us to correct. We quickly put the machine back on George. A look at the fuel gauges revealed that the captain had left the cross-feed valve on, pulling all the fuel for both engines from the port wing! I think we immediately jettisoned our bombs and headed for home. By the time we got there, the tanks had evened out. We came in quite normally. On the next trip we started out for Kiel, but the captain figured that we were experiencing excessive fuel consumption. So, ninety minutes later, we were back on the deck.

I didn't think about this—I was still in the learning stage and didn't know much about things. But on the next trip, our second to Cologne, I learned plenty. I can't remember very much about the German part of the mission, but on the way back—flying up England, everything going well, weather not bad, position known—the captain suddenly put the IFF onto emergency frequency. In about five seconds searchlights came on all over the country, going straight up. Then most of them went out except the ones near us, which proceeded to dip from the vertical position to show us the way to the closest airfield. We followed them around in a great turn until, directly in front of us, was a brilliantly lit aerodrome. The navigator and I wondered what was going on—the navigation was good—but the captain was the captain and we landed. Once on the ground, I asked him what the problem was. He stared at me in a complete flap. "Just be happy you're on the ground!" was all he would say. He was immediately taken off flying.

We had breakfast and at daylight I flew the machine back to our base. I had been kidding the boys in the control tower and they dared me to shoot them up. So when I took off I made a 180 and skimmed back across the tower. Unbeknownst to me the wireless operator had let out the trailing aerial and we wrapped it, weights and all, across the control tower windows. We expected repercussions. Fortunately for me, nothing happened.

Now with 250 hours, more or less, in my log, I was captain of an aircraft! They gave me a machine and I started to put together what was to be the first all-Canadian crew. I didn't quite succeed—all of the Canadian wireless operators on the squadron had re-mustered to tail gunners. They wanted to get out on the end where there was some action!

Jerry must have known that we were coming. The very first night we had a machine, a raider came over and made a direct hit on my Wellington.

Our nursery trip was to Rotterdam, where we were alone on the target.

Art Wahlroth's first aircraft, a brand new Wellington Mk II, photographed at RAF Driffield in May 1942, after a direct hit from an incendiary bomb dropped by a German night intruder. *A. B. Wahlroth*

When we got a bit of flak over the city, my evasive action was so violent that we lost the city completely. Returning to the seacoast, we found the Hook of Holland and followed the Maas River right up to Rotterdam harbour. This time we got our bombs on the proper spot, but we took so much time about it that we were reported missing.

Even with my limited experience, I had come to the conclusion that those who just drove their aircraft to the target and then drove them back didn't live to drive them very long. Our aircrew had mostly come off Whitleys and thus knew how to fly with our Merlin engines. Our ground crew had all come off Blenheims. But nobody knew the airframe. Whether this contributed to our casualty rate I don't really know, but we went through the alphabet at least once, relettering individual identifying letters on replacements for lost machines. The high casualty rate must have been pretty general. So I made a point of learning the Wellington inside and out, from stem to gudgeon. When I got back to Canada in 1944, I checked a list of my Air Training Plan classmates and found that less than 10 percent had returned.

On the day following a raid, at 10 A.M. sharp, "Lord Haw-Haw" would broadcast from Germany, "Gairmany calling, Gairmany calling . . . ," with his plummy British accent. He would then proceed to tell us that eight or nine aircraft had attempted to attack whatever target we'd been on, but that the fighters had driven all but one of them off. And that aircraft had dropped its bombs in the wrong place. Whenever we heard this there'd be one big, spontaneous horse laugh. Actually, one night over Cologne, I counted ninety sticks of bombs on the target. The place was so well defined there could have been no possibility of error.

There was a humorous side to squadron life. Some of the English boys looked upon Canadians as uncouth colonials, and a few of us would foster this impression by going into the kitchen before dinner, getting a small strip of raw meat, and then walking through the mess chewing on it. It tasted like hell. But it sure enhanced our tough, backwoods image!

A typical day in a Sergeant Pilot's life on 405 went something like this: We would wake up in the morning and try to decide whether it was warmer to stay in bed or not. We had iron cots, each with three biscuits (sectional mattresses) and some old blankets that you wouldn't have put on a horse back home. Having risen, we performed our ablutions—washing our face, etc.—in freezing cold water, and with a chill wind making it even more uncomfortable. Fortified with gluey oatmeal or powdered eggs, we went down to the Flight where a list of those on the following night's Battle Order was posted. Sometimes we would wait until the Flight Commanding Officer came along with the gen. Then we would walk over to our aircraft to spend most of the day looking wise and keeping out of the way of the fitters, riggers, electricians, and other ground crew. When they were finished we might do an air test of fifteen minutes to see if everything was right. If your ground crew would fly with you, you knew it was. Then we had to face the ire of the armourers who were impatiently waiting for us to put the thing back on the ground—they wanted to put the bombs on board for the night's mission. The crews of the fuel bowsers would then top up the tanks.

We had a few hours left for sleep, but who could sleep? Finally, we ate a special night-flying supper, with beans as a treat. You can imagine flying at 14,000 feet after a meal of beans. Then we'd gather for briefing. Up on the stage were the CO and various people such as the meteorologists, the navigation specialists, armament people, and the Intelligence Officers. Everyone had his say. We'd learn that the target for tonight was Cologne, or Hamburg, or some city hundreds of miles inside enemy territory, every mile characterized by searchlights and flak or the threat of night-fighting Junkers Ju 88s and Messerschmitt Me 110s. The weather, predicted as clear over the target, generally turned out to be ten-tenths cloud at low altitudes with balloons sticking out of it (at least serving to identify the target area). A brilliant moon silhouetted us against the clouds like sitting ducks.

We would gather up our gear from the flight office: Irving jacket, Mae West, parachute harness, helmet, oxygen mask, and so on. Navigators also collected their maps and charts. And all of us carried escape equipment, issued in case we were knocked down and lived to tell about it. We had maps sewn into the collars of our battle dress jackets and compasses in our buttons. We climbed on board a lorry and were driven around the perimeter track until we reached our machines, where we were unceremoniously dumped out. The CO usually came along to wish us good luck, probably wondering if he'd ever see us again. With him was the Medical Officer, who passed out "bennies," if you thought you needed them to keep you awake.

Like as not there would be Jerry marauders in the neighbourhood and we'd have to do everything in pitch darkness. By that I mean we had to taxi our machines out, guided by a chap with a pair of flashlights. At the runway we would be turned over to another fellow at the far end with another pair of flashlights. Then we would careen down the runway with rudder hard over, one brake on, and the opposite throttle almost fully advanced before we could bring the other one up, and only those flashlights to guide us. Accelerating down the runway with 5,600 pounds of fuel and 4,500 pounds of bombs, we hoped it would last long enough for us to get off. It usually did.

Even though all communication was stopped once we knew we were operating that night, word always leaked out. People from the local village would appear off the end of the runway—the right runway—waving to us as we left. Without fail.

We would turn and climb on course, through all the clouds that only England could produce. We wouldn't see another aircraft for the rest of the night unless we came close to bumping into one. When our turning point came up we'd try to get a ground position, or a fix on the coast when we crossed it. And you know, the water of the English Channel actually looked friendly in the face of what was to come. It wasn't too bad for the pilot who could at least see what was ahead. The second pilot would usually be down in the front, watching to see if there were any flashes of gunfire on the ground and give warning. The wireless operator sat in the cabin, listening or getting fixes for the navigator, but not transmitting except in an emergency. The navigator was busy with his maps and charts, and the tail gunner, isolated away out in his lonely turret, knew what was behind. Sometimes he also had a better idea of what was in front than did the pilot.

This was a typical day. The way I operated was to take off myself, then hand the machine over to the second pilot. I would check with the navigator, watch the compass, and try to relax, sometimes scraping the carrots or shelling the hard-boiled eggs we had scrounged. Generally we saved a bit to eat for the trip home. I would take over the controls before we reached the Dutch coast and, of course, over enemy territory it was my job completely.

Usually we flew across the Low Countries into the Ruhr Valley. The defences we met varied from trip to trip. On one occasion, when we were faced by an intense band of searchlights perhaps ten miles thick, we weaved and dived, went up and came down, hoping they wouldn't get us. If two or more lights caught you a whole cone would develop. Then one of Kammhuber's night-fighting Ju 88s or Me 110s would shortly be hosing us with cannon fire. Alternatively, the whole sky would erupt around us with exploding anti-aircraft shells. Even when they missed, we sometimes got sprayed with shrapnel. Naturally, we got out of there as quickly as we could—to hell with the fuel consumption!

In time this changed. We could be flying over open country and be groped for or picked up by a single searchlight. To avoid them, we would desynchronize the engines to sound like a German machine. In this way it was sometimes possible to pull a searchlight beam from side-to-side. If they were radar-controlled, we would turn the IFF on and off, or onto emergency frequency. But again, if we couldn't get rid of the beam it would soon be joined by others and we would be coned.

All the time we were over enemy territory, we would keep up an evasive pattern of flying. We did this almost in our sleep, the poor navigator trying to keep track of our zigs and zags. Occasionally he suggested one more, one way or the other, in order to keep on track. We very seldom stayed exactly on our course heading. We would turn off five or ten degrees and perhaps climb

Art Wahlroth relaxes with his dog at RAF Hornchurch in 1942. *A. B. Wahlroth*

500 feet, then turn parallel and go up another 500. A few seconds later we would turn back across our track and go another 500 feet up or down before turning parallel again.

Sometimes we got the feeling that we had been on a heading long enough, so we would veer off and quickly and lose some. Then, right where we would have been had we not turned, Boom! Over a period of time one seemed to develop a sixth sense; we were seldom touched. Generally we stayed between 9,000 and 13,000 feet, at extreme range for light flak, which looked something like long strings of Exhibition fireworks but had a nastier bite. Heavy flak came in single, bright, noisy bursts, and was accurate to 12,000 feet up.

When we arrived at the target area there was feverish tension as we tried to map-read our way in. The navigator/bomb-aimer would long since have come forward to accommodate his eyes to the dark after being in his brilliantly lit cubicle. Eventually specialized bomb-aimers were utilized. To guide us there were usually fires on the ground from bombs already dropped, but sometimes dummy fires were set to mislead us. Loops in rivers, or other large distinguishing features on the ground could prove useful in identifying targets.

We were often the first on the target, and in these instances we carried an entire bomb bay of incendiaries to light the place up. Once our target had been identified we would run up on it in the suggested direction, since everyone else was presumably doing the same. The navigator/bomb-aimer down in the nose would direct the pilot by calling: "Left, left . . . right . . . steady . . . bombs gone!" Then we held very steady until a flash told us that the camera had been triggered at the moment the bombs hit. The job done, we got out of there as quickly as we could!

On one trip, just off the target, we were sprayed by a night fighter, not once, but twice! Tracers whizzed by. My reaction was to cut the engines and drop the wheels and flaps, losing a lot of height in a hurry. It was brilliant moonlight and I guess the Jerry could see us. He came back at us and missed again, fortunately. By the time we were rid of him we were quite close to the ground. We flew back across Germany at less than 1,000 feet for most of the way, sometimes at 90 mph, sometimes at 200.

Returning from the target, once we had passed our ETA for the Dutch coast, my practice was to hand the machine over to my second pilot. If we were in cloud at the time, so much the better. Once, returning from a trip to

Dortmund, I had my second pilot take over at this point. He climbed into the seat and I held the aircraft steady while he got his intercom plug and oxygen tube connected. Then I went back into the machine to confer with the navigator and perhaps visit the Elsan.

Eventually I returned to the cockpit and stood beside the second pilot, looking out. We were at about 1,500 feet and had just broken out of cloud over water. Then we ran up over a beach! The south coast of England doesn't have beaches like that—it has big, white chalk cliffs. Inland we saw a rotating white beacon, the like of which I had never seen in England. I told him to get back out over the water. He turned, but lost a lot of height in the process, and was only at about 500 feet when he handed the machine back to me.

He was on his first trip, and no doubt very tense. Consequently he had the machine trimmed nose-heavy and was taking the weight on the control column. He got out of the seat so that I could get in. But instead of following the correct procedure—maintaining control until I was settled—he jumped down onto the bomb-aimer's couch. The aircraft, trimmed nose-heavy, headed for the water! I made a mad grab for the wheel. Planting my feet up the panel—and probably smashing some of the instruments—I succeeded in pulling the machine out of the dive. Just in time! But I bounced the tail turret off the water. Al Lomas, my tail gunner, nearly broke his back!

When finally I got the intercom connected I had a few choice words for my second pilot—about fifteen minutes worth, with no repetition I'm told. Apparently, when I was in the back, the machine had veered around in cloud so much that he had put us on a reciprocal heading. Instead of being out over the North Sea, after passing our ETA for the Dutch coast, we had come back in over the land, breaking cloud over the Zuider Zee. Needless to say, our report on him was such that he stopped flying operationally, as of then.

After this trip I was sent to Driffield, Yorkshire, for a Blind Approach Training course. My crew enjoyed a week's leave. Great Driffield was a permanent force RAF station with a grass field and a Lorenz beam heading northeast/southwest cutting the North Sea coastline at a promontory called Flamborough Head. It was the most northerly point for the very methodical Jerry hit-and-run intruders, who, almost on schedule, came up the coast, turned in on the beam, and ravaged our Yorkshire aerodromes. The word was that RAF had stolen the Lorenz system from the enemy, and we simply assumed they were more adept at using it than we were. We had nonworking instruments in the aircraft and went entirely by sound.

The course was carried out on Whitleys—beasts to fly until you got to know them, after which they were heavy and ponderous but docile machines. I had fought with them through OTU, four months earlier, so I had little trouble, a fact which rather surprised my instructor. The machines were completely blacked out, with black paint applied to the inside surface of windscreen and windows. Only a one-inch by four-inch slit was left for the

Art Wahlroth at the controls of a Wellington bomber in 1943. *A. B. Wahlroth*

instructor to see through. This simulated a totally black night, a very unreal situation that required the pilot to keep his wits about him. But it demanded instrument flying at its best.

For the entire week, twenty-one hours of flying, I didn't see the ground, from the time I took my foot off it until I stepped down on it again. The course was an experience of inestimable value, not only for the technical competence it provided, but for the self-confidence it instilled.

Then I was back with my squadron and crew. The RAF advised us to fly the Merlin engines at zero boost and 2,400 rpm, which gave us something less than eight hours of safe flying. Endurance was further reduced when one considers that we didn't baby the engines—there were times when we opened them right up to get somewhere in a hurry. We also operated at altitude in supercharger.

An engineering friend suggested an alternative procedure. He told me to fly at as high a boost as possible consistent with weak mixture (the throttles had a linkage that automatically put you in rich mixture if you over-boosted) and to drop the revs down until the cylinder-head temperatures started to rise. This worked out so well that we actually had three trips in succession of well over eight hours, at a higher cruising speed. This was sufficient to make the powers-that-be think that we had found a lonely island somewhere and sat on it for a while. But our target photographs proved that we had been where we were sup-posed to be. They tested this procedure, and it wasn't too long before the AMOs came out that this was the way to operate.

Being blessed with a goodly supply of Sweet Caps and chocolate bars, not to mention nylon stockings, I got along quite well with my ground crew. Because our machine had a good serviceability record, the Flight CO began to send new pilots out to fly it on circuits and bumps. My crew and I did not appreciate flying at night in a machine that had been bumping around all day. So, having such good relations with our ground crew, we found it easy to have all the cowlings off and the engines being washed down—day after day. For obvious reasons, we had no maintenance difficulties.

Because of this, and the good petrol consumption, the Wing Commander took my place, put the Gunnery Officer in the place of the tail gunner, and took our machine to Brest on a daylight raid. We had been doing some hush-hush daylight formation practice, leading us to suspect that something special was coming up. The gunner and I weren't honestly sorry to be relieved of this trip.

And just as well—they were shot down over the target at Brest. They had been after the *Scharnhorst* and *Gneisnau.*

I recall sitting at the end of the runway with Al Lomas waiting for our aircraft. Ultimately we came to the realization that our Wimpy was not coming back. Al and I had to go about making up another crew. This time we didn't try to make it all-Canadian.

An aircraft flown by one of the Squadron Leaders came back a good half-hour ahead of all the others. When they landed the crew refused to speak to the pilot. The story came out that, just off the target, he had put the nose down and run away from the other two machines in his flight. Both were shot down. One went into the sea and the other crash-landed near Plymouth. The Sergeant Pilot of this latter machine came back to the squadron about a month later. He went into the Squadron Leader's office and properly beat him up. A lot of us were in the flight common room and could hear it. But we didn't interfere.

While the Sergeant was posted off the squadron, nothing happened to him, and the story never came out officially. When the Squadron Leader got back some weeks later, still with a puffed-up face, he was wearing a DFC.

On one trip we went east, flying over the flatlands of Denmark before turning south into Kiel. This, apparently, was precisely the wrong way to get at that city. Our over-water approach took us over a good part of the German fleet, bottled up there. They greeted us warmly! I can recall twisting and turning, with strings of luminescent flak rising up all around us. Dangling balloon cables seemed to be everywhere. I don't know if we hit anything that night but we sure made the Jerry Navy use a lot of ammunition. I think this was one of the times I had to pump my wheels down by hand because of a hydraulic leak.

One night as we flew down England for Brest, the weather grew thicker and thicker and we received a recall signal. I had a clued-in navigator, who gave me an immediate turn-around, then figured out a correcting course to get us back to base. Some of the others were up a lot longer because they carried on the same heading until their navigators figured out a reciprocal course. We got back and landed safely with our bombs on board. We had taken off our gear, which we left in the flight office lockers, and were walking back to the mess when we heard another aircraft coming in, his engine backfiring as he throttled back on final approach.

Just about the time he would have reached the end of the runway, there was a terrific flash. Believing that every building in the camp was going to be blown our way, we all dived into an open excavation. There was about a foot of water in the bottom. When we got to our feet, realizing that everything was serene, we felt a bit foolish. Apparently someone, to light up the end of the runway for the landing aircraft, had pulled the pin on a flare just as the machine touched down. Everybody got in safely that night, but we were the muddiest!

The closest we ever came to using our parachutes was following a Berlin trip. We had a new navigator, on his first trip. He got us to Berlin, but coming back, he got sick and we got lost. We were shot up over the Frisian Islands. We had no right to be anywhere near them! Finally I took over the navigation, and decided to head north and west, hoping to hit England. We did, making a landfall at a Yorkshire town, Darlington. Then I flew south toward the squadron.

At this point I will digress to relate an incident that occurred a few days earlier. I had, one afternoon, flown an empty aircraft over to Dishforth to pick up some pilots who had ferried their machines there to have new Marconi radios installed. Returning with a load of pilots, a few tail gunners, and very little fuel, I was just coming in for a landing when a Jerry raider dropped a stick of bombs across the runway. I veered off, and the tower told me to stand by. It was getting dark and those bombs had very effectively turned off every light in the whole district. As it darkened there was absolutely nothing to stand by on!

Losing the field completely I went out to the coast, up to Flamborough Head, and turned in on the approximate beam heading which would take us very close to our home field. Again, the tower would only say "stand by," and there was still nothing to stand by on. There was a strong wind blowing me in the direction of the balloons protecting the city of Hull—with my diminishing fuel supply.

Fortunately, we sighted a flare path. I asked for permission to land and it was granted. Then I was advised that it was a short fighter strip, Catfoss, only partially completed. I gleaned that information the hard way when I overran the flare path and started knocking down saw horses and dodging cement mixers. Turning off the runway, I was out of the frying pan into the fire. The main wheels got bogged in mud and the tailwheel, by next morning, was frozen into concrete! We left the machine there.

Naturally, I raised a stink about being left up in the air with little fuel, no navigational aids, and being repeatedly told to stand by on nothing. So it was that this morning, flying down to Yorkshire at about 6,000 feet, with a solid undercast, and calling the squadron on the TR-9, which had a limited range, I received the answer, "We have every light on the aerodrome on." Everyone was ready to jump—there was some very rough country beneath us. The front gunner was standing with his 'chute attached, holding mine ready to clip it onto my harness. But my response to the radio message must have been effective. Some clued-in soul came on with the information that they had a solid overcast at 3,000 feet, with twenty miles visibility. I throttled back the engines, down went the wheels and flaps, and so did we—right through the clouds—and there, right in front of us, was our beautifully lit aerodrome. We went straight in; I don't think I touched the engines at all. We had just turned off the end of the runway when one engine quit. Again, we left the machine right there. In the morning the bowser crew told me that they had refuelled the aircraft with 742 of a possible 750 gallons.

In November of 1941 I was sent on temporary duty to No. 21 OTU, Wellesbourne Mountford, near Stratford-on-Avon, to give the passing-out pupils the latest "gen" on conditions over Germany. I never got back to the squadron. I spent a year on OTUs, then I went to the Middle East to do a second tour on Wellington Xs.

The Vickers Armstrong Wellington Mk II, coded LQ-O, was the machine most often flown by Art Wahlroth. It was one of sixteen aircraft represented on a 1999 series of Canadian stamps recognizing the seventy-fifth anniversary of the formation of the RCAF. © *Canada Post Corporation, 1999. Reproduced with permission. Also reproduced courtesy of Air Force Association of Canada*

Wanderers by Night

Exploits of a Mosquito Night-Fighter Pilot

Martin ("Cy") Cybulski DFC
Squadron Leader RCAF (Ret'd)

Raised in Renfrew, Ontario, Martin Cybulski was attending Renfrew Collegiate when he joined the local militia, the Lanark and Renfrew Scottish Regiment, Black Watch, 52 Battalion. He competed on three occasions for the Dominion of Canada Rifle Championship, winning it once. His excellent marksmanship would later stand him in good stead as a night-fighter pilot.

Another militia course provided him with a grounding in navigation, which would also prove useful. Early in 1940 he applied for aircrew training, taking a course with the Galt Aircraft School while waiting for his call-up. After Initial Training School (ITS) at Brandon, Manitoba, he went on to Elementary Flying Training School (EFTS) at Prince Albert, Saskatchewan.

Recuperating from his wartime injuries, Cy Cybulski attended an air show in Toronto, where one of the aircraft being demonstrated was a de Havilland Mosquito. Leaving fellow patient John Bielby gaping, Cy hopped the barrier and approached the aircraft. The access hatch in the bottom of the fuselage immediately opened and arms reached down to help him swing up into the cockpit. With Cy safely on board, the pilot taxied away and took off. After the sort of aerobatic performance at which the Mossie excelled, the machine returned and Cy dropped to the tarmac, grinning broadly. The pilot had been his former squadron mate, Joe Schultz. After four years in hospital, Martin ("Cy") Cybulski/Ross—the name change was post-war—joined the Ontario Department of Reform, accepting a post at the Training School for Boys in Colborne, Ontario. He died on 26 April 1987, after a lengthy battle with cancer.

learned to fly on the Tiger Moth, starting my flying training on 7 November 1940, at No. 6 Elementary Flying Training School (EFTS), Prince Albert, Saskatchewan. My first forced landing occurred there while I was flying solo. The Tiger's engine suddenly started going clank! clank! clank! and smoke began to pour from the side of the cowling. I was over bush country, well away from the station. Looking for a place to land, I glided toward a farmyard. It had snowed heavily and the stuff lay deep on the ground. Only days previously, I had seen a fellow student come in and touch down too soon in the deep snow ahead of the runway. He had gone right over onto his back, and I could see myself in exactly the same predicament.

So I sideslipped toward the farmer's yard where I could see a haystack and some cattle. I was able to miss them and, at the last moment, I hauled back on the stick and dragged the tail through the snow. I flopped in and bounced, but I stopped before turning over.

The farmer came running up with his son, saying, "I thought you were a gonner!" Then he sent the boy back to the house, to return with a tumbler. "Drink this," he said, handing me the glass. "You look as though you need it!" Now I didn't touch anything alcoholic in those days, but I did as I was told and gulped the stuff down. Wow! Then I asked him if I could use his phone. He didn't have one, but he directed me to a neighbour about a mile down the road. The tracks I made in the snow, happily weaving my way toward that neighbour's house, were anything but straight!

On another occasion, I spotted a horse and cutter travelling along a country road. I decided to drop down and have a closer look. As I skimmed past, the horse reared up, dumping both the cutter and himself into the ditch. No one was hurt, but it so happened that one of our instructors was just above me at 5,000 feet. He spotted me low flying—something I was not supposed to do. When I returned, the CO called me in and, boy, did he chew me out! For the only time in my life, I crawled. I pleaded abjectly. He could have washed me out, and I knew it. But he gave me another chance. A few of my fellow students had had problems barging into one another and, out of our class of thirty-five, only fourteen graduated. It was a touchy time for all of us.

Then I was sent to the Service Flying Training School (SFTS) at Saskatoon, where I was rather fortunate to have the opportunity to fly both single-engine Harvards and twin-engine Ansons. Since I wanted to get on fighters, I appreciated the chance to fly both types. The station had a satellite field at Vanscoy near Saskatoon, where we could come in for practice landings. It had only a hard-packed snow strip—I was not to land on a dry runway until I reached England. Like other fields in western Canada in winter, this one could pose problems. I landed there with an Anson and was making the usual turn at the end of the runway when one wheel dropped into a hole under the snow.

There wasn't another soul on the field—I was stranded there with no help whatever. Afraid I might be blamed for making too short a turn, I gunned the engines, trying to bull her out of the hole, but she wouldn't budge. So I decided on a rather risky procedure. Revving up both engines to takeoff power, I climbed out, taking with me the axe that was kept in the back of the aircraft for emergencies. I began chopping at the frozen snow in front of the trapped wheel. With no warning the aircraft began to move! I whipped around the wing and scrambled inside. Rushing forward, I grabbed the controls as the aircraft picked up speed across the field. I managed to take off safely. I got away with it, but I couldn't help feeling a little disappointed that no one was there to witness my heroics.

One fellow I got on well with, Gord Rawson, was six feet tall, came from Toronto, and was a bit of a joker. On the morning of the day when we were to have our wings parade he was up in a Cessna Crane, about to come in for a landing. Watching him, I realized that he was going to overshoot. He couldn't seem to make up his mind whether or not to go around again until it was too late. He came down too far along the slippery runway and just kept on going until he hit the fence, where he flipped completely over. When he climbed out, almost unscathed, his only comment was, "There I sat—in the back seat—and me supposed to be the pilot!" In our wings parade picture, Gord stands out. He has a bandage around his head, with his little cap wedge perched on top. But he did get his wings.

It was nice to have those wings. We had damned well earned them! At that time there was no embarkation leave. We left Saskatoon on the eighteenth of the month and, on the twenty-eighth, we were due in Debert, Nova Scotia. But I was lucky; there was a smallpox scare and I missed the boat, so I returned to Galt to visit my girlfriend. But I was back down east in time to ship out on the next boat, the SS *Derbyshire*. It took us sixteen days to reach Iceland. Incidentally, to establish a time frame, Hess had landed in Scotland about two days before we arrived. Was it ever nice to get off that greasy old tub and jump into one of those warm pools they have in Iceland, fed by hot springs.

At about that time, a submarine was sunk just off Reykjavik. After ten days in Iceland, we sailed for England. Eventually we arrived at 54 Operational Training Unit (OTU) at Church Fenton in Yorkshire. We flew Bristol Blenheims, light bombers similar to the Bolingbrokes built and flown in Canada. Night fighters were the big thing at the time but some of us would be flying bombers. Fortunately, I had been assessed as having good night vision and, as I had flown both singles and twins, I was given a choice. I opted for night fighters over bombers. It was a matter of choosing between being shot at or doing the shooting, and I preferred the latter. Maybe my marksmanship experience would pay off.

We found it rough on the OTU. German intruder aircraft would come over at night while we were flying in our unarmed Blenheims. As a precaution, we were advised never to maintain a straight course, but to weave in and out. We were also told to use our peripheral vision, to look from the corners of our eyes rather than directly at where we suspected Jerry might be. And this worked. We spotted things we might not otherwise have seen.

I quickly acquired the habit of continually scanning the sky around me. One night I happened to catch a glimpse of a shadow to my right and slightly behind our machine. Immediately I turned hard to port and down. Unfortunately we didn't have any R/T to contact the crew in the aircraft up ahead. The intruder who had been on my tail picked them up and destroyed their machine. We lost about seven aircraft in two weeks, and the fellows became pretty twitchy about going up when there was no means of knowing whether enemy aircraft were in the vicinity.

About this time, I was hospitalized. When I came back, I was teamed up with H. H. "Laddie" Ladbrook, who had instructed the first navigators with whom I had been flying. I asked him why he wanted to fly with me, a Sergeant Pilot, when there were Squadron Leaders around. "Well," he replied, "I remember going up with you and your first navigator. When the exercise was over most of the other pilots buzzed off down to the mess and sat around. But you went back up to 5,000 feet and threw the aircraft about, just to get acquainted with it." That extra bit of enthusiasm, he felt, might give us an edge if anything went wrong, and so he decided to team up with me. That was how we got together. And he was a hot one—one of the originals on radar. I was fortunate to have him as a partner.

We were posted to 410 Squadron initially operating from Heathfield, near Ayr in Scotland. Then we moved to Drem near Edinburgh. We did a lot of stooging around, but there wasn't much enemy activity. We even chased the "Weatherman," a German aircraft that came in from Norway gathering meteorological data, but we never had any luck; he was just too careful.

There was a lot of bombing activity in the Newcastle area—we could see the flames. But no Jerries came up our way. "Let's turn off the R/T," says Laddie, "and take a look down that way." So we headed toward the fires, the search-lights, and the flak bursts and had our look. Blyth and Newcastle were burning, but most of the enemy attackers were already on their way home. When we got back, did we get a blast! Squadron Leader Bennell, our Flight Commander at the time, pointed out how we, an unidentified aircraft, could easily have been blown out of the damned sky. So we didn't do that again—for a while.

Our next move was to Acklington in Northumberland, where there wasn't much activity either. We did put in a lot of night flying—training—which wasn't a bad thing, being in the night-fighting business. By this time we had converted to Bristol Beaufighter Mk IIs. For such a heavy aircraft, their Merlin engines left them a little underpowered. The Beaufighter Mk VI with Bristol Hercules engines was a much better aircraft.

One of the hottest pilots we had on the squadron at the time was Jack Devlin, who would later become chairman of Canadian Breweries Limited. I remember an occasion in April 1942 when he and his navigator, Dave Johnston, had an engine conk out. Then their other engine caught fire. On top of this they were experiencing icing problems. But Devlin calmly glided in, hitting a pole and killing three or four cows. The aircraft exploded and burned, but they walked away from it.

While it is not widely known, there was a certain amount of sabotage on a few squadrons. In one instance, when I was taking off, leading a scramble, I had an engine start to act up. Losing an engine on takeoff in a Beau was usually disastrous. The aircraft would abruptly flip over onto its back and that would be it. With this in mind, I always kept the aircraft at 105 mph while on the deck. When my port engine began to falter as I lifted the nose, I reacted by keeping

Out of their element, a pair of black-painted, night-fighting Beaufighters from
410 Squadron RCAF stand out darkly against the clouds. *410 Squadron Album*

the aircraft low and easing it into the air, clipping the tops of the trees at the end
of the runway. I was able to nurse it around and come back in for a landing. We
switched to another aircraft and continued with the scramble. When I got
back, the Intelligence Officer wanted to know if I had any "bad friends" on the
squadron. "Hell, no!" I said. "I like everyone!" "Well," he replied, "someone
jammed a piece of cloth into your petrol tank!" It could have been a rag accidentally dropped in, I thought. But then he produced a square yard of heavy
flannel. It had been forced into a part of the wing tank that was about six inches
in diameter. As soon as the nose was raised, he pointed out, the fuel line to the
engine would be blocked. It would lose power, and that would have been it
for us!

Another time, coarse iron filings were found in an aircraft's oil. You can
imagine what that would have done to the engine. In yet another instance, after
it had been raining all afternoon, we had a scramble just at dusk. There was no
horizon and it was just like flying through a black wall. We had to rely on our
instruments completely, and when I looked down to check mine, I saw that

Mosquito intruder pilot Cy Cybulski of 410 Squadron RCAF relaxes at
RAF Coleby Grange between ops in 1943. *Mrs. H. Ross*

they were all leaning to one side, sort of tipped over. By this time we were racing down the runway and had no choice but to take off. Once more I went through the tops of those trees. We got down safely and I discovered that someone had filled the pitot static head underneath the lower section of the wing with mud! Again we were lucky. Then one of the other pilots, Bert Miller, borrowed my kite for a night and ended up ditching in the North Sea. Luckily, we were able to save him. Obviously the aircraft could not be checked, but it sure looked like another instance of tampering. There were just too many of these to discount sabotage.

We always felt fortunate in being the first Canadian Unit to be given Mosquitoes, NF IIs. This was in October of 1942, and the fellow who checked me out was none other than Jack Devlin. He was still a hot pilot. Another pilot was Joe Schultz of Vachon, Alberta. With his radar operator, V. A. Williams, he shot down three Dornier Do 217s in a single night, 10 December 1943. I had given Joe his first checkout in a Beau.

Then we moved down to Coleby Grange in Lincolnshire, right in the bomber belt south of Lincoln. Again we did a lot of stooging around. We soon found out that we were training to get into low-level intruder work, and we didn't mind that. It was in March when we were called in, and Ladbrook was handed a computer to help him with his navigation. He didn't even know what a computer was, and that was why we were absolutely lost most of our time over Europe.

On 27 March 1944, after we felt that we were really ready for this intruder stuff, we were told that weather conditions were perfect. The cloud base was at 15,000 feet so that we could nip in and out of it while we knocked off trains or anything else that happened to be around. Our aircraft were now Mosquito Mk VI fighter-bombers. Our three aircraft took off at two in the afternoon and when we reached the halfway point, out over the North Sea, the sun was shining so brightly we could have suffered sunstroke. The other two aircraft turned back, but we decided that, since we were halfway there, hell, we would have a peek and just see what was on the other side.

We continued on, right down at wave-top level so that German radar wouldn't pick us up, heading for the Frisian Islands, just off the Zuider Zee. As I've said, it was to be our first ever trip over Germany and we anxiously watched for a landfall. We were to come in close to Vlieland, a small, narrow island just north of Texel; it wasn't as well defended as Texel. The idea was to skim in close to the island, climb to 5,000 feet, and then go screaming in at high speed. I'll never forget just how dry my mouth was, heading in. On later trips, I always carried lifesavers—just so that I could talk to my navigator.

They opened fire on us as we crossed Vlieland, where we intended to set course for the Zuider Zee and then swing over toward Zwalle. The maps they had given us in England showed a definite outline for the Zuider Zee and in fact for the whole shoreline. We had expected that it would be a cinch to pick out landmarks and fly by compass from each of these to the next. But the intelligence people hadn't told us that the whole damn place was flooded! Ladbrook was having trouble map reading, and this was where that Militia Sergeants' course that I had taken back in Toronto paid off. I was able to pinpoint enough locations to get us into Germany. We weren't allowed to find targets or do any shooting in Holland. We finally found the landmarks we had been looking for, the Ems Canal, the Autobahn highway, and the main railway from the Ruhr Valley up toward Papenburg and Hamburg.

It proved a choice location. The first thing we spotted was a tug pulling two barges. It was clear sailing all the way in, and we dropped the bombs, hitting the barges right on and sinking them. We continued on and came to a railroad junction, where we blasted away at a train in a station and blew it up. It had big warehouses along one side, and we thought that we had better use some of our high-explosive cannon shells and incendiaries on them—do a little damage. We had a good run.

Then we decided to have another crack at the trains. We were skimming in at roof level when I spotted a horse and buggy. Immediately I turned a bit, just as the horse reared up—I didn't want to hit it. When I looked back they seemed to be okay. Maybe I remembered that horse and cutter back at Prince Albert. We were just coming in over the tops of some trees when a camouflaged ack-ack battery suddenly opened up. If they had held their fire for five seconds, we would have been right over them and they would have had us. As it was, the flak came bursting up in front of us. My reaction was hard to port and right around at full throttle. As we turned, Ladbrook was screaming, "Don't give them a full view! Don't give them a full view!" Boy, was my brown spot squeaking!

Where had I heard that expression? Back at Coleby Grange we had the honour of meeting Flight Lieutenant Nicholson, the first fighter VC of the war. He

Intruder pilot Wing Commander Frank Hillock (left), Commanding Officer of 410 Squadron RCAF, and his navigator, Paddy O'Neille-Dunne, with 300 feet of heavy copper wire, obtained the hard way—from between the towers of an enemy radio station at Apeldoorn in Holland. *Air Ministry*

had stayed with his burning Hurricane long enough to bring down a Messerschmitt Me 110 before baling out. He came over from the Church Fenton OTU and proved to be a heck of a nice chap. He was chatting with us, the first Canadians at the station, when he happened to use the term. "The time will come," he told us, "when some of you fellows will find out what that means." We had just discovered exactly what he meant. We did get hit by a bit of the flak, but by then we had spotted a better target, a train heading in toward a heavily wooded area.

We had to come down even lower than the treetops and at an angle. It was our only possible approach, but it was a good one. Our first burst went right into the engine and it exploded. Our next target was a pair of buses loaded with soldiers, and we got in some good shots as they climbed a hill. On our way out, we came across still another train, heading down from Papenburg, wide open. By now we knew where our sites should be and a good long burst blew up that train as well.

Then it was time to head back to England, where we were slated for night-flying duties. In the morning papers there were headlines about a lone Mosquito stirring up Germany. Ignorance is bliss—we had thought it was an everyday occurrence! When we returned from the trip, we had been interviewed by Intelligence and they wanted to know at exactly what time we had sunk those barges, blew up that first train, all that sort of thing. I couldn't tell them. I had been too busy looking after the bombs, the cannon, the machine guns—and just flying the aeroplane. But Ladbrook could. "I've got it all written down here," he says. And he had. All the while things were happening he had been making notes, taking everything down—he was one of those meticulous Englishmen.

Before the invasion of Sicily we were on detachment from the squadron, down to Predannock in Cornwall from where we would fly a dogleg into the Bay of Biscay, then out into the Atlantic, and finally back over to Spain, looking for subs, enemy aircraft, or boats. We flew at low level, as close to the waves as we could get, so that we would be looking up at any enemy aircraft that appeared on the horizon. A lot depended on who saw whom first. One of the fellows got down so low that he hit the top of a wave. At that speed it was like hitting a brick shithouse, but he was lucky and got away with it.

On one such trip, we ran into trouble north of Spain. If anyone had problems it was understood that they had to make it back on their own or else head down to Lisbon in Portugal for a three-week holiday and then back to England. I am dubious about this, but that was what we were told. On this occasion, our port engine began losing glycol and the other one also started to act up. We feathered the port prop and watched the other three Mossies continue on. Now we had to decide: was it to be Lisbon and a holiday, or should we try limping back to England? We opted for England. It was June, and I've never sweated so much in my life! The port engine was down and the starboard engine was flicking red and green, red and green—it couldn't make up its mind. We were at plus six boost and 2,650 rpm, just hobbling along above the stalling point.

Eventually we came to the south coast of England at Cornwall, still just above the waves. "How in hell are we going to get over those cliffs?" wondered Ladbroook. "We sure haven't got enough power in that one engine!" There was only one way we could do it, I figured. There might be just enough glycol left in our port engine for a last kick, although I had been given to understand that having an engine overheat and seize in flight could be very bad. Anyway, we decided to fire it up. It caught, and we climbed over the cliff safely. We pumped along and finally reached our base, where, of all things, they directed us to come in on the short runway.

When you make a forced landing, you try to touch down with as much runway ahead of you as you can manage. If you land too short, you could be out of luck altogether. We managed to hit at about the middle of the runway and, with all our hydraulic problems, I found that we didn't have much left in the way of brakes. "Brake it! Brake it! Brake it!" Ladbrook was screaming. Why didn't he get out and stop it himself was the thought that occurred to me. We

A 410 Squadron RCAF Mosquito fighter-bomber shows off its elegant lines as it takes off from an RAF base in France. *DND UK17550*

tore along and ran off the end, scattering the works-and-bricks people who were busy lengthening the runway. We managed to stop about forty feet short of going over the edge of the cliff and back into the damned English Channel.

In those fighter-type Mossies, the pilot and navigator sat side by side, rubbing shoulders. In fact, I used to wear out my shirt sleeves. Ladbrook was first out of the kite, and he got right down on his knees and, atheist that he was, said a little prayer. When I climbed out I discovered that I was wet completely through—and I don't know whether it was only perspiration! "I'm going to buy your beer for a whole week!" Ladbrook promised me.

The thirteenth of June 1943 was a sad day for all of us. We lost four Mossies. One of the pilots was Dickie Burgess, who had been a heck of a good goalie with the Saskatoon Quakers and was a very nice chap. We weren't supposed to make much use of the R/T, but we did get one message to the effect that they had spotted four Junkers Ju 88s and were taking after them. The next message was that they were being attacked by Focke-Wulf Fw 190s. The 88s had been a decoy to get the Mossies into position, and they hadn't stood a chance. That was the end of them. Our job certainly wasn't all peaches and cream!

Of course there was the trip when we had the skin burned from our aircraft. It occurred on my mother's birthday, 26 September 1943. We were on a special do called a "Mahoud." For this we fixed up our night fighter with a long back-flip on the radar set, as well as a long front-flip. On actual night fighting, we only used a short back-flip; but with a long back-flip we could pick up something extra. We were flying our Mossie NF II, serial D2757, coded 'Q,' and I think we were about the only Allied aircraft over Germany that night. We were supposed to go to northwestern Germany over toward Hamburg, and we were above the clouds under a full moon, a lovely setting. We were waiting for a night fighter to come up on our tail. When he got to within 5,000 feet, we would turn hard and stay with it for a full 360 degrees, by which time we would be on his tail. There was always a lag on the radar screen. By the time the Jerry crew had figured out what was happening, we would be behind them and it would be too late.

When flying a trip like this, we never flew straight and level for too long. We would angle off at 30 degrees to one side for a time and then swing back 30 degrees to the other, then 500 feet down and back up again. But it was so beautiful and serene up there we must have been lulled into a false sense of security.

All of a sudden guns opened up behind us, and I think our starboard engine was ticked. We decided it was time to head back for England. We were humming along nicely when Ladbrook says, "There! There's something back there on our tail!" We knew we couldn't outfly it with our damaged engine, so we used a little craft: I accelerated as much as I could and then throttled back and put the aircraft up on its tail. The German night fighter—we later found out that it was a Messerschmitt Me 410, one of their latest—shot by us and we ended up on his tail. There was a fair amount of jamming from nearby German stations which was affecting our radar but not his and it became necessary to work this manoeuvre about three times. On the third try, we were coming up on him quite nicely when suddenly he pulled the same trick we had been using, hauling his aircraft up practically into a stall. "We're overtaking! We're overtaking!" Ladbrook was shouting. "We're going to go right by him! If we don't get him this time, we've had it!" With the jamming, Laddie wouldn't be able to read his set. So I pulled right back and closed the throttles. Just as we were about to stall, I put the nose down. And there he was, sitting right out in front of us. I remember aiming our four cannon and the machine guns right at where his starboard wing tank should be and letting fly.

There was a blinding flash and after that I couldn't see a thing. Ladbrook had been looking down at his set and didn't get the full impact of the flash, as I had. He was able to see clearly. But even I was soon aware that we were completely enveloped in flames. If I throttled back, the fire would really take hold, so I shoved the nose down, straight down with full throttle!

We dove for about 4,000 feet and I had to have Ladbrook help me get the aircraft out of the dive. Luckily, we had practised something like this—not pulling out of power dives, but having him help with the flying. We would be carrying out night-flying tests in the afternoon, flying into a cloud with him peering into the set. Then I would take off the trim and just let the old aircraft go. "Okay Ladbrook, you've got control. Now bring the damn thing out of it!" We had worked on this and this was one time when it really paid off. We pulled the aircraft out of the dive and were happy to see that the flames had been extinguished. But I still couldn't see very much.

When you go into a steep dive, the compass begins to whirl around and can't be read until it has had a chance to settle down. When we finally got straightened away, good heavens, we were heading back into Germany. The guns opened up again and our port engine was hit—this on top of our already damaged starboard engine and our tattered fuselage!

We finally got turned around, heading for home. But things were pretty rough. Just to keep the aircraft more or less straight, I had to wrap both my legs around the control column and brace them. Keeping our Mossie in the air required maximum engine boost. In this condition, we headed back over the North Sea and were halfway across when I realized how very dry my mouth was.

Whenever we came across the occasional oranges, we would put them aside to take with us on our trips. On our way back from a stint over Germany, they always seemed like a special treat. "Laddie," I said, "let's have those oranges. I could really go for one and we may never get the chance to eat them again." So he reached back for them, only to find that they were frozen solid! When the port engine went, the heating system had gone with it. Later, when I was in hospital, I would wake up crying for an orange. There were times returning from that trip when I wondered if we would ever make it back. The aircraft was so damned loggy! We were all set to bale out. Then we thought of just how cold that North Sea would be.

For the first time ever, I tried three R/T channels to contact England. Finally I sent out a Mayday. I'll never forget the voice of the girl who answered the R/T. "You're heading right for the balloons at Great Yarmouth," she advised us. That was just super. So we limped back out over the North Sea and came in through the Wash. And this was one time when the Army, the "brown jobs" who looked after the searchlights, really helped us. They pointed every light straight up. And since I didn't want to land at a strange 'drome, they headed us back to Coleby Grange. I've been grateful to them ever since.

Coming in for a landing, we dropped like a lead ball. I waited with growing anxiety for the green light to come on. Suddenly it began to shine, letting me know that the undercarriage was down at last—about a second before we touched the deck. When I was able to climb out of that aircraft and had a chance to look at it my knees buckled! It was that bad!

On further investigation, we found that we were even luckier than we realized. Subconsciously, I had been aware of something passing through the kite, but in all the excitement, it hadn't registered properly. We found a hole in the door right beside Laddie's knee, where a piece of cannon shell had come

Cy Cybulski and "Laddie" Ladbrook pose with their charred Mosquito night fighter after a successful combat on 26 September 1943. *DND CF107*

through and then hit the Perspex by my face before falling down at my feet. I have one half of that shell at home and Laddie has the other. For that do they awarded DFCs to both Laddie and me. I still feel that we got the awards because we were too scared to bale out of that burning aircraft into the cold water of the North Sea.

Another incident illustrates the sort of damage a Mossie could safely sustain. Wing Commander Frank Hillock went on a patrol with Paddy O'Neille-Dunne at about 300 feet over the Dutch coast and flew right into the radio station at Apeldoorn. When he realized that he couldn't avoid it, he turned the aircraft on its side and flew between two of the antennae, breaking the cable that stretched between them. They completed their mission and flew back to England with 300 feet of quarter-inch copper wire wrapped around their aircraft. When they landed, the wire was confiscated for salvage. His aircraft was a Mossie NF II DZ726, coded 'Z.'

Laddie and I had another memorable trip on the same night as one of those thousand-bomber raids on Hamburg. We were supposed to go over to Gilze-

Rijan in Holland. It was a very black night and we were coming in from over the North Sea. I knew we were still a fair way out and that we hadn't crossed the coast. But all of a sudden, the guns opened up! Where the hell were we? We had to have strayed over Heligoland, which was just loaded with ack-ack batteries. Back out to sea we went, until Laddie felt that he had worked out the right compass bearing. In again we came, entering enemy territory.

Just then there was a momentary break in the clouds and we were able to look down and see this wide gleaming strip of water. There was nothing like it on our map anywhere in the area where we were supposed to be. Then the guns opened up with flaming onions that seemed to float up to our altitude and explode. We realized that we were looking at the Kiel Canal, a place where we had no business being. But it gave us a point from which we could get our bearings, and we were finally able to reach the 'drome that had been our destination.

They had set up a dummy field to fool attackers like us, and we went to this, dropping a bomb on a railroad junction on the way. When we reached the dummy location, we unsynchronized our engines and flew over to where we thought the real strip was. With our nav lights on and our engines sounding like a Junkers Ju 88, we fooled them into lighting up the real runway. We kept up the charade and made our approach as though we were coming in for a landing. Right over the centre of the runway, we let a bomb go. Every light went out and every gun opened up. But we were off and on our way home.

In a happier story, we had received a report that a couple of our bombers had ditched in the North Sea off the coast of Denmark after one of the thousand-bomber raids. We set out to try and find them, together with another Mossie and a Lanc. We were out for five and a half hours, looking for them, doing a square search over rather rough seas. At last Laddie and I spotted them—four survivors in one rubber dinghy and six in another. Finding them gave me the biggest kick imaginable, a tremendous feeling of satisfaction. Both of the other aircraft had flown over them but had missed them in those big waves. I believe that they were rescued by an airborne lifeboat dropped from a Hudson, the first use of this device.

I have an unforgettable memory of the first time I ever saw flak at night. We were on bomber support and were about two minutes ahead of our ETA, supposedly over Vlieland. Instead we found ourselves over the isle of Texel just off

Den Helder, a big island just loaded with guns. They began firing and I looked down. Good heavens, all those pretty lights! All those different colours! Ha, ha, ha! Boy they were beautiful! Then they came whistling by! I came to my senses and dove off to the right. Down we went until I saw my altimeter register twenty feet below ground level! I straightened the damn thing out and looked over the port side to see the mast of a fishing vessel whistle by. For the next two or three nights I had nightmares of flying down the Zuider Zee, watching masts go by.

When you took off in a Mossie after flying a Beau it was like climbing out of a Mack truck and into a Cadillac. The Mosquito was just so manoeuvrable. Whenever anyone went for his first flight in a Beau, the whole station came out to watch! With the Beaufighter's tendency to swing to the left, the pilot always had to put on port throttle to keep it straight. One very seldom made a good landing in a Beau. And the Mossie didn't have the Beau's vicious trick of rolling if you lost an engine.

Once, when I was on a beam approach course at Wittering, I watched a Mossie coming in on the very long runway there—something like three miles in length. There was quite a solid layer of ground fog and the pilot must have been new at the job. Anyway he seemed to mistake the top of the fog layer for the tarmac and levelled off at fifty feet! Down he came. He didn't turn over like a Beau would have done, he just mushed in. The tailwheel broke off, then one wing separated, followed moments later by the other. The fuselage slid right on by. The two crew climbed out as soon as it came to a stop and walked away.

In another amusing incident, Bud Green, who was later a Winco over in the U.K., was bringing his Mossie down just as the weather closed in. Ours was about the only 'drome still open, and a lot of people were trying to whip in just as fast as they could. With Bud was Dave Ridgeway, his feisty little English navigator. The two of them had accidentally left their R/T on so that what was said in the cockpit could be heard by all of us. At the end of the runway the works-and-bricks people were at it again, doing a job that involved the use of a steam-roller which they had parked just off to the left of the strip. Bud and Dave were coming in fast and we heard Dave snap out, "What the hell's that up ahead? A steamroller! If you're gonna hit the goddamn thing, hit it on your side, not mine!"

I had a friend from Bomber Command, a fellow from my hometown of

Renfrew, who had been unable to make it as a pilot. He had always wanted to fly in a Mosquito, and I offered to take him up and show him around. In Lincolnshire, the country is quite flat with grain fields and you can come down very low. We flew around for a while and then I put the aircraft into a nice little dive, almost to ground level, and headed right for a row of trees, skimming the wheat. We used to challenge each other on the squadron to see who was best at knocking the heads off the stuff. We were aiming right at these two trees. My friend could see for himself that we could never fit between them. At the last moment I dropped a wing and we slipped through. That was how manoeuvrable the old Mossie was.

Speed? We cruised at about 260 and could get up to 400 on the straight and level.

By the way, the original motto of 410 Squadron had been Death in the

Cy Cybulski (left) with fellow Mosquito pilot Joe Schultz at Downsview on 6 September 1946 after his Mossie ride at a post-war Toronto air show. Cy was convalescing from his wartime injuries. *J. Bielby*

Dark, which I guess sounded a bit negative, since it was changed to the Latin *Nocti Vaga*, which means Wanderers by Night.

Now I don't want to hurt the Americans' feelings, but their night fighters had a way of getting lost. One of their aircraft, possibly the Northrup Black Widow, had cannon in the nose, and whenever they fired it they would lose their compass, effectively losing them. They wouldn't have a clue as to where they might be. We would be sent up to find them and bring them back home.

My last trip in the Air Force wasn't in a Mossie but a very unhappy one in an Oxford. Now I should have been wise to the Oxford from a previous experience. When we were down at Predannock and were due to return to Coleby Grange, we had four or five ground crew who wanted to come back with us for their leave. If they took the train, it would have wasted a lot of their time. So I said I would take them back in the station's Oxford. I wasn't supposed to do this, but I told them to climb on board. They brought all their blinking tools with them, something I hadn't anticipated. We started down the runway, with those Cheetahs popping away, the same runway that ended on the brink of that cliff hanging over the English Channel. I had full boost and still couldn't get the tail up, so I stopped before we got too close to the edge.

Now I wasn't going to tell them that I was sorry, we couldn't make the trip after all. So I had them bring all of their gear up to the front of the aircraft and we tried again. I boosted her up with the brakes on and then let her roll. The tail finally came up just before we reached the end of the runway and we roared out over the water. Just as we cleared the edge, a downdraft seemed to catch us and we dropped about fifty feet. I thought all of those tools were going to keep right on going out through the bottom of the aircraft. I don't suppose any of the fellows who were along on that trip will ever forget it. But we got safely to Coleby, although I had to hold it at full boost just for the landing.

On my last flight in an unfortunate Oxford, I was flying all by myself and I felt that it wasn't handling properly, so I landed it to have it checked out. The next morning I took off and almost immediately found myself flying in cloud; I had been looking at my watch and estimating distances. I thought I was at 5,000 feet and that it was time to let down for a look. Actually, my altimeter was way out and I was also twenty to twenty-five miles off course—in a distance of fifty miles. I had no height at all and ploughed into a mountain. They tell me I was very lucky. Amidst all the rock in that range I managed to come down in a bog! I was thrown from the aircraft and again I was lucky. Instead of breaking my neck, as I should have done, I wrenched a nerve in my arm and paralyzed it. I also lost a lot of blood. In fact, I had to have a complete change. They replaced it with so much English blood that I am almost an Englishman.

This happened on Christmas Eve. When I came to in the hospital the doctor said, "You must have bumped into Santa Claus!" His name was Linton and he went on to remark, "The only reason you didn't kick the bucket was because you couldn't—you've broken both legs!" My reaction, while still partially under anesthesia, was, "Boy, that's pretty damn funny!"

After getting away with so much for three years, I would now spend four years and five days in hospital—and undergo twenty-three operations. I almost lost my arm. I had had hopes of making the Canadian rifle team. My useless arm dashed these aspirations and depressed me greatly. On top of this, I overheard someone remark that if a specialist had been able to look at me right after my accident, they might have been able to save my arm. I began saving up my codeine pills to take all at once when I was alone, but one of the nurses was pretty sharp, fortunately, and she caught me. Then one day they had to take me for X-rays and I had to go through the burn ward. That did wonders for my attitude. I saw these fellows with nothing but claws for hands; noses, ears, and eyelids gone, nothing for faces. What in hell had I to bitch about? After that, whenever I started feeling sorry for myself, I had only to remember these fellows to realize how lucky I was. My arm has a quarter-inch screw nail holding it in place.

Desert Kittyhawks

Flying the Curtiss P-40
with 250 Squadron RAF

JAMES E. (JIM) COLLIER DFC
SQUADRON LEADER RCAF (RET'D)

D o gifted athletes make better fighter pilots? Jim Collier's RCAF/RAF fly-ing career would certainly seem to suggest so. Born and raised in the small Manitoba community of Portage la Prairie, Jim excelled in both hockey and football. In 1937, as a nineteen-year-old, he set a Manitoba hundred-yard dash record that would stand for thirty years.

Having a flair for drawing, Jim Collier came east to attend art school in Detroit. When war was declared, he immediately put his career as a com-mercial artist on hold and enlisted in the RCAF at Toronto. After his stint at Manning Depot in the Horse Palace at the Canadian National Exhibition grounds, he was sent to Camp Borden, where he learned to march. For Initial Training School (ITS), he was posted to Victoriaville, Quebec, and then to Portage la Prairie, for Elementary Flying Training.

Since Quebec ITS grads normally went to the Maritimes for flying instruc-tion, to be sent to his hometown was a fortunate posting indeed for young Jim Collier. He flew Tiger Moths at the EFTS there and then progressed to Harvards at the Yorkton, Saskatchewan, SFTS. After mastering the Yellow Peril, he enjoyed the customary thirty-days leave and then shipped overseas. His time at the RCAF Personnel Reception Centre in Bournemouth he recalled as both pleasant and frustrating. "There were just too many men and not enough girls," a sentiment shared by many other young Canadian airmen seemingly stranded in this English resort town.

Following leave at home in Canada after his North African tour, Jim Collier returned to the U.K. This time he was with an RCAF unit, 403 Squadron, of the

Canadian Spitfire Wing commanded by the famed Johnnie Johnson. He served from 26 November 1944 until 15 February 1945. On 25 December 1944, he was credited with the RCAF's first solo victory over a German jet, a Messerschmitt Me 262.

Leaving the Air Force, Jim Collier resumed his career in commercial art, working for several Toronto studios. In the early fifties he and two others launched Art & Design Studios (ADS), where he remained until his retirement. Among those who illustrated for ADS was well-known war artist Don Anderson. Jim Collier died on 26 January 1990, from accidental causes.

B arrack-block wisdom had taught me never to volunteer for anything— invariably you were hooked into something you hadn't volunteered for. But we got very bored after six or eight weeks of hanging around. Daily roll call was our only diversion. One day, when they called for thirty aircrew volunteers for the Middle East, thirty of us were sufficiently frustrated to step forward.

We took nine weeks to sail around the Cape of Good Hope in a convoy.

When we reached Suez, we got off the ship and were immediately asked what we were doing there. It seems that there had been a foul-up, one of many that occurred during the Second World War. They had requested thirty airscrew (single-engine propellers) and received thirty aircrew (single-engine-trained pilots), and they didn't know what to do with us.

Eventually, out of the thirty, six of us got on operations. The rest flew desks in Cairo and Alexandria, undoubtedly a bitter experience for them. I was one of those fortunate enough to go on "ops." After a few weeks of operational training on Curtiss P-40C Tomahawks, getting familiarized with the type, I joined No. 250 (Sudan) Squadron on 22 June 1942 at LG75 (Landing Ground 75) near a place called Sidi Hannish.

It was an area of fairly hard and reasonably smooth sand with a few oil drums spotted around to define the field. Typical of desert airfields, it was windswept, but all in all quite satisfactory. It was hard to ground-loop on desert strips because the sandy surface allowed one's wheels to slide that little bit rather than grabbing as they would on a paved surface.

I arrived on the squadron just in time for Rommel's breakthrough, which pushed us back as far as Alamein. In fact, I flew twenty minutes after I arrived—my first operational flight. Nobody had ever fired at me in anger

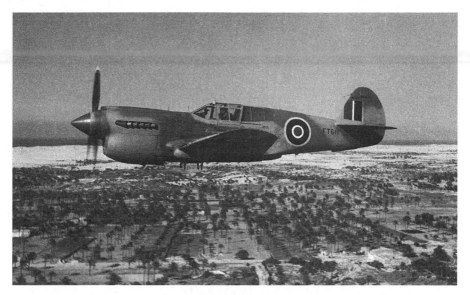

An RAF Kittyhawk Mk I (ET611) in sand-and-earth desert camouflage flying over North Africa. With no squadron designator letters or aircraft identifier, this machine was probably on delivery. The letters LD indicated 250 Squadron RAF. *DND PL15107*

before. I had only the vaguest idea of what was happening. The breakthrough caused a frantic scramble. We dropped back to a field identified only as LG91, about twenty-five miles from Alexandria, in the vicinity of El Alamein. Our backs were against the wall.

Winston Churchill came out and fired up the forces, triggering our growth into an effective Air Group. When good old Winnie showed up we got more Kittyhawks. And he arrived bombed as a billy goat! I know, because I happened to be part of the escort that brought his black Liberator in on the last stretch. We picked him up somewhere on the way from Tobruk. I guess he had been into his favourite brandy all the way from England. When he stepped out of the Lib, the first thing he said was, "I want to shake hands with the pilots who provided my escort." Well, he couldn't shake hands with all of them because most were back along his route. We were fortunate to have been the last ones, and I enjoyed the great privilege of shaking hands with Mr. Churchill. "Oh, thank you, young man," he said.

Drunk or sober, he was a brilliant man. I'm sure that when he had decisions to make, he was sober. But when he was just riding out a long, tedious trip, such as from England to Africa, he could safely afford to get drunk. In any case, he got action. From that point on, the waging of the desert war changed radically. Supplies were sent out and there was a change of command. Montgomery was put in charge and the whole thing was turned around from near disaster to a great victory.

During the retreat we did everything imaginable with a Kittyhawk. We proved it to be the most diversely capable aeroplane ever used in the desert. We provided support for RAF light bombers—Martin Baltimores and North American Mitchells. We did fighter sweeps, which was kind of silly, because if we ever did meet enemy fighters, our six Kittyhawks were likely to face twenty Messerschmitt Bf 109s. We hoped like hell we never had that experience. We also did a lot of groundwork, strafing.

Command was trying to stop supplies getting to the enemy. Rommel's supply lines were becoming increasingly extended, and the more we could disrupt them, the better. So we spent a great deal of time shooting up truck convoys and even shipping in the Mediterranean. Since there was only one road across North Africa, we didn't have to search very hard to find the trucks. If they strayed off that road they soon became stuck in the sand. However, we ran into considerable opposition from German fighters. They wanted to keep us away from their convoys as badly as we wanted to get at them. We were greatly outnumbered, and I would have to say that it was a very low point for 250 Squadron, the RAF generally, and, in fact, for all of the Allied military units there at that time. We were taking a beating. Our communications were so badly disrupted that right hands seldom knew what left hands were doing.

Communications were terrible, and so was intelligence as to where the front lines actually were. When we flew on bomber escort ops, we simply kept going until flak started to come up. That told us that somewhere down there was the enemy and the front line. The bomber crews would then have a target. It wasn't a very efficient way to operate, but that was how things were.

Our squadron was a very cosmopolitan unit made up of English, Irish, Scots, South Africans, Australians, New Zealanders, Rhodesians, one Free Frenchman, and a very few Canadians—the half-dozen from among the "thirty airscrew." It made for a group of young men truly representative of the Commonwealth. Our morale, despite the fact that we were outnumbered, outgunned, and outequipped, was very high. Possibly this could be attributed

Canadians and Americans on 250 Squadron RAF, August 1942. Front row kneeling, left to right: Mortimer, Newton, Prentice, Russell, Collier, Roberts, and Whiteside. Standing, left to right: Tribkaen, Nitz, Chambers, Chap, Martin, Edwards, Warman, Miluck, and Orr. *DND PL10053 via N. G. Russell*

to the fact that, being such a motley crowd of different nationalities, we tried harder to pull together.

After the build-up, during the Allied advance across North Africa, we resumed the same diverse types of operations. The stress remained on ground attack, mostly because the Kittyhawk had proven so effective at it. Our concentration on strafing confused and disrupted the retreating German forces. They would be packed on the roads with hundreds of trucks lined up. Whoever happened to be the leader of the formation would take the first one and, when it became a flamer, the whole road would be blocked. The vehicles behind couldn't pull around it without getting stuck in the sand. The whole convoy would grind to a stop, allowing us to pick them off one by one. I'm not trying to be bloodthirsty—that's just the way it was.

We spent a great deal of time in close support of the army, communicating by signals. They would drop a coloured mortar shell—pink, orange, or blue, the colour of the day, or even the time of day—on the spot they wanted us to hit. We would strafe it heavily. We even carried bombs, using a makeshift Rube

Goldberg sort of arrangement dreamed up by one of our engineers. This involved a little handle that we pulled to release our bombs. We carried two 250-pound bombs, one 500-pounder, or, very occasionally, six to twelve antipersonnel bombs that fragmented on impact. These were used when we were attacking troops moving on foot.

But we weren't flitting about the sky without opposition. We were engaged on many occasions by enemy fighters, Bf 109s in particular, and sometimes but not very often, by Italian Macchi MC-202s. There was also the rare Focke-Wulf Fw 190. We flew in what we termed fluid sixes. We were paired. The leader had his Number Two, then there was Three with Four and Five with Six, or whichever way we wanted to arrange the formation. The leader could concentrate on where we were going, with the other aircraft dropped back slightly, formating on him. Those at the back were the weavers, protecting our tails, and they were pretty good at it. When fights developed, and they often did, we usually ended up in fluid twos. Or we would be spread all over the sky, with each man on his own.

Our standard defensive manoeuvre, when hostile machines tried to get behind us, was an immediate tight turn. With our Kittyhawks, in any air fight, we were almost always on the defensive. Because of the roles we performed and the limitations of our aircraft, we were seldom in a position to launch an attack on another aircraft. Protecting bombers or attacking ground targets, we were almost always attacked from above and mostly out of the sun. So we flew in pairs to try and defend ourselves with one machine above and to the side of the other. The 109s always came in using the dive-and-zoom manoeuvre, to take advantage of their tremendous superiority in the climb. They came in fast, took a run at us, and then pulled up. While we had ample firepower, we didn't have much chance to use it. If we pulled the Kittyhawk's nose up and fired we would stall. After zooming, they would circle above us and come in again. Utilizing our turning circle, which was much tighter than that of the 109 and very slightly better than that of the Macchi, was an obvious tactic and an effective one.

But the Macchis were flown by Italian pilots, who preferred to perform aerobatics rather than fight aggressively. They liked to do rolls, loops, and other pretty manoeuvres. I'm not kidding! They were fine airmen, good pilots, and they had an outstanding aeroplane. But they would never press an advantage or attack with the determination the 109s displayed. Their pilots may have been kind of funny; but my goodness, could they fly! They would have been great at a CNE air show! All their manoeuvres were beautiful but had nothing to do with fighting a war.

I got on a Macchi's tail once and we covered miles of sky. He did a couple of beautiful slow rolls—his nose didn't drop one bit—they were perfect! I sat there, throttled back because he had lost a bit of speed, and waited. I couldn't hit him when he was in the middle of a slow roll. They were lovely and, if I could have talked to him on the radio, I would have congratulated him. I sat there behind him while he rolled again, the other way, to show me that he was accomplished in both directions. Then he did a loop and I followed him around, taking a couple of shots but not hitting him. Then he did another loop with a roll off the top. The roll was just the least bit sloppy, and that was when I got him. It had been the most beautiful aerobatic performance one would ever hope to see. But being realistic, in terms of air fighting it served no practical purpose whatever.

In September 1942, desert transport was whatever was available. Perched on the truck are, left to right: Cairns, Warman, Collier, Tribkaen (in cab), Edwards, and Roberts. *N. G. Russell*

The Italian Macchi MC-202 was one of the Axis aircraft that opposed 250 Squadron RAF. This captured Macchi bears a crudely applied roundel and the AN code of 417 Squadron, RCAF. *N. G. Russell*

When the 109s came in on us, we would wait for a signal from our leader, who would time it just right so that we would turn into them but would not meet them head on. Their nose cannon gave them an edge over our six .50-calibre wing guns. With their height and speed advantage, they came in very fast and shot past us. If they chose to attempt to turn with us, they would go 'way outside of us. If they persisted, with our tighter circle, we could end up on their tails. But they seldom did. It would have been a greenhorn pilot who tried it. In the Second World War a good tight turn was vital in aerial combat between fighters; the tighter you could get your turning circle, the less chance there was of your being hit. Your opponent, you hoped, would grow tired of turning outside of you and would break off. We maintained our defensive attitude until they finally climbed away and tootled off home.

I did manage to fly a captured Messerschmitt Bf 109. Our fitters had put it into flyable condition, but it sure wasn't running at its best. It was a much more stark aeroplane to sit in than our Kittyhawks. Its armament wasn't quite as good as that of the P-40. It certainly wasn't bad, and with its nose cannon, it had one decided advantage: The pilot didn't have to worry about the cone of fire as we did. The fire from our wing-mounted guns was regulated to meet at a point 80 or 180 yards in front of the aircraft. There was no such complication with their cannon, which fired straight ahead. But I didn't fly that 109 much. It had been an unserviceable machine that the Germans had left behind. In fact, it was barely flyable, and we were only put-putting around in it, just having some fun.

I flew with Squadron Leader Neville Duke of the RAF for many months in the desert. He was a great pilot and a great leader. About the Kittyhawk, he wrote, "I would say, if anything, that the Kittyhawk suffered because it was too good in too many unnecessary respects. It was over heavily built, but very strong, and as a result could take a tremendous amount of battle damage and heavy handling." You could thump it down like a ton of bricks or it could be shot up unbelievably. I remember one machine that was hit by return fire from an enemy fighter, exploding the ammunition belts. A great chunk of the wing was missing. If this had happened to a Spitfire or to any other contemporary fighter, I'm sure the wing would have come off. But the P-40 brought its pilot back.

A captured German Messerschmitt Bf 109F, typical of the aircraft that opposed the RAF's Kittyhawk Mk Is, still bearing Luftwaffe insignia and coding. Several such machines were repaired and test flown by Allied pilots. *N. G. Russell*

While the heavy construction had advantages it affected performance adversely.

As Duke said, "It was very sophisticated in equipment and instrumentation compared with the Spartan, weight-conscious British and German short-range fighters." They kept everything down to the bare minimum that was needed for flying short-range fighter missions, improving the power-to-weight ratio and thus the performance. "The P-40 was a relatively long-range fighter carrying a lot of ammunition, but without the weight saving approach in design." There were benefits both ways. I know I was mighty happy a few times when I got hammered and my Kittyhawk stayed in the air. By the same token, there were other times when I wished I could pull up and fire without going into a spin from the recoil of the guns.

The Kittyhawk "was very manoeuvrable and extremely pleasant to fly and the view all around was very good. Because of the aircraft's weight in relation to power available, the climb performance was poor. However, its dive performance and acceleration in a dive was good." In fact it was really something! You could come straight down like a bomb, and sometimes, if you were fighting at an altitude where you had a chance to use this capability, you could turn it to advantage. You could outdive a 109 or anything else the enemy had. But this wasn't normally a defensive manoeuvre we could use—our fights always took place at too low an altitude.

I did have some experience with compressibility, which occurred when one put an aircraft into a very high-speed dive. The aircraft would begin to shake furiously, to vibrate like mad and yaw badly. Most aeroplanes, including the Spitfire, behaved in this way, depending on speed.

"Whilst the Kittyhawk was basically easy to fly, it had one vice: a strong tendency to ground loop if one attempted to make a three-point landing." The problem was later partially solved by increasing the distance between the main wheels and the tailwheel. As for ground-looping, it was nothing serious. I've already explained how landing on a sandy surface allowed our wheels to skid just enough to prevent the aircraft from going over on a wing tip. But it was a difficult aeroplane to set down in a three-point landing on a hard-surfaced strip. We usually flew it on for a two-wheel landing and were careful to keep a wing down if there was a crosswind.

Having flown the Hurricane and the Tomahawk (almost a twin to the

A. W. (Al) Orr, perched on the nose of his Kittyhawk, was also a Canadian pilot with 250 Squadron RAF. At the time, Orr was credited with shooting down a Heinkel He 111 and the partial destruction of a Messerschmitt Bf 109. The photo was taken 10 April 1943. *DND PL10229*

Kittyhawk, lacking only slight changes and improvements), taking off and landing the Kittyhawk was never a problem. It was an easy aeroplane to fly, really. It didn't have serious torque and what torque it did have could be trimmed for quite easily. As with any single-engine aeroplane, torque did become heavy in a high-speed dive. It would cause the aircraft to want to go sideways. One had to develop a strong right—or was it left?—leg to keep it from getting away. But all propeller-driven fighters of the day were like that. All things considered, it was not a difficult aeroplane to fly.

When we dropped the Kittyhawk's flaps, it tipped the nose down. On approach, we used flaps on the turn-in leg, all the way; we didn't just apply them at the last minute, when we were only 100 feet up. We came in at about 100 miles per hour. Our stall speed was definitely under 100, with flaps and wheels down. On the crosswind leg, or on the turn, we always got fancy, doing the sideslip bit.

The Allison engine was a good, smooth unit. It stood up to desert conditions extremely well, better, in fact, than the Rolls-Royce Merlin. The tolerances seemed to be such that a little bit of sand in the pistons helped the Allison where it ruined the Rolls-Royce. Now that is not a fact I would swear to, but Allisons did perform very well under the worst possible conditions in terms of sand. We took off in groups of six or more abreast, which was possible because of the wide-open desert and absence of runways. But this procedure created a fantastic cloud of flying sand. The Allison ate up an awful lot of it, yet kept going.

"Due to the lack of an automatic boost control, it was easy to over boost the engine during combat and during a dive from altitude." We had to keep the throttle back or—if you allowed it to over boost for too long—you could have an engine failure. "As a gun platform the Kittyhawk was excellent and excelled in the ground attack role." It was steady and didn't tend to swish back and forth when you fired. Armament of six .50-calibre guns in the wings was effective. At the Tomahawk stage of its career, it had a couple of .50s in the top of the engine cowling firing through the propeller and only four .30s in the wings. However Curtiss dispensed with these fairly early on, when they developed the P-40E Kittyhawk. With its stability you could draw a bead on a ground target. It was there and, after you fired—it wasn't!

The Kittyhawk was too heavy and lacking in performance and agility to match the Spitfire, for instance. You flew the Spit with your fingers; the Kittyhawk you flew with your fist. It just could not match it or the 109 or the Macchi 202 in overall performance, particularly in the climb. Now I am not running down the P-40; it was a marvellous aeroplane for what it had to do and where it was at the time. Yet its only real dog-fighting asset was a tight turning circle. If we turned hard enough and kept the Kittyhawk shuddering on the stall, the Messerschmitts and Macchis just couldn't get inside for the deflection necessary to hit us.

In the desert, the Kittyhawk was a lifesaver. While in terms of overall performance, it doesn't seem to have stacked up against the opposing types, it was the principal single-engine aircraft defending the Suez Canal. That was what it boiled down to. The Kittyhawks did all of the things we asked of it, some of them exceptionally well. And it stood up amazingly to punishment.

The Kittyhawk's takeoff performance in hot desert weather was okay. Our takeoff run, while I can't remember specifically, wasn't too long—about two hundred to three hundred yards, which wasn't bad. Taking off in the desert was no more difficult than in Canada. We took off in groups because we couldn't sit around idling in that heat. We always started up one flight at a time. Our six aircraft would take off, strung across our so-called airfield—those patches of sand with oil drums around them. They had been carefully surveyed by our engineers before being selected and there were no soft spots into which a wheel might suddenly drop and cause the aeroplane to cartwheel.

If we stayed on the ground too long idling, our Allisons would overheat fairly quickly—we had to get into the air fast. We scarcely needed a warm-up period. We could almost put on full throttle immediately after start-up. We had to check our magnetos and that was it; the engines were probably already at near operating temperature just sitting there in the desert sun. It was pretty damn hot. Of course, it depended on the season. The weather could be cool, especially in winter, somewhat like our Canadian fall. And it was always cold at night.

Finding our way around the desert was not as difficult as one might expect, although we had very few landmarks such as roads, railroads, or towns, and there was nothing much but sand. The entire battle of North Africa was fought along a relatively narrow strip of land between the coast and Sahara Desert. No one could even have moved there let alone fought a war. The Qattara

Depression in the south formed a natural barrier. There was only one road, the main highway that ran all the way across North Africa.

It was two lanes of hardtop, but in pretty bad shape. And, of course, both sides had been planting mines in it or beside it. If you ever went off the road to allow another vehicle to pass, you were liable to be blown up. That road was really our only mark. If for some reason we wandered too far south, we simply flew north until we picked up the Mediterranean coast and discovered exactly where we were. We always knew where our airfield was in relation to the coast, and the road was never too far. Command had to get supplies up to us. Although we flew in gasoline and certain food items, most of our supplies came by motor transport.

I earned my DFC on a dive-bombing, strafing raid on an aerodrome at Al Dabah, near where we were stationed at the time of El Alamein. It was the closest German base and they worked it pretty hard, while we tried equally hard to slow it down. On this particular occasion, the Group Captain dreamed up the idea of going out really low over the Mediterranean—way out—and then coming in and climbing as hard as we could. By the time we reached the coast, we would be at sufficient height to roll over, dive-bomb, and strafe their field. We hoped to destroy some of their aircraft and supplies. And we did. But somehow or other, their radar picked us up, even when we were out low over the Mediterranean, and they gave us a very warm reception. In fact, they pasted the hell out of us! Consequently, we got split up. We did our strafe but ended up spread all over the country and had to straggle home alone.

Separated like that, we were very much on our own. When this occurred, our practice was to get down on the deck till the propeller was almost touching the sand. While our earth-and-sand camouflage was effective and the aircraft itself was hard to see from above, the bright African sun cast a strong shadow. So we tried to hide the shadow by tucking it under our aircraft.

On the way back, I picked up the Wing Commander who had been leading that particular show. He was being hammered by three 109s when I showed up out of nowhere. There he was and there they were! I was trying to help him and was getting shot up myself when suddenly, for some unknown reason, they broke off: they must have been out of ammunition or low on gas. By this time, turning in ever diminishing circles, I had lost the Wing Commander, so I set out due east for home.

As I skimmed low over a dune, I spotted a Kittyhawk down in the sand. It hadn't been down long; there was still a dust cloud floating away at a distance of about a quarter-mile. The pilot was out and waving his arms furiously. "Boy," I thought, "here's my chance for the big DFC. I'll pick him up!" It had become almost automatic: if one picked up a downed pilot in the desert under these circumstances, it seemed as a matter of course that a DFC would arrive with our next allotment of "V" cigarettes.

It wasn't an easy thing to do. I would have to land in uncertain sand, lower the seat, throw away his parachute, settle him on my lap and get the aircraft off the ground again. And I could never be sure of the sand, of just how soft it might be. Then, with two of us squeezed into the cockpit, I would have to fly back. I'm not sure, but I think it had been done more than once.

I went down and did a little test. I dropped my wheels and ran them along the sand, just touching it. It felt good and looked good. I came around on a last little turn with my wheels and flaps down. I was just settling onto the ground when WHAM! I was hit by bullets from all over the place! I hadn't been keeping a lookout. Concentrating on getting down, I suddenly found myself being hammered by three 109s. Was it the same three from my previous scrape? I didn't know. But, sure as hell, they were there! They knocked the daylights out of me and set me on fire. Fortunately it was only a small fire that burned for about ten minutes and then went out. It made a helluva lot of smoke and luckily not much else. I was hit in my hip by some cannon shell fragments. I thought for sure I was going to need an amputation if I got back. Luckily, it turned out to be nothing much and, in fact, was embarrassing. The doctor had me bend over while, with a pair of tweezers, he picked bits of metal out of you can guess where.

That was the end of my attempt to pick up our downed pilot. Happily, and to my great relief, these fellows did the same thing as the previous 109s. They pulled up into a neat, tight formation and went home. For some unknown reason they let up when they had a sitting duck situation—three 109s against one shot-up Kittyhawk. Their tactics had been the standard dive-and-zoom with me doing the tight-turn bit. While they had hit me, they obviously knew I wasn't down. Again, maybe they were low on fuel, ammunition, or both. And the Wing Commander did get back. He was shot full of holes, but he got back.

On our rare fighter sweeps we did have some freedom of movement, but we very seldom fought as fighter against fighter. And we were never aware of the identities of any of the opposing pilots. While we had all heard of Adolph Galland, we never knew any of the individuals flying those 109s. It was an impersonal thing—we never related to the pilot in the other aeroplane. We were trying to shoot down the machine, not the man in it. That was certainly my feeling and probably that of most pilots. If the enemy pilot happened to get killed, that was tough luck. If he bailed out, then good luck to him. He might even be back tomorrow shooting at me!

When we were sent out to protect a group of bombers, we had to use restraint—no scurrying off and getting into fights. We simply tried to drive attackers off and then get back into our protective positions.

Weather was seldom a problem. While there were occasional freak rainstorms—which you might think rather strange in the desert—they came once in a blue moon. They were a flash thing, with apparently tons of water coming down. Our camp or a neighbouring village might be flooded. But an hour later there would be little indication of what had happened. The water just disappeared into that big blotter that was the desert.

Sandstorms were a problem, and they could extend up to 10,000 feet— seemingly of almost solid sand. We had to use guide ropes to get around camp, from our tents to the mess tent where we ate Spam garnished with sand dressing. Without a rope it would have been easy to get lost and just wander off into desert.

We could see such a storm coming, like a huge dark wall. As far as I know, no one in our fighter group was ever caught in one. But one could escape from sandstorms by flying out of them. They seemed to be a kind of front that moved in one direction. If we were flying faster than it was moving, we would escape it. Again, I've never heard of any pilots who had that experience, although it must have happened.

In my military flying career, I had four force-landings and one bailout. I was shot down five times in all. What was it like to crash land in the desert? Perfect! If I picked the right spot, I could slide in, wheels up, and I would only bend the prop. Maybe that was why we needed all those airscrews. We would never drop the wheels unless we were trying to pick somebody up. There was no point endangering your life if your aeroplane was dead anyway. Since landing in the sand was so easy, you might as well take the safe, wheels-up way.

Jim Collier of 250 Squadron RAF with his Curtiss P-40E Kittyhawk Mk I, fitted with a 250-pound bomb. The diving hawk insignia, inspired by the label on a beer can, was soon to be joined by a more glamorous Scheherazade painted by Flight Lieutenant Collier, an art school graduate. *DND PL10228*

When I was shot down, I hadn't seen anything coming. I was busy trying to get behind an enemy when I was hit from behind. My Number Two had been diverted. Someone attacked him, leaving me with no one to yell "Hey! Look out! There's somebody up your tail!" All of a sudden, I was hit, but it was in the engine and not that serious. This happened to me a couple of times. The fan up front stopped going around, obliging me to force-land and walk back from behind the German lines. On the other two occasions in Africa, I was fortunate to be over our side—just enough. The final two times, I was shot down flying Spitfires over Europe.

The instance when I had to walk back from enemy territory makes an interesting story. I returned about thirty-five miles, hiking across the desert at night and laying low in the camel scrub during the day, covered with sand. I had lots of water, two bottles in the aircraft and a third on my hip, as well as an escape kit. I wasn't terribly uncomfortable—maybe a little hot. I had an evader's compass made from a couple of buttons which I put one on top of the other. It told me where north was. I didn't navigate by the stars—I couldn't read them. But I could read the little slot on that button. I didn't attempt to move during the day because I stood out like a signpost—a little black figure walking across the desert—visible for miles and miles. The Germans couldn't have missed me. But in the cool of the night I could walk.

Any of our aircraft shot down in the desert were salvaged if at all possible. As I've said, my Kittyhawk was fairly far in, but we were well up around Tunis, moving quite quickly, so it was only a matter of a day or two before the Army had covered the thirty-five miles I had just had to walk. A salvage crew was able to pick up my Kittyhawk and put it on a trailer. Fitted with a new fan and plugs—they had been shot off, causing my engine failure—my machine was flyable. I don't think they even bothered to repair the few scratches on the bottom.

Our amusements were simple. Australians, New Zealanders, Englishmen, South Africans, and Canadians, we would all get together and get smashed in a convenient bar. There might or might not be a fight, the bar might get broken up or it might not, just like the movies. We didn't do anything particularly unusual.

Everyone has seen pictures of No. 112 Squadron's Tomahawks and Kittyhawks with shark mouths painted on the front. They were the only ones in our wing who sported this device. Chennault's Flying Tigers later used the same decoration on their P-40s in the Far East. Most people think that the shark-mouth design originated in China with the American Volunteer Group. The AVG pilots had simply seen pictures of 112's aircraft, taken in North Africa, and adopted the design. Hollywood got to China first with the film *God Is My Co-Pilot* based on the book by AVG pilot Colonel Robert L. Scott.

We in 250 envied them the glamour of having those ferocious shark teeth on their machines. So we painted other crazy things like skulls and such on ours. My own machine bore a representation of Scheherazade, the Sultan's beautiful mistress in *One Thousand and One Nights,* who kept herself alive by telling him a new story on each of 1,001 successive nights.

I was tour expired, after 201 hours and 15 minutes, on 1 June 1942, almost a year after I joined the squadron. My operational flying, which made up that total, didn't include air tests, practice flying, or any other kind of flying that

Group Command didn't consider to be operations against the enemy. I had leave from 1 June until the twenty-fourth, when I joined 73 Operational Training Unit (OTU), located at Abu Sueir, Egypt, almost on the Suez Canal, halfway between Cairo and Alexandria. It was a peacetime RAF station and boy, was it posh living. It had been there for years and years, and they had everything. I became an instructor on combat flying. The students in my classes were a changing mixture of Turks, Egyptians, New Zealanders, English, and South Africans. I was there until 1 December.

At that time, I was very fortunate in coming under a new policy that had just been introduced. After a tour of operations and a tour of instructing, I became eligible for thirty-days leave in Canada, excluding travel time. Even if it took us two months to get home, I still got thirty-days leave.

A Spitfire Pilot's Story

"You Flew Most Aeroplanes, But You Wore the Spitfire"

BILL MCRAE, FLIGHT LIEUTENANT RCAF (RET'D)

B ill McRae was one of the fortunate few who succeeded in achieving the dream of most young airmen of sixty years ago: to become a fighter pilot and fly Spitfires. Born in Aberdeen, Scotland, he came to Port Arthur (now Thunder Bay) in Northern Ontario as an infant and grew up there. Enlisting at the Lakehead, he was sent to Brandon, Manitoba, Manning Pool. He did his guard duty and marching at Portage la Prairie, where the station was still under construction. He was among the first airmen in town. Initial Training School (ITS) at Regina came next, and then back to No. 14 Elementary Flying Training School (EFTS) at Portage, operated by the Winnipeg Flying Club with Tiger Moths—and civilian instructors, as was the case at most EFTS fields. For advanced training, Bill was posted to Camp Borden on Harvards and Yales.

His trip overseas—in May of 1941, on a peacetime banana boat, the SS *Nicoya*—was an adventurous one. The convoy was attacked by U-boats and, of thirty-one ships, nine were lost. Four young airmen were passengers on the *Nicoya,* but only Bill McRae would survive the war.

In England, Bill completed his training at an Operational Training Unit in Wales, flying elderly Spitfires, followed by an operational posting to 132 Squadron, then forming at Peterhead in Scotland. About a year after his arrival in the U.K. he found himself sailing for South Africa aboard the battleship HMS *Nelson*. Eventually he arrived at Takoradi in West Africa, where he would spend almost a year ferrying Hurricanes across Central Africa to RAF units in the Middle East.

Returning to the U.K. for a second tour, he was almost immediately posted to 401 Squadron, RCAF, flying Spitfire Vs. His harrowing convoy experience

91

still fresh in mind, not receiving the customary leave in Canada did not bother him. With his new squadron, he flew bomber escort ops, occasional sweeps into France, and various other assignments. When 401 re-equipped with Spitfire IXs, they began experimenting with dive-bombing techniques. At this point, Bill picks up the story—a few months before 401 moved to an airfield at Beny-sur-Mer in France, just behind the Allied lines.

After the war, before leaving the RCAF, Bill flew a Norseman on mapping operations in the Canadian North with 413 Photographic Survey Squadron. Returning to civilian life, he embarked on a career with Canadian Industries Limited, representing their Explosives Division. His love of flying led him to buy a sleek little Globe Swift—not a Spitfire, but still a lively performer.

The final days of February 1944 were filled with escort jobs. On two occasions, we picked 800 USAAF Fortresses returning from Germany, and what an impressive sight it was with this many machines leaving vapour trails against a clear winter sky! It must have been a fearsome sight for the German people. During the first week of March 1944, we escorted 108 USAAF Marauders to bomb the Laon airfield. We also escorted home 800 to 900 Fortresses and took another 108 Marauders for a second visit to Creil marshalling yards, a key rail junction not far from Paris which had the distinction of being the most-bombed marshalling yard in France.

This last trip produced some action. I was flying Number Two to Jack ("Shep") Sheppard, 'A' Flight Commander, with Bill ("Gristle") Klersy Number Three. I can't recall who was Number Four. Shep spotted a Focke-Wulf Fw 190 flying at ground level near Beaumont-sur-Oise. We dived down and soon caught it, Shep and I closing in while Gristle covered from above. Skimming the treetops, with me on his right and almost line abreast, Sheppard closed to about one hundred yards directly behind the Fw before he began firing. He must have been overtaking too fast, because he suddenly throttled back and for a moment I was slightly ahead of him. I saw that by turning in a few degrees I could get a small-angle deflection shot. Turning slightly toward the 190, I got him in my sights and was about to press the gun button when he suddenly decelerated—either from Shep's fire or in an attempt to cause us to overshoot. Sheppard, now in imminent danger of collision, banked steeply in my direction. To avoid Shep, I was forced to turn steeply away. Swinging back, I was just in time to see the 190 hit the ground at high speed, in a flat attitude, as if it was trying to do a wheels-up landing. It bounced back into the air. The engine tore out and flew off on its own. Then the rest of the machine hit the ground and exploded.

Klersy started to rejoin us, then called out that he had spotted another low-flying Fw 190, and the four of us gave chase. Gristle reached it first, and we watched while he destroyed this one in much the same manner as Sheppard had the first. We climbed back to rejoin the rest of the squadron, still covering the bombers, just in time to be bounced by about a dozen Messerschmitt Bf 109s. After two of them were damaged by Cameron and Cummings they took cover in clouds and we lost them. This was a rewarding and exciting trip, but once again I had had no chance to fire my guns.

During the first week of April we were doing "practice" patrols over invasion ships, probably actual invasion units being moved south from shipyards farther north.

Bill McRae sits in the cockpit of his Spitfire Mk V at RAF Redhill in June 1943, waiting for the start-up signal. A member of his ground crew rests on the wing. The apparent white stain on the cowling is nose art, rare on a 401 Squadron RCAF aircraft.
W. R. McRae

Then we were told to pack our things; we were moving to Tangmere, but first we were off for a dive-bombing course. With only a change of clothing and our razors stuffed into the Spitfire wing panels, the squadron went to Fairwood Common in South Wales, not far from Swansea. For five days we continuously practised dive-bombing and low-level bombing.

We bombed with 12-pound smoke bombs, hung from a rack beneath the belly, diving at a target about fifty feet square anchored out to sea. With the procedure we were required to follow, the target was no longer visible when the bomb was released. In my opinion this was ineffectual. We went into the dive from a half-roll, or wing-over, lining up the gun sight with the target. When we were ready to drop, we pulled the nose of the aircraft slightly through the target, simultaneously releasing the bomb. This was necessary to avoid having the bomb hit the propeller, or so we were told. I recall hitting the target once on the course. But there is only one entry in my logbook recording any hits by anyone

At RAF Staplehurst, Kent, in August 1943, 401 pilots relax around their 100-octane heater. Seated, left to right: Evans, Stevens, Tew, Studholme, McRae, Wing Commander Keith Hodgson, Saunders. Standing, left to right: Kelly, Sheppard, Klersy, Hayward, Bishop, Maybee, Buckles, LAC Pudge (ground crew), Squadron Leader "Jeep" Neal. *RCAF via W. R. McRae*

on operational targets; on 9 May we claimed eight good hits on a Noball north of Le Touquet.

I arrived at Tangmere on 18 April flying the Auster with Doc Jones, the squadron doctor, and Dinghy, his dog, as passengers. The tents had been set up for us, ready to move in. The next day we went on our first operational dive-bombing trip, our first experience carrying a 500-pounder. The target was a Noball ten miles northwest of St. Pol. As I had been doing on the practice drops, I half-rolled from about 10,000 feet and picked up the target, trimming to keep pressure off the control column. At about 3,000 feet, I began the pull-out and released my bomb (I thought). Then I needed all my strength, plus full nose-up trim, to recover from the dive, blacking out as I did so. I believe the V_{ne} for the Spitfire was supposed to be around 450 mph but a quick glance at the airspeed indicator in the dive had shown well over this.

After everyone had bombed, we set out for home, and I noticed several of the others banking and skidding around. I thought they were looking for something on the ground, but I could see nothing down there so thought nothing more of it. When we got back I asked about this and was told, "Oh, we were just looking to see where your bomb hit. It was hung up and fell off on the way out." Had it not fallen off, I wondered if they would have told me before I landed!

This was the first of several potentially dangerous situations I experienced arising from bomb-carrying with this particular aircraft. Initially, if unable to drop our bomb, our orders were to head back to England, point the machine out to sea, then bail out. After a couple of our pilots did this, I guess the powers that be decided it was wasteful and we were now instructed to bring the bomb back.

We continued to escort bombers as well as dive-bomb on our own. On 27 April, while bombing a bridge on the Cherbourg peninsula, we had our first dive-bombing casualty. I had made my run and was circling to watch Bill Cummings make his dive. He went into the dive normally, but then appeared to steepen up to absolutely vertical, even past the vertical. With a strange feeling of detachment I watched as he continued on straight into the ground.

Later, when we moved to France, Bob Hayward found the remnants of the machine, and Cummings's grave. From the evidence Bob found it is almost certain that this incident was the result of a phenomenon yet unknown, at least to us, the effect that very high speeds had on the elevator controls of the Spitfire. At the time we believed that Cummings had been hit by flak and rendered unable to recover, but another incident soon gave us reason for concern.

On the next dive-bombing show, Gerry Billing made his dive in the manner I have described, released his bomb, then found himself unable to pull out. He tried everything he could think of, to no avail. Finally in desperation he applied full rudder, regaining control in a violent skid as he was flying through the debris from the bursting bombs. He managed to get home, badly shaken and with an aircraft twisted beyond further use.

Following this incident and the investigation that followed, we changed the dive procedure. I no longer trimmed the pressure off in the dive; instead I held the machine in the dive with sheer force. Then, after dropping the bomb, I released the forward pressure on the control column. The stick slammed back into my stomach and I would momentarily black out. When I recovered, my machine was hanging on the prop back at the starting level. Rather drastic, but this was better than flying into the ground. A subsequent study made mention of these harsh elevator movements as the probable cause of wing wrinkling and in some cases structural failure.

There were disturbing rumours going around about Spitfires shedding ailerons in the dive. We were told that, at extremely high speeds, the trailing edge of both ailerons tended to lift, not differentially as they were designed to do for normal control, but both together. Travel beyond a certain limit would tear them off, with drastic results. To provide us with a means of determining this failure point, white and yellow lines were painted on the inboard chord of the ailerons. With the control column centred, the white line would usually appear during the dive. If the yellow line appeared we were in the danger zone, and should reduce speed. At the same time we were supposed to keep on target—and make sure we didn't fly into the ground!

Probably recognizing that our 500-pounders were not penetrating concrete buildings, we were given the task of testing 1,000-pounders. Bob Hayward got the job and I went along, formating on him in the dive to observe the results. Instead of falling clear when released, the bomb seemed to turn 90 degrees, then tumble along the belly of the aircraft as it passed over. When Bob landed, the underside of his machine was crushed almost back to the tailwheel. That ended the experiment as far as we were concerned.

Bill McRae in front of a cannon on a Spitfire Mk V at RAF Biggin Hill in the winter of 1943–44. *RCAF via W. R. McRae*

Toward the end of April, 127 Canadian Wing with 403, 416, and 421 Squadrons under the leadership of Wing Commander Lloyd Chadburn joined us at Tangmere. With as many as seventy-two Spitfires in the air at one time it made the circuit interesting. Throughout May, the wing continued to dive-bomb various targets. On one of these, Squadron Leader Norm Fowlow, leading 411 Squadron, blew up in the dive, having either put his bomb through the prop or had the bomb hit by flak.

I had my final showdown with my tank and bomb-rack problem on 19 May. The target was a railway junction near Dieppe. Because of the proximity of Dieppe, and the exposure to its flak batteries had we climbed back to altitude, our usual tactics were changed. Instead of climbing we were to continue on down in the dive, crossing the coast at ground level. I went into my dive in the usual way, released my bomb, or so I thought, and kept diving to just clear the cliffs and level out over the water. I ignored the light flak coming from Dieppe, but all of a sudden there was a tremendous updraft. Looking over my shoulder, I saw a huge waterspout directly behind me, where I had been a second before. I thought they must be lobbing really heavy stuff at us from Dieppe, but we were soon well clear and I forgot about it.

When we got back, my Number Two told me what had happened. It was not flak; my bomb had hung up again, and as I levelled out sharply just off the water, it had fallen off and exploded.

That did it. I went storming to the Engineering Officer demanding that something be done, a new aircraft or something. What I got was a plunger, a rod sticking through the floor with a knob on the end. I was supposed to stamp my foot on it and literally kick off the hang-up! That is assuming some-one told me it was hung up. I thought this Rube Goldberg remedy was con-ceived for me alone, but I learned later that this was a common solution to a problem not unique to me. Fortunately I never had to use this contraption. Ten days later Spitfire 'L' was pulled off the line. It would be the eve of the inva-sion before I got another 'L'-coded Spitfire.

On 20 May, we were on a low-level sweep across northern France, looking for trains. It was a hazy day with poor visibility. Suddenly, looming out of the haze a bit to our left and slightly below rose a tall, ghostly white shape. As we got closer and passed it I realized it was the Vimy Ridge Memorial. I felt a wave of emotion, looking down on that bit of France where so many Canadians had given their lives two years before I was born. I was brought out of my reverie with a start when an 88-mm shell burst just above and ahead of me. There was a thunk as a piece of it ripped a long gash in the panel over my port cannon magazine. Jerry was letting us know that he was once again in possession of Vimy Ridge.

I won't forget 3 June, for Fate spared me that day. I was still waiting for a new 'L' and had been assigned another machine for a sweep over the Cherbourg peninsula and the area where U.S. paratroops would be landing three days hence. I was strapped in and ready to go when Cy Cohen, who would be flying as my Number Two, came over to ask if I would switch aircraft, since the one I had was normally his. I said sure and we switched. The sweep was uneventful, and we were on our way back across the channel at low altitude when Cy called that his engine had quit. When I looked around he was gone. We all turned back and searched for as long as we had fuel. Although there was a green patch on the water from the dye in his Mae West, there was no sign of him. Perhaps he had bailed out too low, or had been unable to get out. There was no parachute on the water. Looking down on that green patch sent shivers up my spine. It should have been me.

A sure sign of an impending move to France was our move out of the tents so that they could be prepared for transport. We could now enjoy a short spell of relative luxury in the permanent mess at Tangmere. An even surer sign was a visit from General Eisenhower, who gave us a disappointingly uninspiring pep talk. On 5 June I tested my new Spitfire, coded YO-L, just in time for it to be painted with the black-and-white invasion stripes for my first trip on D-Day, the following morning.

After dark that night we could hear wave after wave of heavy bombers droning over us on the way to France and also the unmistakable sound of Dakotas. This meant paratroops or gliders. I was awakened about 3 A.M. by a WAAF bringing me a cup of tea—we never got that service in our tents! Due to the rotation system, I was not on the first trip, but I was on the second patrol of the morning. Enough has been said elsewhere about the unforgettable sight of the invasion fleet and the hundreds of aircraft filling the sky. It seems incomprehensible that Hitler could have believed this mighty effort was only a feint, and that the Allies could have a similar or larger fleet in reserve for the real thing farther north

Throughout the Normandy campaign, our operations were categorized as either beachhead patrol or armed reconnaissance. The former initially meant patrolling over the actual battle area; later they were usually flown on the enemy side of the lines. All were intended to intercept any attempt by the Luftwaffe to penetrate the territory we held. But of course we would also attack ground targets if they presented themselves. At first these patrols were in wing strength, later reduced to squadron strength. Finally, after we moved to France, we patrolled as four-man sections, maintaining continuous coverage from dawn to dusk.

Armed reconnaissance was basically the same as our old sweep, except that our primary target now was anything that moved on the ground. We flew as a squadron, with one section attacking the target while the rest covered.

My four hours over the beach on D-Day came as a sort of anticlimax, since the Luftwaffe failed to appear. We were over the Canadian and British beaches and from what we could see things were going well, with tank engagements well inland toward Caen.

Bill McRae with his Spitfire Mk IX at RAF Tangmere in England in May 1944, shortly before moving to the continent. *W. R. McRae*

On the second day the weather was bad, with a solid low overcast at about 2,000 feet. Our wing had been cruising back and forth in the St. Aubin area for some time, over the Canadian beachhead, and our time was just about up. Swivelling my head around to watch my back, something caught my eye; it was a Ju 88 which had just popped out of the clouds behind us. I called out to Cameron, who began to turn the squadron around just as the Junkers hit a ship's balloon cable and crashed into the sea.

Then about a dozen more bombers emerged from the cloud and attempted to bomb the beaches. I found myself directly behind a machine that looked vaguely like a Short Stirling, but with only two engines and German markings. I was familiar with the Junkers Ju 88, and this was not one. Then I realized it was a Heinkel He 177, a type we had not encountered before, but which was later used extensively for night attacks on the beachhead. This machine had four engines mounted in coupled pairs in two nacelles. Similar in appearance to the Ju 88, it was much larger, having a wingspan of 102 feet.

I was less than two hundred yards away and it looked like a sure thing. Placing my gun sight on the wing between the left engine and crew's glasshouse, I pressed the gun button. I had no sooner done so when I had to release it. An American Thunderbolt shot out of the clouds ahead, narrowly missing me. I suppose he had followed the bomber down through the clouds. I watched helplessly as he fired his six .50-calibre machine guns and the German went down. I was furious; I had waited three years for this opportunity, only to be robbed by an American who was not supposed to be in this area.

The sky was now a jumble of aircraft. With at least thirty-six Spitfires and possibly twelve Thunderbolts, all chasing about a dozen Germans in the confined space between cloud and balloons, it was a miracle there were no collisions. When we got back to Tangmere and tallied the score, it was 401 six, 412 three, Americans one (at least), and balloons one. Few if any of the bombers escaped, and it would be a glum dinner table in the German mess that night. They certainly had a lot of guts, pressing on with an attack without fighter protection in the middle of that hornets' nest.

My next trip was on D+4, covering Stirlings and Halifaxes dropping supplies by parachute. That evening we went on an armed reconnaissance of the Chartres/Evreux area, carrying a bomb. Finding no targets, we brought the bombs back for our first landing in France at B-1 near Courselles, one of the two refuel and re-arm strips the engineers had laid down. Johnny Johnson's wing had been the first to land there that morning; we were the second wing to land in France. Carrying a bomb, I took great care to make a very good landing on this hastily prepared steel mesh runway. Enough cannot be said for the planning and dedication of the engineers who had bulldozed this strip. They laid down the matting and brought in a supply of long-range tanks and Jerry cans of fuel in only three days following the first man stepping ashore. Here we put on drop tanks and took off on another trip, from which we would return to Tangmere.

We continued carrying out patrols from Tangmere until 20 June, when we moved permanently to B-4 airfield at Beny-sur-Mer. Just prior to leaving Tangmere we had our first look at the weapon we had been attacking for months, the Noball, now called V-1 or buzz-bomb. I stood and watched several buzzing their way toward London. This was a terrible weapon because it was indiscriminate in its target. Aimed roughly at London, it flew until the engine quit, then dived straight down. When the sound died you looked for cover if it was near, because the blast effect was extensive.

Beny-sur-Mer was about two miles from the beach and eight miles from the line in front of Caen. We found our tents already set up in a line, with a larger mess tent at one end and the usual primitive latrine and shower facilities right out in front. Behind our line of tents was a stone wall, behind which was a newly started cemetery. Our first chore was to set up our cots, four to a tent. The first night we realized that something would have to be done to protect ourselves against the red-hot fragments of our own flak that came raining down on us.

The Germans were dropping flares to illuminate the beachhead in an attempt to find targets to bomb, and this brought a fierce response from our anti-aircraft gunners. One of my tent-mates and I took the truck to a former German radar post and removed a number of long 2 x 10 planks. We dug a trench in the floor of our tent, lowered the canvas beds into it, head to head, then laid the planks across the top. On top of this we put sandbags. The whole set-up covered each of us from head to shins. With this arrangement we had no trouble sleeping, even with the flak sizzling down, sometimes through the tent.

Beer was almost nonexistent on the beachhead, and whisky was rationed.

The beer problem was soon solved when someone got the idea of flying it across from England in an unused drop tank, then siphoning it into a barrel in France. This worked until someone used the tank for gasoline. Then the armourers managed to fasten the barrel itself on the bomb rack. This arrangement worked well, until one day a reporter from the London tabloid the *Daily Mirror* saw it and used it as a front-page story. Soon after, orders came down: no more beer flights to Britain. We would have killed that reporter had he ever shown his face again, but of course we ignored the order.

Our first trip from Beny was to dive-bomb a couple of bridges on the east side of the Orne, following which Scotty Murray destroyed a staff car. There followed patrols and armed recces and on the twenty-fifth a squadron scramble. Enemy fighters were reported around Caen but faded into the clouds at our approach. The weather was terrible, completely overcast with about a 400-foot ceiling, and we almost got ourselves tangled in the balloons off the beach on our return.

The eight 401 Squadron RCAF pilots who each shot down an enemy aircraft in a dogfight with more than a dozen Bf 109s and Fw 190s over Beny-sur-Mer, France, on 27 July 1944. Left to right: Squadron Leader Charlie Trainor (on his first mission leading 401), Johnson, Havers, McRae, Halcrow, Bell, Morrison, and Wyman. *RCAF via W. R. McRae*

Several of the landing craft had been sunk just offshore, with their balloons still flying, anchored to the sunken hulks. When the cloud was this low the balloons were in the clouds and their cables invisible. Eventually we got permission to shoot them down.

There was another squadron scramble on the twenty-seventh. Wing Commander George Keefer was leading the squadron, with me as his Number Two, and Cameron was leading one of the flights. We were hardly off the ground when we saw about fifteen Bf 109s near Caen. They took to their heels with us in pursuit. Our throttles had been kept wide open since takeoff, but with the head start they had we were closing very slowly.

One by one, the squadron started dropping off, and I thought they were having engine trouble because of the hard run. Finally there were just Keefer, Cameron, and me in the chase. Then I heard a bang and my engine slowed down appreciably; I figured my supercharger had gone. I had been keeping close to Keefer, but now I could not keep up and was starting to fall back when he must have decided to give up before we ran out of fuel—we had no drop tanks. He called to say he was turning back, but before doing so, he let go a long shot at a lone straggler well behind the main bunch but still about six hundred yards ahead of us. To my surprise, and probably George's, the 109 began to smoke and the pilot bailed out. This was a testament to the usefulness of the new gyro gunsight. Cameron didn't seem to hear the recall, because he kept going.

Later, as Keefer and I were on our way home, we heard him on the radio calling for help, but there was nothing we could do. The 109s had turned on him when they saw they were being followed by only one madman, and he was circling as tightly as he could at treetop height while they each in turn had a shot at him. Finally they gave up. He could see them landing at a nearby field, probably Beauvais. Although I noticed no flak on that trip, we later discovered that every one of our machines had been hit one place or another.

Some sources give the impression that there was no opposition from the Luftwaffe in France, but this was not entirely the case. Formations all the way from twelve to forty were not unusual, with the larger formations usually stepped up above each other at different heights. It is true that they were not encountered on every trip, and it was pure chance what type of a show we had. We could come back from a trip that was entirely uneventful, except for the flak that was omnipresent. Then another section would go out to essentially the same area we had just left and run into hordes of Germans. In one such incident, the squadron was busy shooting up transports when it was bounced by twelve Fw 190s. In the fight that followed four 190s were destroyed, but we lost two of our own. One was our 'A' Flight Commander, Scotty Murray, who bailed out and managed to evade capture. He was replaced by "Hap" Kennedy, a Malta veteran with twelve victories to his credit.

With the small area of the bridgehead and the proliferation of airfields in it, there were almost too many aircraft. On one patrol I chased formations that turned out to be Spits, Typhoons, Mustangs, and Thunderbolts, but saw no Jerries. That same day, on other patrols, the wing shot down a total of thirteen, of which 401 got six. With aircraft dodging in and out of cloud it was necessary to use restraint and be absolutely sure of your target. But this was not always the case, and our first pilot killed in France was shot down by the Americans.

From the moment of our first landing in France, dust had been a real problem. The single runway had been bulldozed out of a wheat field, and the steel mesh covering it kept us from sinking into the mud when it rained—and it rained often. But when the sun came out, the area became a dust bowl, and gun stoppages were becoming serious. The armourers had their work cut out finding a covering material to keep the dust from infiltrating through the empty cartridge ejection chute and yet give way when the empties were ejected.

The single taxi-track was too narrow to allow the usual zigzag taxi procedure and there was a rash of accidents with aircraft taxiing into the one ahead. Eventually, this problem was solved by having an airman ride the wing to give hand signals as we taxied out and back.

There was little to do at Beny-sur-Mer except work and sleep. We did on occasion get out to one of the village cafés, where wine and very young Calvados, the local brandy, were available. The cafés were usually filled with Army types, who now recognized the value of the Air Force. Usually one of them would come over and ask what we flew, and of course we answered "Typhoons." This brought an immediate drink on the Army! They appreciated the great job the Typhoon pilots were doing in attacking German ground targets. From our field we could see them climbing for height, then a short distance beyond we could often see them going into their dive. Their trips were very brief, very frequent, and very dangerous. I take my hat off to them.

We were never better informed than we were in Normandy. Monty Berger and his deputy, Flying Officer Stewart, had set up the Intelligence tent near our dispersal area. This had the usual easel and blackboard on which the day's operations were displayed. Each day he had the latest front-line information shown on the map in red to give us a rough idea of where things stood and how the battle was progressing. In actual fact it was virtually impossible for us to determine from the air where our territory ended and the Germans' began. There was no front line as in the First World War. Even the presence or absence of flak could not be taken as a guide, since both sides often fired at anybody who got too close.

One day we were all grouped around Monty, listening to his spiel, when the ground began to shiver slightly, then the easel began to rock, and finally the blackboard crashed to the ground. We all thought "air raid" and were rushing out of the tent just as the first huge bang hit our ears. Another pilot and I eyed a large pile of dirt near the tent, which we figured had come from a slit trench. Both together we dived over the pile to land in a little hollow about six inches deep. We both thought it so funny that we couldn't stop laughing. Getting to our feet we could see that, if it was an air raid, it was not on us. Some distance down the road from our field we could see an immense mushroom cloud of smoke.

We learned later that an ammunition dump had gone up; they were in just about every available space not otherwise occupied. Apparently they were unloading and piling German mines that had been cleared, when one detonated. This set off the pile, which in turn set off piles of other things. It was quite a show. Flying Officer Stewart had just passed the spot before it blew. As the other pilots began to emerge, we saw that several had dived under the gasoline bowser, about the last place I would want to be in a raid!

On 1 July, I was out with Hap Kennedy, Gerry Billing, and one other, patrolling the Bayeux-Carentan area of the American front. There was a sudden flurry of flak, and Gerry began to stream glycol. We saw him crash land in what looked like tall grass on the German side, and while we didn't see what happened to him after he got down, we had good reason to believe he was okay. Moving a little farther west we finished out the patrol.

On the second, we dive-bombed a bridge near Caen. After I bombed, we were jumped by Bf 109s, and the rest of our bombs were jettisoned. Hap and Gristle each caught and destroyed a 109. Later that day it was another armed recce in the Falaise area, where half a dozen trucks were destroyed amid a hail of flak. The following day, the Boss was brought down in the same area, doing the same job.

With Hap Kennedy now promoted to Squadron Leader after only a week or two as Flight Commander, and Klersy replacing him as Flight Commander, we were out again later the same day to cover a flight of medium bombers while they pulverized Villers-Bocage where the Germans were blocking the advance.

The seventh was a dull day with a solidly overcast sky. I was leading Yellow Section, flying my usual machine, 'L' (MK560), on the second of two four-man patrols I had led that day, with a newly arrived pilot named Horsburgh as my Number Two, Tony Williams Number Three, and Art Bishop Number Four. After about an hour patrolling the area north and east of Caen we were returning to base at 5,000 feet, about 500 feet below the cloud base.

Suddenly twelve-plus Bf 109s, flying in line abreast, slipped out of the cloud almost directly over our heads, going in the opposite direction. Two seconds earlier and we would have met head on. I had a gut feeling that this formation was not alone and hesitated a few seconds before turning our backs on a possible second group, then wheeled my section around and went after the 109s that had passed us. We had not been seen, obviously, since they continued to cruise blissfully along in line abreast at reduced speed, and we were soon within three hundred yards of them. With this gut feeling still bothering me I called back to base to have them scramble a second section.

We were at two hundred yards, directly behind and slightly below, when I called for each man to pick his target and then opened fire at the Jerry I had lined up. Immediately they all broke hard left, putting themselves in a sort of line-astern formation. I rolled in behind my target and got him lined up for a large-angle deflection shot. With the bead of the gyro gun sight on his left wing root, I opened fire with all my guns. With this first burst, three seconds according to the camera gun record, I could see my cannon shells exploding at the wing root and up the side of the fuselage ahead of the cockpit, but he continued to hold his tight turn. I fired another short burst, and this time the flash of cannon strikes went up the side of the fuselage and into the cockpit area. Large pieces were shed, a flicker of flame showed, and he snap-rolled out of the turn and went down in a right-hand spin, trailing flame.

I let him go because now there was a second one directly in front of me, but at long range, frantically trying to reach the safety of the cloud base. I knew I couldn't close before he disappeared, so I let off another three-second burst just as he reached the cloud. I followed him into the cloud, turning out a few degrees so I wouldn't collide with him. The cloud was not very thick and I soon came out on top, where I circled in the slim hope that one of them might make a mistake and show himself. But they were adept at using cloud cover for escaping, and in this instance they succeeded.

My section had not followed me through, so after checking the fuel situation, I ordered them back to base and followed on my own. When I got back, Williams and Bishop confirmed seeing my 109 spin in and crash near Lisieux; the pilot did not bail out. I was relieved to have this confirmation, without which I likely would not have been credited, because the camera gun film showed an aircraft at a large deflection angle and close range, but not the hits.

My hunch had also proven right. The section of four scrambled at my request ran into about twenty Bf 109s and Fw 190s near Lisieux. Sinclair went after a 109 at low level and chased it into the side of a hill, where it blew up without his firing a shot. This section also claimed an Fw 190.

It was no secret how desperate I had become for a "victory." Oddly, I felt no elation at this success, only a great feeling of relief that the drought was finally over. I could understand how a professional hockey player might feel, finally scoring a goal after having played for years without even a shot on the net. It was only three weeks short of three years since I had first joined an operational squadron.

This was the eve of Operation Charnwood. At our briefing the next morning we were told that the plan was for the tanks to break out to the north of Caen, then turn east and run until they were out of fuel. The appearance of so many Jerries so close to our base was unusual, probably triggered by the clouds of dust that had been rising all day on the seventh, as a continuous stream of Sherman tanks passed the end of our field moving up to the Orne. That evening there was to be a massive bombing attack on Caen by 450 Lancasters.

Rod ("Smitty") Smith had learned that there was a forward vantage point overlooking Carpiquet airfield, still in German hands, from which we could watch the bombing. We found a spot alongside a Canadian Bofors unit, within a mile of the German positions. The Lancs began to stream in at about 8,000 feet. We were so close we could see the bomb bay doors open and the bombs falling. Soon the target was obscured in a cloud of dust and smoke. The Germans were pouring up light flak, and many of the bombers must have been damaged, but all managed to get away safely as far as we could see, except one.

This Lancaster crossed the target in the main stream. His bomb bay doors opened, but no bombs dropped. Then it swung out of the stream in a wide 360-degree turn and went back in for a second run, but this time it was down to about 4,000 feet. The flak poured into it like coloured water from a hose, and soon it was burning. The bombs were dropped. Then the nose went down, steeper and steeper, until the machine disappeared from our sight. We waited for the ball of fire, but to our disbelief the Lanc reappeared in a steep climb, up, up, and over in an elongated loop, then dived into the ground and exploded. Had I not seen it I would not have believed an aircraft that size could perform such a manoeuvre, even in its death agony.

About this time Air Vice Marshall Broadhurst, in charge of all the air activity within the beachhead, arrived in his personal aircraft, a German Fieseler Storch which he had brought back from Africa. With this machine painted bearing black and white invasion stripes, and of course RAF roundels, his flitting back and forth in the beachhead was a common sight for us. Now, as it began to settle down in a field about two hundred feet from us on the other side of the road, the Bofors crew swung their gun around with every intention of shooting it down. I'm certain they would have done so had we not been there to dissuade them. They were arguing quite logically, "Anybody can paint on black-and-white stripes—that's a German aircraft!"

In July, there was frequently an early morning fog, which soon burned off and lifted to broken cumulus. Jerry became quite adept at using this cloud cover for hit-and-run attacks. When the Army spotted them they would call for help and one of the four-man sections always sitting at the end of the runway would be scrambled. On one occasion I was leading a section scrambled to the vicinity of Bayeux. We could see where the Jerries were by our own flak, which, incidentally, did not stop when we arrived, so we were obliged to fly through it. As soon as we arrived on the scene the Jerries broke off in pairs and dived into the cloud. I told my guys to break off and search singly, which they did and had more luck than I did. Two Bf 109s ahead of me popped into cloud as soon as I opened fire. Wheeling around another cloud I saw an Fw 190 appear out of a cloud straight ahead of me, streaking across the open space to the next one. I took a long, full deflection shot at fairly close range as he crossed but could not observe the results.

In the meantime, one of my section had destroyed a 109, and another claimed to have probably destroyed one. Next day, my trips were uneventful, but on other sorties the squadron destroyed two Bf 109s and two Dornier Do 217s, bringing the squadron's score since forming to over the one-hundred mark.

Early in the month, George Keefer left us as his tour had expired, and he was replaced by Dal Russell, the second time during my tour that Dal had led the wing. On the eighteenth, Wing Commander Keith Hodgson was replaced as Commanding Officer of the airfield by Group Captain Gordon McGregor. McGregor was an original member of No. 1(F) Squadron RCAF, predecessor of 401, and later went on to become President of Trans-Canada Air Lines. My aircraft was withdrawn from service due to flak damage not repairable on the unit; until a replacement was received I would be flying 'E.'

A Canadian Spitfire Mk IX on a temporary steel mesh runway in France.
RCAF via N. G. Russell

The day after Caen fell, a couple of us took the jeep up to the front, hoping to get into the ruined city. We stopped to talk to a Canadian Bofors crew who discouraged us from going any farther, saying there were still snipers active. While we were standing talking, twelve Bf 109s came lazily over our heads at about 1,000 feet, carrying drop tanks, and here we were on the ground with our aircraft five miles away! The Bofors crew immediately got busy, and at the first shot the Germans dropped their tanks and tried to turn back. We were busy ducking the tanks, which were dropping all around us, falling-leaf fashion. Although I had a very healthy respect for German flak gunners I had always been somewhat skeptical of our own. This crew sure changed my opinion.

In a matter of seconds they had downed three of the 109s. One made a crash landing just behind us, in our territory; the second came down between the lines. The third took a direct hit, completely severing his tail. Down he came like a stone. At about 400 feet the pilot got out and his parachute opened. We were inwardly cheering for the German at this point and were relieved to see the chute open. But then the Canadians opened up with a heavy machine gun, the chute collapsed, and the pilot plummeted into no man's land.

We didn't like the ideas this would give German troops watching from the other side, so we voiced our disapproval. This brought a snarl of "Whose side are you on, anyway?" from the Army. They had a point, so we let the subject drop. After all, they had accomplished more in three minutes than I had in three years. About this point the Germans demonstrated their disapproval by dropping mortar shells around the battery, so we moved on. A short piece down the road we saw the 109 that had belly-landed, about one hundred feet off the road. We were tempted, but noting the warning signs reading "Verges cleared (of mines) to six feet," we decided not to investigate.

On 26 July, with me back in my new 'L,' Hap led us on a long-range recce around Orleans. At one point we dived down to investigate a horde of unpainted machines that turned out to be Lockheed Lightnings, the first I had seen. On the way out, crossing the German fighter base at Dreux, we were greeted by a sudden burst of heavy flak, and Hap began trailing that telltale stream of glycol. Someone called to tell him he was hit. Hap was absolutely unflappable, and in his usual quiet drawl answered that he knew, adding that he was waiting to get farther away from the German airfield before bailing out.

I kept an eye on him and could see his machine was close to burning. We were at least one hundred miles behind the lines and there was no chance at all of his getting home. I pleaded with him to get out while he had time; eventually he did and we saw his chute open. He was one of the many pilots who succeeded in evading the Germans until the war passed him by. In fact he was back in England in time to share a cabin with me (and others) on the voyage back to Canada. When I returned to Beny-sur-Mer and checked over my new machine I found a hole right through the radiator casing, but somehow it had missed all the coolant pipes.

Charlie Trainor, a Flight Commander in 411 Squadron, took over as our Squadron Leader. About 6 A.M. the following morning we were returning from our first sortie with Charlie leading, a recce in the Argentan area. I spotted a number of aircraft above us, which from their formation were obviously German. They were flying toward us, so were looking into the sun. I reported this to Trainor, who could not see them immediately. He asked me to take over and lead the squadron toward them. I did so, and after a while he picked them up and took over again.

As we climbed up, under, and behind them we could see there were about fifteen Me 109s and Fw 190s carrying drop tanks, which indicated they had not yet been engaged. We were within four hundred yards without being detected when Trainor called, "Every man for himself," or words to that effect. We waded in. This time there was no cloud to escape into. When I was about three hundred yards behind the 109 I was overtaking, he dropped his tank and broke hard to the left, turning so tightly that his machine left vapour trails from both wing tips. I was able to turn inside him but could not lead enough for a shot. After a few revolutions he suddenly rolled level, throttled right back, and seemed to stop in mid-air, obviously trying to make me overshoot and end up in front.

Thinking about it afterwards, I marvelled at how the brain automatically assesses a situation and tells you what to do. The instant he slowed down I knew what his intention was and I too had my throttle fully back. The Spitfire both accelerated and decelerated slower than the 109 and I could see that a collision was inevitable if I did not turn away. To turn in any direction would mean losing sight of him and possibly allowing him to turn in behind me. I rammed on full rudder and kept the machine from rolling with the ailerons. In a gut-wrenching skid, I shot out to the right, straightening out when I was clear of his wing. But I was still slowly sliding past him, so I fishtailed vigorously until our relative speeds stabilized. Now I was in formation with him, literally, wing tip to wing tip.

We stared at each other across the thirty feet or so that separated us, both hanging on the verge of the stall, which I believed would happen to him first. Then in a flash he opened his throttle, and before my engine would respond he was four hundred yards ahead of me. I soon overtook him, but this time did not try to get too close.

From straight behind I fired a burst. Immediately something detached itself, and as it sailed past my left wing, I could see it was his cockpit canopy. I fired again, and this time what looked like a brown sack emerged. It soon displayed arms and legs—he had bailed out! As he flew past my wing I could see his parachute starting to open. I broke sharply to the left, both to check my rear and to keep him in sight. I was alone.

It always amazed me how the sky could be full of aircraft one minute and empty the next. Although my Number Two, again Flight Sergeant Horsburgh, stated later that he saw the pilot bail out and his parachute open, I think he must have seen someone else's victim. He certainly was nowhere in sight when I wheeled around, nor did he rejoin me for the trip home. This did not surprise me because we had been cleared to act on our own.

I was determined to have confirmation of this kill, so I decided to photograph the parachute. I wheeled around and lined up with the chute, but before I could press the camera gun button I had to turn steeply away—I had almost flown through him! Then I realized my throttle was still wide open. Throttling right back I gave myself some more room and this time had him nicely framed, keeping the camera going until I had a full-frame picture of pilot and chute.

He must have needed a change of underwear when he got down, expecting any second to hear the last thing he would ever hear, my machine guns. Now, for the first time since the fight started, I checked my instrument panel. The fight had started at 15,000 feet, and I was shocked to see I was now at 3,000 feet. This was no place to be on my own, so I climbed out of light flak range and headed for home, continuously rubbernecking to the rear. The final score for this operation was seven 109s and one 190 destroyed—for no loss, the best single-trip score to date, at least during my time with the squadron.

Just before the end of the month, Wally McLeod, who was currently leading 443 Squadron and whose DSO had just been announced, dropped in to our mess tent. He told me he had a personal goal of destroying twenty-five aircraft; his score was then twenty-one. Unfortunately he never got another and was himself shot down and killed about a month later, leaving me the only survivor from our original draft.

The month of July closed out with an evening escort job of a large force of Lancasters bombing the German garrison in Le Havre, almost on our doorstep. Apart from the usual flak, which scored a direct hit on one of the bombers, this was a quiet milk run and, although I did not know it yet, my last with 401. The next day an Anson took me back to England to pick up a replacement Spitfire, NH353. When I landed back at B-4, Squadron Leader Trainor summarily announced that my tour was complete.

This news was so sudden I was stunned; just as my fighting career seemed to have taken a turn for the better it came to an abrupt end. We all believed, wrongly, that the end of the war was near and we wanted to be in on it. To use the hockey player analogy again, I felt like a professional player who had held up his end throughout the season and the semi-finals, only to be benched just as the finals were about to begin.

It hurt even more when I moved just a mile or so down the road to a holding centre, where I was still in touch with the squadron pilots and got the daily news of the slaughter at Falaise, making the end seem closer than it would prove to be. Yet I had flown sixty sorties in the last sixty days, during which our squadron alone had lost eleven pilots. I could not deny myself a guilty feeling of relief at getting a rest.

During my time with 401, eleven pilots had died and seventeen were missing, more than the equivalent of a full squadron. Happily, almost all the missing pilots would eventually show up, either as evaders or released POWs.

Including my previous two years in Africa, I had been flying continuously with operational units for three years. I had flown a total of 240 sorties, excluding all African flights other than PR sorties. I had logged close to nine hundred hours on Spitfires and Hurricanes.

Mosquitoes over Burma

Photo-reconnaissance in the Far East

JOHN J. (JACK) WINSHIP DFC
FLIGHT LIEUTENANT RCAF (RET'D) WITH NORMAN MALAYNEY

The operational history of the de Havilland Mosquito in the European the-atre during the Second World War is well documented. Operating day and night over heavily defended areas by pilots who exploited its exceptional performance, this aircraft achieved a legendary reputation. A less publicized but equally important role was played by pilots who employed this aircraft in the photo-reconnaissance role, particularly in the China-Burma-India (CBI) theatre. Here, long distances were flown over sparsely populated plains and mountainous jungles, photographing enemy installations and troop movements.

Jack Winship flew photo-reconnaissance (PR) missions with 684 Squadron RAF from India, part of a little-known Canadian contribution to the war effort in the CBI theatre and Southeast Asia (SEA) using de Havilland Mosquito aircraft.

Born in Winnipeg, Manitoba, Jack Winship enlisted in the RCAF and was sent to Edmonton Manning Depot in November 1941. From here he went to No. 5 EFTS, High River, Alberta, to fly Tiger Moths and later Cessna Cranes at No. 10 SFTS, Dauphin, Manitoba. Graduating from the program as an "above average" pilot, Jack Winship was invited to become an instructor. To avoid this, he accepted a posting to No. 1 General Reconnaissance School (GRS), Summerside, PEI, for navigation training on Avro Ansons. Completing the course, he was again slated to become an instructor at a Hudson-equipped Operational Training Unit (OTU). Jack avoided this by exchanging postings with another pilot and was dispatched to England for advanced training for photo-reconnaissance duties at No. 8 OTU, Dyce, Scotland.

graduated as a fledgling PR pilot from the course at Dyce and was posted to No. 1 Photo Reconnaissance Unit, RAF Benson, near Oxford. When new aircraft arrived from the factory, they were immediately assigned to one of the awaiting pilots. Here, I teamed up with navigator Peter Haines and received all-blue Mk IX Mosquito MM254, which I was instructed to fly to 684 Squadron in India, my new assignment. Many pilots who preceded us never reached their destination because of accidents. We were instructed to "follow the blue trail" to India; you couldn't miss it—so many Mosquito aircraft had pranged en route!

The unpredictable weather forced postponement of our flight to Portreath, in Cornwall. In England, when the weather comes down, it seems like a blanket over everything. It was foggy and wet, and snow began to fall. Ground crew continually swept snow from the wings just in case we had a break in the weather. Our luggage was placed in the rear of the engine nacelles; there was no room in the fuselage. The bomb bay was neatly packed with spare parts, cameras, and equipment needed for the squadron in India.

Finally, on 11 December 1943 at 1600 hours, the sleet ceased and the sun temporarily broke through a clearing in the clouds. Peter and I received orders to take off and quickly became airborne, ascending steeply along the shafts of light streaming through the break in the overcast. After climbing above the cloud layer, we suddenly confronted and nearly collided with a huge barrage balloon. I radioed base asking if balloons were supposed to be here at 5,000 feet. "No!" the tower operator replied. At their request, we orbited the errant balloon so that a fix could be obtained and a fighter aircraft dispatched to shoot it down.

Arriving at Portreath, we were delayed for several days due to a technical difficulty. We were finally given instructions to prepare the Mosquito for an early morning takeoff. Two aircraft were scheduled to leave: our Mosquito and an American A-20 Havoc. Both were classed as good all-weather aircraft. The Havoc took off ahead of us. The American pilot flew his aircraft off the end of the runway and crashed into the sea. Then I received clearance for takeoff.

We became airborne without difficulty and flew south over the Bay of Biscay for Gibraltar. The miserable weather consisted of continuous sheets of rain. Instructions previously issued required us to maintain an altitude of

A Mosquito PR 34 banks steeply, revealing its distinctive planform. The two circular camera ports in the forward fuselage and one aft are apparent. *Via N. Malayney*

4,000 feet in clouds flying on instruments throughout the flight. Peter Haines was top navigator in his class at Dyce and we experienced no difficulties during the IFR flight skirting around Spain to reach Gibraltar.

On approach to The Rock, oil began to stream along the starboard engine nacelle and the propeller went into coarse pitch. I immediately feathered the engine. Gibraltar radio sent a course correction, directing us in by radar. Still flying in cloud, I descended slowly out of the overcast onto the deck. We waited for the Gibraltar radio operator to supply additional landing instructions, but none came. The previous briefing stated The Rock had a large arrow on its face indicating direction of the landing pattern. Skimming over the wave tops, we saw no arrow as the base of The Rock loomed out of the mist.

Circuits were generally in a right-hand direction. As we flew around the towering Rock, a stream of Liberators confronted us head-on. Obviously we were circuiting in the wrong direction. At this very moment the radio operator came in very loud and clear. Apparently, he had attempted to contact us but The Rock blocked the transmission. Because of our location, they panicked, informing us we were number one in the landing pattern. I continued the wrong-way circuit still on one engine, descended in a shallow turn over a sea wall, and safely touched down on the runway. Previously, several fellows had overshot and gone off the end at the far sea wall.

After a brief Gibraltar sojourn for engine repairs, Peter and I were airborne again, having received a specific heading and altitude to fly. We flew from Gibraltar over the Mediterranean until reaching a lighthouse near the North African coast. Here we orbited several times to allow ground radar to identify us as friendly, then flew on to Castle Benito, located near Tripoli. The war in Africa had ended by this time and the desert for miles all around the Tripoli area was littered with the burnt carcasses of tanks, vehicles, and equipment.

En route to Castle Benito we again experienced propeller trouble and performed another single-engine landing. Unfortunately, the local ground crew did not have proper tools for the necessary repair. A few damaged aircraft already sat parked here and I was urged to leave my Mosquito and catch a flight back to England. But this I had been told not to do—not to sign the aircraft away. Ground crew suggested tools might be available at Cairo West. So I thumbed a ride on a Dakota and left Peter to guard our aircraft. At Cairo, after much searching and negotiating, I obtained the necessary tools and hitched a ride back to Castle Benito. When the work was completed, we took off, heading for Cairo West on 27 December 1943.

After a brief stay in Cairo we flew to Habbanniya, located near Baghdad, where some of our personal effects and aircraft equipment were pilfered from the Mosquito. We left Habbanniya, made a refueling stop at an island near Saudi Arabia called Muhurraq, and then departed for Karachi. On arrival, our aircraft was checked over and we spent a week waiting for further orders.

Our squadron was located at Kamilla, near Calcutta, but on 12 January 1944 we were directed to fly to Cawnpore. I was eager to begin flying with an operational unit. This news deflated my mounting enthusiasm.

Arriving at Cawnpore, we spotted an aerodrome in the middle of the city. For the life of me, I couldn't imagine how I could land on that tiny field with its very short runway and tall buildings at both ends. The warm temperature dictated increased landing speed—there would not be the lift the wings generated in cooler, more dense air. And there was no headwind to slow me down on landing. I descended slowly, barely squeezing the aircraft onto the strip.

Photo-reconnaissance Mosquito pilot Jack Winship (left), and his navigator, Peter Haines, at a location in India. *J. Winship*

Rapidly using up the available runway I contemplated a ground loop to avoid crashing into a chain-link fence at the far end.

We taxied to the control tower where the Commanding Officer, beaming with elation, immediately shook our hands. He congratulated us on the terrific landing. We had been expected to land at a larger airfield located several miles beyond the city outskirts. "You can't get a Mosquito in here," he added. The runway we had just used was far too short!

They had planned to tow our Mosquito from the larger airstrip to this smaller one to perform modifications on the aircraft. Not knowing any better, we had landed at the research facility by mistake and saved them the time and trouble of hauling the aircraft a relatively long distance by road. Thus, they were delighted at our arrival and made us feel very welcome.

It was another five days before we performed an air test. Initially, I made a brief flight with one of the engineers, Flight Lieutenant Owens, to determine if I could land the Mosquito again on the small strip. I had no fear of getting off; it was landing that was questionable. I took off without trouble and landed again safely. Completing this twice successfully gave me confidence in my abilities.

The RAF planned to attach a 90-gallon, external fuel tank under the fuselage similar to the long cylindrical-type used on the Hawker Hurricane to provide the Mosquito with additional fuel to extend its range. They did not know how it would affect the flight characteristics and that was why we were there. When the modifications were completed, I flew out and back into the strip with the empty tank strapped to the belly. The tank did not hinder performance. In fact, the aircraft seemed to handle better with it attached. To test the aircraft with the tank fully loaded, we were required to fly to the larger airstrip and top-off there with fuel.

The military wanted to investigate the effect of jettisoning this belly tank, and asked if I would make a slow, low-level run across the strip at Cawnpore and jettison the tank while ground cameras recorded the separation.

Well, the night before the test, I met an Army Major at the officers' club. He had heard about the test and wanted to observe. But he was afraid he would miss it, being preoccupied with work in his laboratory. I told him I would beat up the field on the first pass to forewarn him that the test was about to begin.

Next morning, on the first pass, I beat up the field at low level and full throttle. They always wanted us to perform this thrilling spectacle for the local Army types. It also allowed time to ready the equipment. We came in low and slow the second time, allowing for good photo coverage. I pressed the release button but didn't feel anything jettison. Flight Lieutenant Owens lifted the bottom trap door and reported the tank was still attached. We were by now nearing the end of the runway. I pulled up gently and gradually, so that the tank would not shake loose but when Owens looked again, the tank was gone. Quickly, I made another pass and peered down at the field, but no one was in sight. Everyone seemed to have vanished. I landed immediately to investigate what had happened.

It seems the belly tank fell away when I put the aircraft in the climb. It hurtled straight toward the Army Major standing in the doorway of the large building surrounded by a high wire fence with a guard at the gate. A series of large stone steps led up to where he stood. The fuel tank bounced off the ground and skidded through the gate, straight to the foot of the stairs. Seeing the tank hurtling toward him, the Major ran into the building for protection. That night he met me at the mess and admiringly remarked, "That was bloody

The first Mosquito PR 34 arrived at Karachi, India, on 1 June 1945 after a record-breaking flight of twelve hours and forty minutes from RAF Benson in the U.K. *Via N. Malayney*

wonderful!" He believed I purposely dropped the tank so it would skid to his stairs!

But, with the tank hung-up, the Army technicians failed to obtain good photos of the release. We performed another drop test and this time secured good photo coverage.

At about this time, the CO from 684 Squadron, Wing Commander W. B. Murray, flew to Cawnpore in a B-25 Mitchell and asked that Peter and I proceed immediately to the unit. I wanted to go, but the Cawnpore CO, Squadron Leader Campbell, said no, we would have to stay and complete the test program. My CO was quite angry and flew to Headquarters Command in New Delhi to demand our immediate release. Later he returned and instructed us to remain and perform the tests. Eventually, on 24 February, with testing completed, a Mitchell aircraft arrived to transport Peter and me to the squadron at their new location at Dum Dum on the outskirts of Calcutta. My modified Mosquito (MM254) remained at Cawnpore.

Peter and I were finally with an operational unit and it was only a day before we performed an aerial photo survey of Imphal, situated in a valley with an airstrip under the protection of the British Army. Imphal was under siege by the Japanese, who surrounded the area.

Next day, Army Intelligence officials arrived and shook our hands. We had provided them with the first perfect survey of the area. We had flown a beautiful line-overlap and didn't miss a patch of area anywhere. We assumed this to be the norm. But we never achieved another perfect survey; we performed very good ones but nothing to compare with that first sortie. Beginner's luck!

Most flights were photo surveys flown from forward areas we called "bomb lines." They consisted of landing strips bulldozed out of the jungle. We flew from Dum Dum across the Bay of Bengal and refueled at these strips, most often at Ramu. We flew long, five- or six-hour trips that consumed a fair amount of fuel.

Initially we flew south, down past Rangoon, to the Bangkok area of Siam. The first pilots who flew to Bangkok received the DFC for the long flight over enemy-held territory. The Japanese responded to the over-flights by firing at them. Later, we flew farther south, extending our range to obtain as much photo coverage as possible.

Toward summer, the monsoon season arrived, with increasing high cloud development that created terrible flying conditions. It became imperative to have sufficient fuel for the return flights. Often we landed with the tanks nearly dry. If half the fuel was consumed on the outward journey, the aircraft returned lightly laden and achieved better speed and mileage. Thus, if half the fuel supply remained on the return flight, we were safe—unless we encountered bad weather.

I was still a green pilot when an event occurred that provided more than I really wanted in terms of adventure.

On 5 April 1944, Peter and I flew from Dum Dum to Ramu in MM294. After all tanks were topped-up, we set out for Kaugean, located near the eastern border of Siam. Our procedure was to first consume fuel from the main tank in the bomb bay to provide room for transfer of petrol from the wing drop-tanks. Each external tank held 50 imperial gallons. Therefore, we needed to consume more than 100 gallons from the main tank before transferring fuel.

When I attempted to transfer fuel, a red light indicated a vapour lock, so I switched back to my regular tank again. According to the manual, you are to return to base. You don't fly around with 50 gallons of fuel in either drop-tank. Now, I had had vapour locks before and after a while, as things cooled, the lock usually disappeared, allowing the transfer of fuel to the main tank. I had never returned early from a trip and did not intend this to be my first aborted mission.

We had good altitude, 35,000 feet, and a terrific tail wind. Peter computed a hundred-mile-an-hour-plus tail wind—we couldn't believe it! Apparently, we had climbed up into the jet stream to attain this terrific ground speed.

We continued our flight. Everything by then was cooling down and I was ready to transfer fuel from the drop-tanks when I noticed the port engine temperature-gauge needle climbing. I looked out and there was this horrendous plume of vapour issuing from the engine—a colossal cloud. Startled, I realized it was my coolant. I immediately feathered the prop and shut the Merlin down before it could overheat and seize.

Then it dawned on me that this was the engine I needed for transferring fuel. The Pesco pumps were located on this engine and we required them to pump fuel from the drop-tanks. We were approximately two and one half hours from Ramu by this time and had covered nearly 800 miles. Peter immediately gave me a reciprocal heading. I made the turn with the single engine.

A Mosquito PR IX of 684 Squadron RAF taxies out for takeoff at Dum Dum, India, in late 1943. *Via N. Malayney*

The drop-tanks were now of no use. We badly needed the 100 gallons of fuel but not the added weight and increased drag of the tanks. So I pressed the jettison button and they both flew off.

The aircraft would not stay at 35,000 feet on one engine, so I preserved airspeed by maintaining a slow rate of descent. Peter continued plotting a course and managed to transmit an SOS signal on the key. We were too far to reach Ramu by VHF radio. And the generator was on the feathered engine. We had to be careful to keep the batteries strong for as long as possible considering the circumstances. Using the VHF radio would have drained them. Peter dropped the trailing aerial in an attempt to secure any response to our distress signals but received no reply. But that was not our main worry. Had we enough fuel available for the return to Ramu?

According to the manual, we were not going to make it. Peter suggested flying on to China, which was closer than Ramu. I had doubts about this; we would have to fly through mountainous areas having very few airstrips, and I didn't know if the natives in the area were friendly. My plan was to fly as close to Ramu as possible, then crash-land in a riverbed, get our escape kit out, and try to work our way back to the coast. Even if it took months, I was determined to reach our lines. Young and foolhardy as I was, I didn't realize how grave the situation was or could become.

The aircraft was gradually losing altitude when all of a sudden it gave a shudder and the starboard engine starting running rough. Peter began preparations to bailout, thinking we had now lost both engines. I told him to sit tight for a moment. Suddenly it dawned on me: the supercharger cuts out after you descend to an altitude where the air is of increased density. The cut out was like losing an engine. Immediately, I opened the throttle to retain my boost. With boost restored, I managed to maintain the aircraft on an even keel at 14,000 feet with no difficulty.

I kept the engine running slightly hot and it behaved properly. The radiator-inlet was controllable and, when opened, caused drag. I made adjustments, opening the inlet enough to maintain speed and engine temperature barely below the danger point. The over-burdened Merlin seemed to run smoother when it was hot.

The feathered prop started to windmill slightly. It had not feathered completely and now caused the aircraft to wallow, resulting in a loss of airspeed. I unfeathered the prop, held the starter button, and the engine turned over. Then I punched the button again to get the prop feathered. I was able to trim the aircraft and found it flew beautifully with both hands off the wheel.

But our greatest worry remained our fuel supply. According to the manual, we would be approximately 100 gallons short, running empty a few hundred miles from base. And ahead there were mountains to cross.

We took a direct route, passing over known enemy airfields, still maintaining 14,000 feet. Japanese aircraft were parked on the fields located around the Irawaddy Valley plain below. We did not produce a contrail, but I'm sure they must have heard the droning sound of our engine on the ground. If an enemy aircraft did come up, all we could do was dive for the ground and attempt to fly as far as possible.

We flew over the enemy aerodromes, escaping detection, and then sighted the bluish hue of the far distant Adaman mountain range. We were doing 200 mph, surprised that the aircraft could maintain this speed on one engine.

We did not realize our SOS had not been received at Ramu but had skipped and gone all the way to Calcutta. The squadron Wireless Officer was working on a receiver when he suddenly heard the SOS coming through. He immediately wired Ramu and asked for their contingency plans. They replied that they had received no message. Learning of our predicament, they dispatched Spitfires to escort us back. By this time, we were flying over the inhospitable Adaman mountain range at 14,000 feet; this was why I had wanted to maintain altitude. If we ever had to dive down, it would be difficult to regain this altitude or to navigate our aircraft through the remote valleys and around the high ridges.

But everything went well and fuel expenditure proved less than anticipated. We consumed 90 gallons an hour when the manual said it would be around 125 gallons. We encountered no head winds—a fortunate circumstance, considering the terrific tail wind we had experienced at high altitude on the outward journey.

It took slightly over four hours to reach Ramu, still with some petrol in our tanks. As we approached the fairly short strip, another Mosquito pilot entering the circuit heard our radio conversation with the field. He orbited, and followed me to make sure I maintained my airspeed on one engine. Ramu had two runways called Reindeer One and Reindeer Two located next to each other. Fighter aircraft used one while the other was for Mosquitoes. Suddenly, the pilot in the other Mossie began yelling that I was landing on the wrong strip. "Hell," I responded, "wrong strip or not, it's the one ahead of me!" But he was mistaken and we landed on the correct runway.

On a previous occasion, I made a single-engine landing at Ramu after an op, and on another flight they brought me in downwind and I overshot. We had to have the aircraft towed out of the mud by truck. But this landing was the best I had ever made. A single-engine experience like this requires full attention during descent, easing the aircraft onto the runway with great care. Whenever I made single-engine landings, they were always perfect. It was when I had good conditions, two healthy engines, and was lax that I had made "ropey" landings.

We had been in the air over six and a half hours.

After safely landing, I felt embarrassed at having gotten myself into this predicament. But the following day, a Mosquito arrived with my Flight Commander, Squadron Leader B. S. Jones. He came running from his aircraft, shook my hand vigorously and congratulated me on a terrific job of bringing back the aircraft. He was very enthusiastic. Slapping me on the back, he said everyone was worried I would never make it back. He brought a spare part to repair my aircraft for the return flight to Dum Dum. Later, I was told a burst glycol hose had caused the vaporization of engine coolant.

It was near midday when I landed at Dum Dum and taxied to the dispersal area. Men came out of the officers' mess and congratulated Peter and me on our single-engine flight.

The only one who did not pat me on the back was the CO himself, and rightly so. After lunch he called me into his office and tore a strip off me for not returning immediately. From day one, we had never got along—stemming from the instance at Cawnpore when he had wanted me to return to the squadron and the other CO would not release me. But I had had to take orders from whichever superior was issuing them at the time. Somehow he felt it was my fault.

Later, I received a Mention in Dispatches and came to realize it wasn't a bad effort. Peter computed that we had flown a distance close to 790 miles on one engine. The Dispatch lists the flight as 760 miles.

Not long after this flight, I had another memorable experience. One late afternoon, I entered the officers' mess and noticed a fellow in civilian clothes— a sweater and flannel slacks and, like a typical Englishman, a little scarf around his neck that was tucked into the sweater. I introduced myself but did not pay much attention to his reply. In an RAF mess, only military personnel may purchase drinks, so I offered to buy him one.

We were engaged in conversation when the CO walked in. "Oh Geoffrey," he said, "I didn't know you were here yet." The CO asked the civilian if we had met, calling me by name. The civilian then began asking me about my single-engine flight. He was none other than Geoffrey de Havilland. New aircraft were ferried to our unit and he had brought a Mosquito all the way from England. He asked me what I did and how the aircraft behaved. He wasn't really quizzing me, only wanting to know how far the Mosquito would go and how it performed. Geoffrey de Havilland was a gentleman: unassuming, very quiet, soft-spoken, and not saying very much—mainly listening. I presume the information I provided was passed on to other pilots.

Mosquito MM254 that I left behind at Cawnpore was complete with modification and ready for a long-range test. Another pilot and navigator were sent to fly it back to Dum Dum, but they refused to take off from the short strip. The aircraft had to be towed through the city to the larger airfield on the outskirts. I was happy to see my aircraft complete with belly tank attached, but the CO said I had not logged enough hours on Mosquitoes. The long-range test would be performed by another, more experienced pilot.

At dawn on 19 March 1944, MM254 was ready for takeoff. I guess the pilot was a bit nervous carrying the extra fuel, for he opened the throttles too quickly, causing the aircraft to veer off the runway and crash. It disintegrated into a million pieces of plywood but fortunately did not catch fire. How the crew escaped alive, I'll never know. That was the end of my beautiful aeroplane. So much for experience.

Another Mosquito Mk XVI, MM392, was flown to Cawnpore and towed into the short strip. When modifications were completed, Army authorities cabled Dum Dum requesting that Peter and I perform the testing. No, said the CO, and sent two other officers. They refused to take off from the short strip; the Army had refused to tow the aircraft to the larger airfield. They kept insisting that Peter and I come up there. Finally, the CO relented and on 14 July we flew by Mitchell to Cawnpore.

The research staff were elated at our arrival. It was a homecoming event with a special party held that night in the officers' mess, where we were wined and dined. The next morning, the Mitchell returned to Dum Dum and my CO ordered Peter and me to return with it. But again the CO at Cawnpore instructed me not to leave until all testing was completed. We went through the entire squabble again, with telegrams going back and forth and threats of court martial if I did not return.

We remained for five more days carrying out several test flights from the short strip. By now I was quite confident and accomplished at performing this task. During our brief stay, the authorities treated us like royalty and we dined at the Cawnpore Club with the higher echelons of military brass. Reluctantly—the test program completed—we returned to Dum Dum with our modified aircraft.

Another long-range test was planned, but they were sending another pilot. Again they would not allow me to fly the modified Mosquito. The pilot for this flight was hesitant, claiming not to know enough on the intricacies of the fuel-transfer system. I took him into the cockpit and went through the entire drill necessary to use the tank. He insisted that since I knew the procedure and the aircraft I should perform the test flight. He found it quite a complicated system—changing tanks and cocks—transferring fuel from one tank to another. I found it elementary. Undoubtedly, he was worried because of the previous crash. I explained to him that the aircraft had improved flight characteristics with the belly tank attached, and did not swing to the left as much on takeoff.

That night at the mess, I had a few drinks too many and expressed my dissatisfaction with a few sarcastic utterances within the CO's hearing. Eventually, the CO and Peter had enough of my obnoxious behaviour and left. I remained behind until the bar closed at 0100 hours before returning to my quarters.

In the early hours of morning, I remember someone vigorously shaking me and telling me to get up—I had to make a test flight! I thought someone was joking with me until I recognized the Intelligence Officer, a straight-laced fellow. I told him in most disparaging terms that if the CO wanted me, he would have to haul me out of bed himself. Shortly, the CO appeared and ordered me to gather my flying equipment and report to a vehicle waiting to transport me to the aircraft. Staggering around with a terrific hangover, I struggled into my clothing and carried myself and equipment to the vehicle, where Peter was waiting.

We were driven to the Mosquito, and I immediately connected the oxygen mask to help sober myself. It was now the monsoon season and the weather was terrible. Low grey clouds nearly touching the ground covered the aerodrome with sporadic drizzle. With the oxygen mask on and engines running, I performed the cockpit check. Takeoff was from Alipore, located on the southern side of Calcutta from Dum Dum.

The flight went smoothly; we flew on instruments continuously in cloud throughout the test. When the belly tank ran dry, I pressed the release button, but it remained attached. I put the nose down and then did a sharp pull-up, and heard a loud bang. My first thoughts were that our tailplane had been smashed by the jettisoned tank. Peter looked rearward searching for any visible damage, but none could be seen. The controls functioned perfectly. What had happened?

Annoyed at the tank's failure to release I had pulled back hard on the control column, pitching the aircraft upward. The tank came loose and bounced off the fuselage, leaving a long jagged scar across the side. I should have been gentler. The flight lasted over six hours. All else considered, the aircraft functioned properly and the flight was uneventful. The squadron initiated modifications; belly tanks were attached to other Mosquito aircraft.

On 11 August, Peter and I flew Mosquito MM392 (K) to Trincomallee/China Bay located on the east side of Ceylon. Here the CO informed us that he and another navigator would fly the aircraft to Sumatra. When the next day arrived, the CO developed a case of jaundice and required hospitalization. The other navigator became a bit hesitant about the mission. So Peter and I received permission to perform the long-range flight.

It was 15 August when we took off at 0805 hours and flew across the Bay of Bengal to a place called Nancowery situated in the Nicobar Islands just north of Sumatra. We carried roughly 850 gallons of petrol plus the 90-gallon tank under the belly, so we had a lot of fuel on board. It was a long trip, well over a thousand miles, across water all the way. Navigation was strictly on instruments and dead reckoning. At 30,000 feet if you have a break in the cloud cover, you will sight an island and right away know your location. We were a little off track but not much. Due to cloud cover, photography was only possible at Nancowery, taking photos of several airstrips and the harbour, where four ships were visible.

The weather on the return flight was good. We searched the horizon for cumulus clouds, knowing they formed over Ceylon. If all that could be seen was a haze, you began to wonder if you had passed the island. We returned on course with no problem, and the trip took seven hours and twenty-five minutes. We now knew the fuel parameters for long over-water trips.

Peter and I made a second flight on 26 August in LR464 (R) to the Nicobar Islands. But, due to overcast, we changed course for northern Sumatra, where we photographed a new airfield at Padang Tidgi and Samalanga and the town of Sigli, which had never been photographed before. We took off at 0645 hours and landed at 1450 hours. After these initial flights, other squadron pilots flew the long-range missions with the external belly tank, extending their coverage down the Sumatra peninsula. The Mosquito's extended range also assisted in providing PR support for missions flown by B-29 aircraft of the USAAF's 50th Bomb Wing stationed at China Bay, Ceylon.

Originally, we operated Mk IX Mosquito aircraft—the newer Mk XVI was just coming into squadron strength. They carried more fuel and covered

A 684 Squadron RAF Mosquito navigator, Flying Officer Davidson, prepares to board his aircraft at Alipore, India, in 1944. *Via N. Malayney*

greater distances. With the Mk XVI we surveyed Rangoon, Bangkok, and all parts in that area. These trips later became milk runs.

The Mk XVI had semi-pressurized cockpits and improved Merlin engines. On brief occasions, we reached 40,000 feet, but at this height nitrogen bubbled in your body joints and we encountered problems with the bends. We refrained from such high flights unless absolutely necessary. At such high altitudes, oxygen leaked up from around the face mask and burned our eyes, causing them to become bloodshot.

Compared to American machines, British military aircraft were uncomfortable. We were jammed tightly into the Mosquito with no co-pilot or autopilot, and our flights were gruelling, lasting six or seven hours. The pilot sat on a folded dinghy that was part of the seat. Strapped down on top of this equipment for long periods of time, our legs became numb—very noticeable when we strained to climb down from the cockpit and attempted to walk. We flew as far as we could with our fuel and usually came back nearly empty.

The weather was at times more fearsome than the enemy. We flew frightening trips during terrible storms, especially through cumulo-nimbus clouds (CBs). Generally we took off early in the morning and, at 30,000 feet, we wound our way through the canyons between menacing thunderheads with peaks at times towering to 45,000 feet and higher. It was dream-like, coursing among the billowing white clouds, so peaceful and sublime. We might fly out nicely, but by afternoon, on the return leg, the CBs would have grown and closed in. We seldom had sufficient fuel to detour around them—it would have taken us hundreds of miles out of our way—so we screwed up our courage and flew through them.

The upward air currents were most violent on entering and exiting these clouds. The updrafts shot us skyward as though on an elevator, even with both engines throttled back. At times, treacherous turbulence tossed us upside-down. With no visual horizon, it required gut instinct and instruments to right the aircraft. I cannot express what a fearsome experience this was. Hail battered and slashed the leading-edge fabric, causing it to peel back and flutter from the wing. The carburetors began to ice up and the engine would just about die. Then we came out of the clouds into the warm sun! Such weather, and possibly bad judgement in terms of fuel, were, I believe, the prime factors in the loss of some aircrew.

Most trips were flown at high altitude, relatively safe from flak. I do recall flights over Bangkok when we did receive flak bursts. Later, we flew several low-level missions, and one in particular comes to mind, an on-the-deck run in the eastern part of Siam. We were to survey the entire length of a particular mountain road and its vehicular traffic. The Mosquito had forward-facing cameras mounted in the external wing tanks. The clouds were low, covering the mountaintops.

We flew down through the overcast, then straight and level along the road with cameras on, taking photos. We shut them off as we banked the aircraft through the canyons, following the twisting turns of the road. When we were again level, we resumed photographing the road. We occasionally came across long enemy truck conveys. The Japanese immediately jumped from the trucks and scurried into the dense brush and ditches for protection. They thought we would strafe them. We, in turn, figured they would open up on us with AA fire. We continued along the entire length of the road until the canyons closed in with cloud. Immediately we ascended into the bright sunshine. After our return to base, the photos were developed and laid out on a table, where they looked like a giant snake.

The last trip I made with Peter Haines was on 1 February 1945. I didn't realize how good a navigator he was until he was posted away toward the end of his tour. Several other navigators volunteered to fly with me so that I could complete my tour. I found most of them to be quite nervous, especially when I dove down, slicing through the clouds into the winding valleys for visual inspection at low level, when taking pictures. Fearing for their lives, these navigators always wanted to get out of there.

Not Peter—he never complained. He was an A-1 navigator and had had top marks in his class in the GR course. He had been pleased to learn that I had completed the same program, commenting "You're a Gen Man too!" He was good with charts. Flying in clouds and relying on dead-reckoning, he would be exactly on target. We would be away for up to six hours at a time, and when he brought us home, if he said so, I knew we were descending out of the clouds over water and not mountains. We were a good crew.

On 5 February 1945, I made a flight with Group Captain Wise, the CO of No. 171 PR Wing, comprising 681 and 684 Squadrons. He asked if I would volunteer to take him up and demonstrate the Mosquito's flying characteristics.

I inquired why he didn't ask another more experienced senior pilot.

"No," he said, "I want to go up with you as I understand you get off pretty short and handle the aircraft very well."

So I allowed him to flatter me into the flip. In the air, I moved out of my seat and slid into the navigator's position, allowing him to sit in the pilot's seat and fly the aircraft and experience the feel of the controls. We flew a couple of circuits and bumps, but of course I landed the aircraft. He then asked if he could be checked out in this aircraft to annotate his logbook that he had flown a Mosquito. I told him to go right ahead. Then he asked me to go with him.

"No," I said. I would not fly without being in full control of the aircraft. And he couldn't command me to do so. But finally, after his polite appeals, I relented. But I requested that he obey my commands to the letter. It was a good thing I went with him. Accustomed to flying Spitfires, which glide quite well, he throttled the Mossie back too far and failed to pay attention to the airspeed. If too low, it will cause the aircraft to drop like a stone. I instructed him to apply more throttle and he brought the aircraft in for a ropey landing. He decided to

An RAF D.H. 98 Mosquito PR 34 (RG203) of 684 Squadron RAF's Cocos Island detachment in July 1945. *Via N. Malayney*

do one more circuit. He felt that, without two landings, he wouldn't really have been checked out in the aircraft.

I've never sweated so much in my life. There was nothing I could do except talk calmly, telling him that he'd better open more throttle and watch the landing because the aircraft had a tendency to swing left. I had no rudder control and was unable to do anything to help him. My anxiety level increased. But I continued talking quietly and calmly, trying to correct his flying. And his second landing wasn't too bad. Pleased with himself, he bought the drinks that night.

Little did I suspect that, because of this brief flight, he selected me to become an instructor on Mosquito aircraft. I was dejected. I longed for something more exciting, but RAF policy prevented pilots from stepping from one tour into another. They needed experienced pilots to train new flyers arriving in the CBI/SEA. Although I did not want to instruct—it was at the bottom of my list of non-op flying—I eventually ended up an instructor.

I was nearing the end of my tour with 684 Squadron and the weather was terrible. Many pilots became ill with malaria, dysentery, and other diseases. I was flying missions for both A and B flights, packing in a lot of trips. Normally, between flights there were a few days off for rest, but I continued flying one mission after another until 29 February, when I completed my tour with 684 Squadron.

I was temporarily posted to Yalahanka near Bangalor, then on to the Central Flying School (CFS) at Amballa, located north of New Delhi. I took an instructor's course on Oxford aircraft, which I detested. We had to parrot words while performing sequences again and again on these aircraft. I accumulated many hours on these flights of short duration. In the Mosquito we flew six- or seven-hour trips, whereas at the CFS, one-hour flights were generally the rule.

I narrowly missed being killed during a flight-sequence stall flown with a fellow instructor. We were flying at 4,000 feet, performing sequences until we lost altitude, ending up at 2,000 feet. The fellow piloting the Oxford wanted to return to base early and initiated a stall sequence at this altitude, which was much too low, allowing little height for safety margin. He was in the stall position when he suddenly called me to lend him a hand. I thought he was joking but the aircraft fell off on one wing and we were in a spin heading for the ground. I had figured he was an experienced pilot and could handle the situation. Between the two of us—opening the throttles and feverishly kicking top rudder—we manoeuvred out of the spin with precious little space between us and the ground. The other pilot was trembling, sweating, and scared. That was when I knew he had not been joking. Getting into such predicaments was sheer stupidity.

From the CFS, I was posted to 672 Conversion Unit at Poona as an instructor on dual-control Mk III Mosquito aircraft. Never having flown a Mosquito from the right seat before, I had to accustom myself to the different perspective. I had a stubby little throttle that proved difficult to move. As the trim was located on the pilot's side, the student had to adjust this under supervision.

Normally I took up a new pilot and executed several bumps and circuits, then slid over to the right-hand seat and observed as he performed several takeoffs and landings. Most were experienced Wellington and Beaufighter pilots training for transition to Mosquitoes. Usually they converted easily, except for the Beau pilots who were accustomed to the aircraft swinging to the right because of the torque they had had to contend with. In the Mosquito, it was the opposite. On takeoff, differential throttle increased left engine power more than the right, until the aircraft was heading smoothly down the runway. As the tail lifted into the air stream and the pilot gained better rudder control, he applied both throttles fully. The Mosquito unstuck at 120 mph and climbed at 170. Once at altitude, you throttled back both engines to cruise.

I don't know why, but soon I became the only instructor checking out new pilots on dual-control. The CO, Wing Commander W. B. Berry, a fine fellow and Battle of Britain pilot, allowed me a free hand at whatever I wanted, so I had the run of the station. The control tower often made requests to give the place a beat up, even at night with my navigation lights on. Occasionally, I feathered one engine and did a few passes. It was all permissible.

Poona had a large RAF aircraft-maintenance depot. There was a restricted area on the far side of the base. At this time, pilots were ferrying in Hurricane aircraft that were being phased out and replaced by Spitfires. I was asked to taxi the Hurricanes across the field. I jumped into an aircraft, ran up the Merlin, and zigzagging, taxied down the roadways to the opposite side of the field to an area set behind some trees. Here I found that instruments were being removed, and then a huge steel ball dropped on the aircraft, crunching it to a heap of scrap. Beautiful Hurricanes in good condition were destroyed and pushed aside by a bulldozer. There were hundreds of these aircraft smashed and piled up as scrap metal. It was heartbreaking to watch this happen.

RCAF personnel in the CBI/SEA were recalled to re-form in Canada and join the Americans for the invasion of Japan. Canadians passing through Poona asked me how I could keep on flying since orders from Canada had come through grounding all RCAF personnel in India. My CO said he knew nothing of such orders. Besides, they had no one else to instruct pilots on the conversion course. So I continued flying. Previously, I had volunteered for the Pacific and soon orders arrived ending my flying in India.

My last day at the OTU was 8 July. I boarded a train for a staging area near Bombay and waited there for a ship, which took over two weeks via the Suez Canal to reach England. I returned to Canada on VJ Day, 14 August 1945, my birthday.

Mitchell Tactical Operations

Flying B-25s with 226 Squadron RAF

Robert H. (Bob) Fowler OC

B ob Fowler was awarded the McKee Trophy in 1974, appointed an Officer of the Order of Canada in 1975, and inducted into Canada's Aviation Hall of Fame in 1980. His accomplishments as an engineering test pilot with de Havilland Canada—first flights on the Turbo-Beaver, Twin Otter, Buffalo, Dash 7, and Dash 8, as well as the initial air testing of Pratt & Whitney Canada's PT6—have been deservedly recognized.

Less well known is his wartime RCAF career as a medium bomber pilot with 226 Squadron, an RAF unit flying North American B-25 Mitchells with the Second Tactical Air Force.

A native of Toronto, Bob learned to fly at nearby Barker Field, cycling there for flying lessons when he could afford them. After six hours of dual instruction, accumulated over several months, he soloed. Then he joined the RCAF. Although he proved that he had had flying instruction by showing the recruiting officer the receipts for his flying time, he still went through all of the stages of the BCATP system with training on Tiger Moths at the Windsor Mills, Quebec, Elementary Flying Training School. For his Service Flying Training he was sent farther east, to Moncton, New Brunswick, on Ansons, and from there a short distance down the road to Pennfield Ridge for Operational Training. In the first volume of *Flying Under Fire,* he recalls a harrowing training flight in a Ventura out of Pennfield. He begins his story here after a rapid but extremely rough passage to England aboard the liner SS *Louis Pasteur.*

After completing forty-eight missions with 226 Squadron, Bob did a stint ferrying aircraft and instructing, becoming acquainted with the Douglas A-20 Boston in the process. Returning to Canada and civilian life, he studied law for a year at the University of Toronto. But flying had gotten into his blood and, after obtaining a commercial pilot's licence, he joined Dominion Gulf to pilot a Grumman Goose on aerial mineral-survey operations. His next move was to Spartan Air Services. In *Skippers of the Sky* (Fifth House, 2000), he describes what it was like to fly a Second World War fighter, the Lockheed P-38, on high-altitude aerial mapping operations in northern Canada.

In 1952, he accepted a test-flying position with de Havilland Canada; in 1987, he retired as Chief Engineering Test Pilot.

Many wartime squadrons maintained a Line Book, in which any story or line that sounded doubtful or exaggerated was recorded. Any squadron member caught stretching the truth was assessed a quid, which, with many other pound notes collected in this way, eventually funded a late-night, food-parcel-and-beer bash in one of the Nissen huts. Since a piece such as this would have bankrupted me, I will try to describe things I saw rather than things I did.

After finishing the Operational Training Unit (OTU) on Venturas at Pennfield Ridge, New Brunswick, we were posted to Halifax and sailed on the *Louis Pasteur* in late 1943. Six days later, when we arrived in England, it was 1944. At sea we received word that the *Scharnhorst* had been sunk, which did a lot for morale on the ship. After the roughest six-day crossing the *Pasteur* had yet experienced, we docked at Liverpool. We disembarked just after dark and spent our first night in England on a blacked-out train, heading for Bournemouth on the south coast. Arriving in the early morning, we were billeted at the RCAF Personnel Reception Centre, from which all RCAF postings and overseas movements were made.

We ran into friends there from our SFTS who had been cooling their heels since we had received our wings at Moncton. In February we did a four-week Commando and Escape Course at Sidmouth, Devon. We learned to throw grenades and how to kill people with knives, guns, and bare hands, along with other things my mother would never have approved of.

The escape course was followed by a two-week posting to 1538 BAT (Blind Approach Training) Flight at Croughton, Oxfordshire. We flew Oxfords on the SBA (Standard Beam Approach) System, and the training was second to none.

One very foggy morning near the end of the course, when I thought I could safely sleep in, one of my hutmates roused me with, "The BAT Flight loves a morning like this, they will be the only ones flying." And he was right. I could hardly find my way to the hangar, but that morning we were taught, with commendable cool, to land on a sodium-flare-potted grass strip without seeing the ground until after the wheels touched down. We were cautioned to keep the old Oxford straight on the ground using the directional gyro, and not to look up until the tail was down. We had done this on good days, but actual fog pointed up the practical value of the training. I once asked if they flew in fog with every BAT course. No, I was told; we were one of the lucky courses, first because landing in fog was prohibited, and second because it was just not possible to order up fog for every course.

A month after completing the BAT course, we were posted as a crew to No. 13 RAF OTU at Finmere in Buckinghamshire, for conversion to Mitchells. Finmere was a 2 Group unit where pilots and crews were trained on Bostons, Mitchells, or Mosquitoes. Mitchell training supplied the three Mitchell squadrons of 139 Wing at Dunsfold, and 137 Wing at Hartford Bridge, composed of one Mitchell and two Boston squadrons. Like Pennfield, Finmere was quite a jump forward. We soloed in three flights, taking less than four hours. The second aeroplane of any size I had flown, the Mitchell, with its tricycle undercarriage, was considered a fairly modern aeroplane.

Powered by two Wright Cyclone R-2600 engines of 1,750 hp, more than 250 hp less than the Ventura's R-2800s, the Mitchell could carry a 4,000-pound bomb load, which was 1,500 pounds more than the Ventura's 2,500 pounds. The Mitchell had been designed from the outset as a bomber, and was a very successful aeroplane.

The Mitchell's nose-wheel was the first of my experience. At first we weren't sure that tricycle gears were here to stay, but we quickly learned that the Mitchell could almost land itself on the main wheels—the nose-wheel inherently settled to the ground, restrained slightly with the elevator. The tricycle made takeoffs and landings much simpler and safer than with the Ventura.

The only thing I didn't like about the Mitchell was the separation of front and rear fuselage by a bomb bay that almost reached the ceiling. This effectively removed the pilot and observer from the two gunners in the rear. It was possible to squirm over the bomb bay in either direction, but the trip could take a fair bit of time depending upon one's size and agility—and how scared you were.

Pilot visibility was very good, and the pleasant handling qualities made the Mitchell a superior aeroplane for formation flying. It was good in crosswinds, and its single-engine performance was much superior to the Ventura's. The Mitchell had powerful but very sensitive toe brakes. If you watched a Mitchell taxiing you could quickly tell how much experience the pilot had on the type. Low-time pilots caused the nose to bow down every time they touched a brake pedal. After four or five flights, we learned to handle the brakes smoothly.

Since we had to be able to get a lot of aeroplanes into the air quickly, we picked up a few new formation techniques. We took off in twos, with one aircraft behind the other just far enough to avoid collision should either lose an engine. Landing in boxes of six, we liked to get two aircraft on the runway at the same time. Later, when we landed in a stream, we strove to have one machine taxiing off the upwind end of the runway, with two more on the pavement rolling toward him, and a fourth close in on the approach. It looked a little crowded, but with the bomb load and most of the fuel gone, a lightly loaded Mitchell was very sprightly.

At Finmere we were introduced to a remarkable device called the Mark XIV Gyro Stabilized Computing Bomb Sight. The Ventura carried the old Mark IX sight. I was told that in the early days of the war, if the bomb-aimer knew the wind speed and direction, some of them preferred to sight between the tip of their index finger and thumb.

With the old sight, anything within 150 yards of the target was considered good bombing. With the Mark XIV, 50 yards was routine from 10,000 to 15,000 feet. Many times during their training with the Mark XIV at Finmere, our observers did better than that, even with very short bombing runs. The Mark XIV was also quite accurate for bombing in a turn. We had one lead observer, Dougie Farquar, who invariably bombed in a turn. He was very accurate.

The accuracy of the Mark XIV was made possible by a device then called a computer. When we first heard the word we didn't quite know what it meant. In this case it was a box about eighteen inches high, twenty-four inches wide, and three inches deep, mounted vertically on the left wall in the nose com-

North American Mitchell Mk II (B-25C) of 226 Squadron RAF. The tricycle landing gear and stub engine exhausts are visible here. *UK11855 via R. H. Fowler*

partment. For its time, it was a very decent mechanical analogue computer. After a series of lectures, we wrote a quiz on the computer so we would at least be knowledgeable about the observer's task.

With computers in short supply, only the Number One and Two aircraft in each box carried them. At Finmere, all observers were trained in the use of the full computer system, and also in a manual mode using a slide rule. The results in either mode were excellent, and bombing accuracy was very much improved.

Almost a month after D-Day we were posted as a crew to 226 Squadron at Hartford Bridge. Before the Allied invasion of Europe, the mission rate had been steady but not brisk. After D-Day, there was an overabundance of targets. As a result, medium bomber crews in 2 Group finished a tour, one way or another, fairly rapidly. A first tour had been thirty-five trips, but when we arrived on the squadron, it had been raised to fifty trips due to increasing losses, and to crews completing tours more quickly.

We weren't the new boys for very long. We reported to Wing Commander Dennis Mitchell, the Commanding Officer of 226. He told us it might be a while before we could get on a trip, but to get all our kit together and be ready when we were needed. Mitchell (appropriately named) was an outstanding CO. He was very direct and you didn't need to decipher anything he said. Much later he would become Air Commodore Sir Dennis Mitchell, Commander of the Queen's Flight.

"The first thing is to get you out for a formation check flight with one of the senior pilots leading." There were a number of conventions to become familiar with, and it was important that we understand how the squadron operated in the air. We ran the familiarization flight that afternoon. We did about everything that could be done in formation with a Mitchell without a word being spoken. It seemed more professional to stay with a leader without being told what he was about to do. If he surprised us with a move, we weren't paying enough attention. Formation flying was satisfying when nothing was said until it was time to open the bomb doors.

The Wing Commander's office, the squadron administration offices, a briefing room, and the two Flight Commanders' offices were housed in two large, interconnected, H-shaped Nissen huts. They also housed a nondescript ready room, where we could keep dry when it rained, snooze, play cards, or shoot crap, "as long as you do it quietly."

The next day we hoped we might at least see an op take off, and by midmorning, the Intelligence Officer's van, with its motorbike escort, could be seen coming across the north end of the airfield, which usually meant a trip was on. 'B' Flight Commander Squadron Leader "Paddy" Lyle asked, "Where's Fowler?"

"Yours and Wyjad's (a Canadian pilot with whom I had trained at Moncton and Pennfield) are the two junior crews," he said, "and we need one of you for this trip. We will have to toss to see who goes." He tossed, and I "won."

We barely had time to be issued parachutes and American life jackets. We each signed for a .38 Smith & Wesson with a full ammunition pouch, flak suit and flak helmet, plastic escape pack, and waterproof money pack. The money pack contained occupation money or scrip, along with Dutch guilders and Belgian and French francs in case we fell into the hands of friendly Europeans who wouldn't accept scrip. The slightly curved transparent escape pack was about eight inches square, an inch thick, and fitted nicely into an inside battle dress pocket. With that little plastic pack, you could catch fish, shave, purify water, take pills to keep awake for seventy-two hours, suck on high-calorie candies, or dine on high-calorie chocolate and biscuits. There was also a tiny compass to show us where north was. As circumstances dictated, we could swallow it or slip it into our rectum or navel, whichever seemed appropriate.

The Smith & Wesson was a better revolver than had been previously issued, and some senior guys were envious, so much so that we thought we had better wear them into the briefing like everyone else. Considering we had hardly been on the squadron forty-eight hours, things were moving right along.

The Squadron Intelligence Officer arrived with his armed motorbike escort. The crews filed into the briefing room and sat four to a table, with the DR guarding the door on the outside. The Intelligence Officer, Flight Lieutenant Bob Lawrie, in peacetime a Glasgow barrister, opened the briefing. He rolled a blanket back from a large map showing most of the U.K. and

A North American Mitchell Mk II (B-25C) of 226 Squadron RAF over typical English countryside. *UK11852 via R. H. Fowler*

Western Europe. Starting from our base in England, a piece of blue yarn ran to a pushpin on the channel coast, then southeast to another on the coast of France, then to another pin just south of the French coast, from where it headed back to the U.K. by a slightly more direct route.

At the point where the yarn turned back to the north, there was a cluster of black pins. I leaned back to the pilot at the table behind, and asked what the black pins were for. "They're heavy flak positions," he whispered. "Each black pin is three guns—or five." He couldn't remember. At every briefing thereafter, I was very interested in the black pins. The Flight Commander of 'A' Flight took over the briefing and welcomed our crew to the squadron, which I thought was very nice. "You'll be flying the last position in the last box," he said. "Back there you'll see everything—it would be a pity to miss anything on your first trip."

The target, near Abbeville, was a Noball, which had nothing to do with balls, but was the codename for a V-1 buzz-bomb launching site. On numerous subsequent trips, our targets were similar sites and destroying them was sometimes secondary to our main purpose of attracting German fighters. This was always made clear in the briefing. Even though we had a large close- and high-cover fighter escort, I was sure my mother would never have approved of the RAF using her little boy as bait for German fighters.

Well before Liberators and Fortresses of the U.S. Eighth Air Force arrived in broad daylight at 25,000 feet on their way to targets inside Germany, at 10,000 to 12,000 feet, we would look pretty juicy to Hun fighters. If we could lure them into the air to chase us, expert wisdom said that they would be hard pressed to refuel, re-ammo, and get off again before the Libs and Forts had picked up their own escorts of Mustangs and Thunderbolts and were well into the Fatherland. It was a good theory, but most times the Huns had a go at both of us.

At my first briefing I remember thinking, "I've finally made it to the war!" The idea of being fighter bait was something I hadn't anticipated, but it was a great thrill just the same. I looked around and was surprised that nobody else looked very thrilled. With forty-nine trips to go, my own outlook would undergo significant change during the next few months. Once the briefing was finished the crews seemed to be in a great hurry to get out of the briefing room for a QNP (Quick Nervous Pee), or even a QNS!

At Pennfield, I felt lucky to have been selected by my crew. I had laboured under the disillusion that they propositioned me because I was such an

Bob Fowler pilots his bicycle in front of a Nissen hut at RAF Hartford Bridge, home of 226 Squadron RAF, in the summer of 1944. *R. H. Fowler*

intrepid pilot. But my main attractions, they said, were that I didn't drink, didn't do much saluting, and didn't try to act like an officer. I didn't know whether to feel complimented or not.

Our observer, Russ Hunter, was the best looking guy in the RCAF. We thought that God had intended to make Gregory Peck look like Russ, but Hunter got the looks and Peck just had to make do. Our wireless air gunner was Wilf Stanger, a big guy from Winnipeg, with a scar across one eye where somebody had cross-checked him. It definitely made Wilf look like he should be handled with care. Our air gunner was Gord Owen from Toronto. Gord was married and a father, and it was not until some time later that it occurred to us that Gord's concerns were not quite as lighthearted as our own.

At the end of that first briefing we were issued two packages of gum, a Mars Bar, and a Cadbury's Chocolate Sandwich. "This is great," I remember thinking. "We get all these goodies just for dropping bombs on Huns!"

Before the briefing was finished, the observers were given an edible flimsy listing a number of codes and challenges covering the period of the day. The pilots took no notes except for a small list of key times. The first was lorry time. Woe unto him who was not ready to board the big Bedford truck when it came to take the crews to the dispersals. Like a tram conductor, the driver called off the letter of each aircraft as he stopped to drop off a crew. Next came engine start time, when every engine in the squadron was fired up. For a few minutes, the smoke from oil and priming fuel from twenty-four or sometimes thirty-six Wright Cyclones dropped visibility close to zero.

Next was run up time, which quickly improved the visibility. Then came taxi time, when the box leaders in each dispersal began to move, followed by the aircraft in their respective boxes in the sequence listed on the Battle Order. Each pilot knew the letter of the aircraft he was to follow. You watched for that aircraft, and space was provided for you to join the line behind it. Very courteous.

This put each box in the right order when their turn came to enter the runway, which occurred at box line-up time, when the first six Mitchells taxied onto the runway. With two tons of bombs and another two tons of fuel, the amount of runway they occupied made what remained of the six thousand feet look rather short, particularly for the first two aircraft. In 1944, two thousand yards was a fairly long runway.

All of this took place right on time, with no talk. Though it sounded far-fetched, we were warned that a Jerry listening aircraft on the other side of the channel could hear anything we said. After the radio talk I had earlier become accustomed to, it seemed very polished that a good number of aircraft from three squadrons could get off the ground in complete radio silence.

The road from Basingstoke to London went right through Hartford Bridge aerodrome parallel to the main runway, but separated from it by a few hundred feet of grass. Six Mitchells on the runway, with many more waiting on the taxi-way, all with engines running at high rpm to prevent spark plugs from fouling, was a noisy spectacle. A civilian car travelling through the airfield would some-times stop, and if we were lucky, a pretty girl or two would tie kerchiefs over their heads, and sit on the grass to watch. "What the hell am I doing in this thing? I should be down there on the grass with the girls," I thought.

Being the last aircraft in the last box, we did indeed see everything. When the first flak bursts arrived, there were a few clipped remarks on the radio. One said he had a fire, but thought it was out. The flak filling the sky looked to be quite far ahead, and we thought there must be another operation of some kind up there. But in minutes we were surrounded by bursts.

A voice on the VHF said, "Orange box, bomb doors open." That was us, and along with the rest of the box, we opened the bomb doors. The lead navigator was transmitting corrections to his pilot, and to the rest of the box. All I had to do was hold a good position on Number Four aircraft on my right. The run seemed to go on for a long time; in truth it might have taken all of ten or twelve seconds. It was quite a surprise when we heard several loud bangs. "If you hear bursts, you've got holes," we had been told.

The lead navigator finally called "Bombing, bombing, GO!" and the bombs began to slip out of the bay of the Mitchell in front of us, down past our nose. The odd bang could still be heard, and over the intercom, Russ observed that we had taken some hits. I asked him if he had been hit. "I'll tell you later," he said.

In box bombing, the lead navigator in each box transmitted the heading corrections he gave to his pilot, and the box responded as one aircraft by stay-ing tight on the leader. When he called "Bombing, bombing, GO!," all six navi-gators pushed their bomb release buttons together. The leader usually aimed to undershoot the target slightly, and the correspondingly slight lag in response from the other five observers tended to lay an optimum pattern across the target.

After the bomb doors were closed, we began an almost leisurely climbing turn to the right. This caused us to slow down, and felt wrong, but the flak gradually fell away. This was one of my first practical lessons in tactics. The natural instinct to dive away from a target was a bad one. As we climbed away, we could hear other boxes on their bombing runs. Levelling off, we made slow turns every ten or twelve seconds accompanied by changes in altitude to keep ahead of the time the Wehrmacht anti-aircraft predictors required to read our heading and altitude.

The French coast fell away and it wasn't long before we had the white (make that grey) cliffs of the U.K in sight. With no fuel leaks we could smoke, so the crew lit up. I have never smoked, and have always felt it would be better for one's health to eat the fags. But the smell of cigarette smoke in an aeroplane

North American Mitchell Mk IIs of 226 Squadron RAF outbound in loose box formation. *UK13311 via R. H. Fowler*

brings back a sweet nostalgia that I'm sure stems from the return legs of forty-odd Mitchell trips.

This was the time to tie into the gum and chocolate bars, and I found that my flak helmet was an excellent tool for shattering cold chocolate bars on the co-pilot's seat. I couldn't believe that on this first trip we had actually been hit by flak!

When we reached Hartford, we re-formed into a starboard echelon on the downwind leg, and then did an intervalled peel-off for a stream landing. We were the last aircraft to turn in on the approach. When I selected the undercarriage down, nothing happened. A quick look at the hydraulic pressure gauge showed it to be zero. I pulled out of the circuit. With no hydraulics, the only option I had was to open a valve to the emergency hydraulic system. From then on it was the observer's job to pump the gear down with the emergency hand pump located on the forward end of the lower bulkhead in the nav compartment. Russ pumped for all he was worth until eventually the undercarriage indicator showed all three legs down and locked. This would not be the last time he pumped the wheels down.

The emergency procedure for extending the flaps called for twenty-seven turns of a crank. I liked flapless landings and decided it would be easier to leave them up.

Before he climbed into the co-pilot's seat for the landing, Russ got my attention and held up his navigator's bag. It had a cluster of holes where the green fabric and the paper of the maps inside had been subtracted by pieces of flak that had gone through the bag when he had it with him in the nose. The same burst took the heel off one of his Wellington boots.

Of course, with the main hydraulic system out of commission, the brakes did not work. I learned that the emergency brake handle did indeed apply the brakes on both main wheels at the same time—they went on so abruptly that it was impossible not to leave a lot of rubber on the runway.

After shutdown the ground crew gave us hell for all the holes in their lovely aeroplane.

In the briefing room, the Wing Commander asked us if everything had gone well. New crews, he explained, normally were not sent to places like Abbeville on their first trip. But they had needed a crew. Danny Wyjad had gone on the trip as co-pilot with another crew.

In the early summer of 1944, trips took from an hour and a half to two and a half hours and were flown mainly to targets in northern France. After the breakout from Normandy, as the war moved east and north, we began hitting targets in Holland, and by the end of September, a round trip to Germany sometimes took more than three hours.

In addition to target illumination trips, we hit buzz-bomb sites, fuel, oil, and ammunition dumps, marshalling yards, power stations, road junctions, road and rail bridges, harbours, and concentrations of troops and armour.

Occasionally, when Allied ground forces ran into strong German resistance, they called on us. We were supposed to be off the ground within thirty-five minutes of the time the request was received. We were sometimes briefed to bomb on red smoke markers which would be fired into the German lines by Allied artillery just before we arrived. On one such trip, the Army fired the markers into the German positions too early. The Huns quickly caught on, and shot red markers back into our lines. When we arrived with bomb doors open, the whole target area was a mass of red smoke. We were feverishly recalled just before putting a load of bombs into the middle of it all—at least half of which was Allied territory.

A number of our night ops were flare-dropping, or target illumination operations, where our job was to keep a target area lighted while it was bombed and strafed by Mosquitoes, Bostons, or other Mitchells.

Our Mitchells were not configured for night operations. We had unshrouded exhaust stubs around the engine cowlings, and the long blue flame from each stub could be clearly seen at night. We had no window covers in the navigator's compartment, where he needed lights for most of the trip. Presto, black-painted windows! But much of the light could still be seen through the painted windows. And light leaking around his curtain into the cockpit significantly degraded the pilot's night vision.

In the cockpit there were a number of different-coloured indicator and warning lights. They were very bright at night, and only a few were fitted with iris dimmers. This was satisfactory for flying in the U.K., but they ruled out much chance of seeing other aircraft in the dark. Then somebody had a great idea. All you had to do was chew up a lump of gum and put a little wad over each light, then dig a fingernail into it just deeply enough to identify its colour.

Danny Wyjad, another Canadian (RCAF) Mitchell captain with
226 Squadron RAF. The bandaged hand and face were the result of
a motorcycle accident. *R. H. Fowler*

This "mod" worked well, but scraping the gum off the next morning for a day-time op was a messy job.

Our .50-calibre Brownings were loaded with red tracer and, if fired at night, scared the hell out of everyone. For some time after firing, all one could see was a continuous stream of receding red balls.

Night trips were considered a break from daylight ops—it was nice not to fly in formation. We felt that nobody knew we were there. Sometimes we would get fairly close to the ground. After the war I visited a number of places in Europe and was appalled at some of the hills and high-tension wires on our former night routes.

We knew nothing about night fighters, nor what to do about them. So, in the best RAF tradition, we were briefed by experts on how night fighters operated, and how to cope if we were attacked. One sunny day the crews from our three squadrons at Hartford Bridge were transported by bus to Dunsfold, home of our sister Wing, No. 139.

Group Captain Paul, their Commanding Officer, walked onto the stage and welcomed us. He announced that it would be our privilege to be briefed by none other than Wing Commander John Cunningham and Wing Commander Robert Braham, the two most decorated Allied night fighter aces of the war. He introduced them. After a while a blond head appeared around the curtain on one side of the stage. Then it disappeared, replaced by another blond head, which also disappeared. We could hear muffled conversation behind the curtain.

"You go, John."

"No, Bob, I think you should go first."

Finally somebody must have given them a shove, and they were both on stage, looking surprisingly young. Theirs was the most self-effacing presentation one could imagine. They suggested that we ask questions. We did. Salient points were: Keep changing height and heading—making the night fighter put his nose down might cause your blip to get lost in the ground clutter on his radar scope; heading changes would make it difficult for them to re-acquire us, and if he did get us back on his scope, he would want to get close enough to make visual contact before opening fire; by corkscrewing all over the sky, we could make it tough for him to get a visual fix.

But, "If your air gunner spots something close behind you, for heaven's sake make sure it isn't a Beaufighter or a Mosquito before you start shooting! Once certain, put a few good bursts where you last saw him—night fighters are a scary lot, unaccustomed to being shot at." Both men were sure that they had been fired on by British aeroplanes.

There were more British than German aircraft in the air at night during that phase of the war. "If you see his muzzle flashes, spray him with everything you've got. It will scare hell out of him, particularly your tracer loads, which will ruin his night vision." Night fighters never used tracer.

"If an enemy fighter does get a shot at you, corkscrew and lose height." Corkscrewing was an evasive manoeuvre that required skidding the aircraft to one side with rudder, then pulling the nose up and skidding across the top to the other side, then pushing the nose down again. "Do this at a relatively low frequency, but fairly violently—at least until the crew gets sick—then reverse the process."

It was important to keep your nose down. As the night fighter closed with you he would want to get below to identify you. While you lost height, it was tough for them to stay lower, particularly if you got near the ground.

Finally, "If an aeroplane stays with you and keeps shooting at you, when all else fails, fire the colours of the period. Don't even worry about firing the right colours, fire any colours. The German chaps won't want to be court-martialled for shooting down a friend. While they look them up, you corkscrew to hell out of there"—first-hand advice from two outstanding individuals who were very determined nonheroes.

On 26 August 1944, we flew an op to Rouen, where the Germans, who were moving north, had massed tanks, fuel trucks, transport, and every other sort of vehicle on the south bank of the Seine. They were queued up for miles, waiting to get across on barges and a few pontoon bridges. We visited them in the afternoon. When we left, the whole area was in flames. Smoke rose several thousand feet. The Huns had a good number of 88-mm guns with which they put up a lot of very accurate flak; but the trip was very successful.

When we returned to Hartford Bridge, one of the first things we did was check the new Battle Order to see who was on the next trip. As the saying went, "We live and die by the bloody Battle Order." We were certain the odds would have us going back to Rouen that same night. We were one of ten aeroplanes scheduled for that particular night.

As we turned south at about 5,000 feet, we could immediately see the twinkle of a very bright light ahead. We thought it might be an aircraft crash or something burning on the ground. As we continued south we could dimly see the channel coast going by underneath. The twinkle was noticeably brighter but was still further south. A ship on fire in the channel? The French coast became visible, and we could see this twinkling fire growing larger and brighter. It was well south of the coast. Maybe it was an aircraft crash in France?

I was beginning to wonder how much farther south Rouen was when Russ said, "Okay Bob, about three minutes to the target." Barely another minute later, "Bomb doors open, bring it left a bit." The course change to the left pointed us directly at what was now an enormous mass of flames on the ground down in front of us. It was the same area south of Rouen that we had visited in the afternoon. The south bank of the Seine had become an enormous conflagration we had been able to see all of the way from Hartford Bridge!

Just prior to brakes off, Mitchell crews that have been stood down wave to other crews about to take off. *R. H. Fowler*

We were not supposed to keep diaries, nor were we to record dramatic operational details in our logbooks. Some aircrew recorded details of every trip, and a few had entries in their logs censored when they were handed in for monthly signing. As a result, most of our entries tended to be terse; remarks were sometimes added later, after the signing for that month. A number of us did keep notes and diaries, which did not have to be signed by anyone.

Wars are largely fought by amateurs. It was inevitable that some technical and operational ideas that at first might have seemed well thought out were not always successful in practice. In wartime, there was seldom the luxury of a perfecting period, and the consequences of too hasty introduction could sometimes be expensive. We encountered two particularly costly examples—in terms of lives and aircraft—in the summer of 1944.

After D-Day the Mitchell squadrons of Second TAF were engaged in essentially two kinds of night operations: conventional bombing and target illumination, called TI ops. We carried eight bundles of parachute flares, seven flares to a bundle. A bundle would be roughly a foot and a half in diameter, about four feet long, and consisted of one flare in the centre, with six more clamped around it. The bundles were hung on each side of the bomb bay, in the same way we carried eight 500- or four 1,000-pound bombs.

Each flare bundle was held by two one-inch-wide strips of perforated strap-iron. One end of each length of strap-iron was secured to the aircraft with a small metal loop which locked into the hooks of the electrical release shackle in the bomb bay. To drop a bundle, the loop-ends in the electrical shackle were released. The bundle fell free, pushing the two strap-iron bands downward out of the way. When the parachute opened, it ignited all of the flares in the bundle.

When the parachutes opened, they seemed to light up the whole of western Europe. Any thoughts we might have had of stealth or being alone in the sky were immediately gone. Suddenly there were aeroplanes everywhere. Every Mitchell was an Me 110, and every Boston or Mosquito was a Ju 88.

TI trips usually required several runs over the target area, dropping two bundles on each run, and timing each drop to avoid a burn-out or dark period before we dropped the next pair of bundles. It seemed to take a very long time to get rid of the load.

Smoke from flak bursts was not as obvious as in daylight, but we could clearly see the flashes. Searchlights occasionally picked up an aircraft. It happened to us only once. Being rather low, it was fairly easy to dive steeply and then to pull away from the beam. It took a very long time to get away from the lighted area.

When we returned from any op, before leaving the dispersal, we routinely checked the inside of the bomb bay to be sure that everything was gone. After TI trips, the bomb bay was a tangled mess of strap-iron. On a preflight inspection, everything looked very neat, but in the course of a flight, as each pair of flare bundles was dropped, they left four dangling strap-iron strips. This meant that on each succeeding run, the bundles carried higher up in the bomb bay had to fall through an increasing snarl of straps.

Following the loss of one 226 Mitchell on a TI operation, the navigator was picked up and returned to England. He reported that, when they released the last pair of bundles, at least one of them must have hung up in the bomb bay, where it ignited, causing a massive pyrotechnic fire. The pilot ordered everybody out, but only the navigator made it. After this, the strap-iron was scrapped, replaced by a very neat self-coiling roll-up of light spring steel enclosed in khaki webbing. While it carried a flare bundle in the same way as the strap-iron, when a bundle was released, the loose ends automatically recoiled into neat rolls about the size of a roll of toilet paper. Losses on TI trips were reduced. It was gut-wrenching to think of the crews that had likely been lost to the strap-iron lash-up—which was undoubtedly applauded at its inception as being cheap, easy to make, and adequate.

Another procedure that seemed eminently sensible and ensured there would be no hung-up bombs over a target was later found to have lethal potential.

On daylight- or night-bombing trips, after the observer made the bomb load live by turning on the fusing switch, he opened the bomb doors by pushing the bomb door control lever downward with his right hand, which he then kept on the lever. His left hand held the release switch, triggering an intervalometer to drop the bombs at a preset interval.

When the time came to release the bombs, the observer pressed the tit and watched the intervalometer panel to be sure that a green light came on as the first of the bombs was released. This told him that everything was functioning properly. If the green light did not come on, the intervalometer had failed and would not release the bombs. The prescribed procedure called for him to immediately push the bomb door lever through to the jettison position, which mechanically released all of the bombs simultaneously. The bombs were thus jettisoned live over the target.

A pilot flying in the rear vic could easily identify a jettisoned load coming out of an aircraft in front of him if he saw the eight bombs come out of the bomb bay in a tight clump, oftentimes touching each other. Bombs released by the intervalometer came out in a uniformly spaced vertical stream.

On 23 July 1944, along with Mitchells from 139 Wing at Dunsfold, we attacked a target using a very accurate radio/radar navigation system called "GH" which allowed us to bomb through cloud. The GH trips were unpopular due to the need for a somewhat protracted bombing run, giving the Huns more time to find our range with their heavy flak. We were behind and to the right of another box of Mitchells with our bomb doors open when one of our crew yelled, "Look over on the left!"

What had been a box of Mitchells was all pointing in different directions. One appeared to be on fire and was almost on its back, and another banked

After standing down, Mitchell crews relax. Left to right: Marv Green, Bob Fowler, and Johnny Irvine (in flak jacket)—all Canadians (RCAF members) in the RAF. *R. H. Fowler*

away to its left trailing smoke and fuel. They had just flown through a wide scattering of smoke and burning debris that, moments before, had been the box leader's aircraft. The explosion and debris caused severe damage to other aircraft in the box. We could only take in the scene for a few seconds before it slipped behind us. The sky was littered with pieces of Mitchell—large chunks of wing, even one outer panel with the engine and propeller still attached—and a cloud of vari-coloured, vaporized fuel, oil, and smoke.

We had never seen anything quite like this. With no sign of flak, we thought we'd been jumped by fighters; but none had been seen or reported. At least one Mitchell had exploded and might have taken another with it. Weeks later, we learned that this was partly true. Once again an observer was able to bring back a description of the apparent cause.

This observer, in Number Four position directly behind the leader, sustained serious injuries from the debris, but his aircraft returned and he survived. His last memory prior to the explosion was of a jettisoned bomb load beneath the leader's Mitchell, probably jettisoned due to an intervalometer failure. In the jettisoning, one bomb in the load had likely contacted the detonator of another, setting off the whole two tons.

As a result of that observer's key report, fused loads that failed to release properly were no longer jettisoned in the vicinity of other aircraft, nor were they brought home. Whenever possible, after leaving the formation on the way home, hang-ups were dropped, safely defused, into the channel.

One Mitchell from the Dunsfold Wing, after many attempts to free a hang-up, decided to land. Moments after it touched down in a very smooth landing, it disintegrated. It is shocking to think of some of the procedures that would not have passed normal scrutiny but were adopted simply because "there's a war on."

On the morning of 17 September 1944, some unusual aircraft visited 226. One was a pristine, specially painted Spitfire, and another a very special intruder Mosquito. Both were parked in a prohibited area, but instead of being shot on the spot, their crews were warmly welcomed by the Wing Commander. The 342 Croix de Lorraine Free French Squadron, our neighbour, was also visited by a very shiny Black Widow. And a number of staff cars arrived that certainly didn't belong to Hartford Bridge.

Out of these aeroplanes and cars emerged some interesting bodies: an Air

Commodore and a variety of Army officers with red staff tabs on their collars. I was told that our own Basil Embry came in the Mossie. Occasionally, he visited the Wing and even went on the odd op. On such a trip he usually wore a Flight Sergeant's battle dress—apropos an incredible escape from Germany. This particular morning he was an Air Commodore.

Before lunch, 'B' Flight's Supernumerary Flight Commander, Squadron Leader Jim Betts, called me in to say that our crew had been put on the next op. When I pointed out that we were not on the current Battle Order, he responded, "You are now." When I mumbled something about doing box leading and being slowed down a bit, Jim looked me in the eye and said, "Please Bob, just shut up and relax!" Since Jim was one of the good guys, and I usually did what Squadron Leaders told me to do, I shut up and tried to relax. But I got a dirty look when I gave the news to my crew.

The wool on the map went to the east, south of London and the estuary and, after crossing the Belgian coast, it went to hell-and-gone into northern Holland. Many visiting ranks were standing at the back. One of them, I think a General, opened the briefing by saying, "Today you will support the largest airborne invasion in history."

As the briefing wore on, we began to appreciate the size of this operation. Everybody was taking part, the British First Airborne Division, and the Polish Fifteenth Airborne Brigade, plus a huge American effort. An enormous force of gliders and paratroops was to be dropped near the town of Arnhem in northern Holland. West of Arnhem was the small town of Ede, one of many nearby locations where retreating Panzers and other German armoured units had stopped to rest and regroup before continuing their dash to the Fatherland. Our boxes were to bomb the concentration at Ede.

Some of our Mitchells were to carry designated guests, and when our name was called, I was directed to Major Clegg, a British Army Intelligence Officer, who was to occupy our co-pilot's seat. Clegg was a fine type, and when we met, he seemed a little concerned about our experience. At one point he asked how many "bombing missions" we had done. When I told him this was number thirty-nine, he said, "My word!" Later, he told me that we had seemed rather young. Very perceptive was Clegg.

Our box was led by Commander Witholt of the Royal Netherlands Naval Air Service. He was another Supernumerary Flight Commander, who later became Commanding Officer of 320 Royal Netherlands Naval Squadron, one of three Mitchell squadrons in 139 Wing, our sister wing at Dunsfold. Withholt was quite familiar with the Arnhem area.

Takeoff was at 1300 hours. After crossing the Belgian coast, we passed south of Breskens on the lower Schelde, where we saw a variety of aeroplanes. We had never seen so many aircraft in the air at one time on any of our previous ops, and all seemed to be going to the same place. It was the first time I had seen Lockheed Lightnings on operations. They were mainly occupied with shooting up ground positions. Far outnumbering the fighters were waves of Dakotas, along with Stirlings and Halifaxes pulling gliders. Dakotas not pulling gliders were packed with paratroops or parachute-delivery cargoes. Our route to Arnhem turned us north while we were still west of the American drop zones south of Nijmegen. The gliders we saw in greatest numbers were mostly Horsas and Hamilcars.

Over the flooded area of Holland we saw increasing numbers of glider tugs and other aircraft in trouble; several were trailing smoke. Some gliders were down in the water where the only dry land was a few elevated roads. As we got closer to Arnhem, with so much activity in the air and on the ground, it was like arriving halfway through a movie.

A number of open fields west and south of Arnhem were packed with gliders. Many had landed in different directions, and several appeared to have collided. Other areas were covered with parachutes of different colours, and more parachutes were still being dropped in sticks, mainly from Dakotas.

There was no time to stare. Maintaining a tight position in a six-plane box allowed only snapshot glances at the activity on the ground. Our air gunners were occupied with searching the sky for fighters, and our observer gave a running assessment of our chances of successfully getting our bombs onto the target.

As I remember the day, the weather was fairly decent, with a broken layer of cumulus below us. Since 1944, I've read accounts that described the weather at Arnhem on 17 September as very bad. There might have been a few tenths of cumulus at about 8,000 feet, which had the potential of being a bombing nuisance; but the weather was quite good. Weather on subsequent days was indeed bad, which made support and resupply of the landings very difficult.

At 10,000 feet, through the breaks we could see what looked like the main glider and parachute drop zones on our left, but when we turned west toward Ede, we found a solid pan of strato-cumulus over the target area. When the call came to open our bomb doors, we could see the target shortly before the edge of the approaching cloud slipped under us, cutting off any further view of the aiming point.

We closed the bomb doors, and made a wide orbit away from the target area while changing height to evade flak. There were fighters in the general area, but I saw no German aircraft near us. When we did see an occasional Hun, it was being chased by a horde of fighters. The orbits we made over Ede gave us a little time to take in the activity on the ground. There were occasional calls from aircraft in trouble, and their discipline was amazing. Hearing calm voices describing desperate situations, often with grim humour, while we killed time waiting for the cloud to move off, increased our impatience.

Our crew gave running descriptions of glider situations they saw in the air and on the ground. We later learned that in some cases the tangles of gliders below looked worse than they actually were—some of the larger gliders could be dismantled to unload vehicles and heavy wheeled pieces. Paratroops going down in widely scattered areas, and parachutes of different colours, gave the scene on the ground a totally chaotic appearance. Major Clegg was clearly thrilled with it all, giving me the impression that he was pleased with what he saw. He busily made notes and sketches in a pad on his knee. To us, the scale of the operation was incredible, and we were amazed that anyone could make sense of the apparent confusion in the drop zones.

After what seemed like ten orbits of Ede, we finally got our bombs away and climbed to the southwest. We had lost visual contact with the other boxes. When we got back to Hartford, the Wing Commander was impressed with our repeat runs; it was thought, with good reason, that Commander Witholt had been very conscientious. Considering that our crew was not supposed to have been on the trip, we felt lucky to have seen such an operation first-hand and to have returned without picking up a single hole.

Jim Betts knew, before the briefing had been called, that the Arnhem operation was on. Knowing that our crew was nearing the end of its tour, he was sure we would be keen to go on the trip. But he couldn't tell me that when he put us on the Battle Order.

Getting the Picture

Memories of a Photo-reconnaissance Unit Spitfire Pilot

WILLIAM K. (BILL) CARR CMM, DFC
LIEUTENANT GENERAL CAF (RET'D)

B ill Carr's war was a lonely but extremely vital one. Like Bill McRae, Jim Collier, and Bill McKenzie, he flew single-engine fighters—Spitfires. His flights were always solitary, and deep into enemy territory in an unarmed, camera-equipped aircraft. The aerial photographs he and other PRU pilots obtained provided the intelligence needed to establish enemy positions, esti-mate enemy strengths and weaknesses, find targets for bombing strikes, assess the effectiveness of earlier bombing, and generally plan strategies.

A native of Grand Bank, Newfoundland, Bill Carr graduated from Mount Allison University in 1941 and immediately joined the RCAF.

Completing Elementary Flying Training at 22 EFTS, Ancienne Lorette, Quebec, on Fleet Finches, he earned his wings on Harvards at No. 2 Service Flying Training School (SFTS), Uplands (Ottawa). After taking a Navigation General Reconnaissance course in PEI, he went overseas to take an Advanced Flying Training course on Miles Masters at Watton in England. Next came Photo-Reconnaisance Operational Training on PRU Spitfires located at an OTU at Dyce, Scotland, from where he was sent to 540 PRU Squadron on Spitfires at Benson. His next posting was to 683 RAF PRU Squadron in Malta. For his photo-reconnaissance work in Malta and Italy he was awarded a DFC.

After the war, Flight Lieutenant Carr flew a Norseman with 413 Photo-graphic Survey Squadron on mapping operations in the Canadian Arctic. Flying an accompanying Norseman was Bill McRae. In 1956, promoted to Wing Commander, he commanded 412 (VIP Squadron), flying such notables as Queen Elizabeth, Princess Margaret, Prime Minister John Diefenbaker, and

General Charles de Gaulle. He oversaw the establishment of the RCAF's first scheduled twice-weekly trans-Atlantic jet service, flying de Havilland Comets.

In 1960, Group Captain Carr was sent to the Congo to establish and command the first-ever United Nations Air Force. This organization included crews from fifteen nations, flying seven different types of aircraft, and developed into an efficient and effective facility for the support of UN operations throughout the Congo.

After a distinguished Service career, which involved the founding and command of the new Canadian Forces Air Command, Lieutenant General Bill Carr retired from the military in 1978. He was then appointed Senior Vice President of International Aircraft Marketing with Canadair and later Bombardier. He retired in 1993 and became an aircraft marketing consultant. He resides in Ottawa and, since his retirement, has been Honorary Colonel of 412 (VIP) Squadron. Bill Carr was inducted into Canada's Aviation Hall of Fame in 2001.

It was a sodden, foggy, and cold day in June 1943 at RAF Portreath, the departure airfield for aeroplanes headed for North Africa and the Middle East from the U.K.

We had just heard that conditions were dismal over the route via the Bay of Biscay and far out to sea southward off the coast of neutral Spain and Portugal; the powers-that-be had decided that none of the twin- or four-engine aircraft I had seen when I landed the day before would be heading out until the weather improved.

I had resigned myself to a dreary day in the Nissen-hutted shantytown where I knew no one, when the Briefing Officer asked if the Spitfire pilot was in the room. Having seen no other single-engine fighter aircraft on the field when I landed the day before, I presumed I could be the pilot he was looking for. I spoke up. "You can go!" he said.

I wasn't the only one surprised. But I wasn't about to let their decision seem anything but normal for a photo-reconnaissance Blue Spit pilot. No way would I let on to this bunch that I had anything but a no-sweat reaction to the decision. If the truth were known, I had the same self-doubts that I suspect other pilots might have, even at the confident age of nineteen.

I was flying a Mark XI PRU Spitfire to Malta. And to think a Spitfire—with one engine—could go to Gibraltar when they—enjoying the safety of more than one engine, with a navigator and a radio that worked—couldn't, was not only news, it was a wonder.

I went to the Route Planning Operations Room as directed, got maps, escape kit (including emergency money for use in case of bailout), donned my Mae West over my khaki battle dress already fixed with hidden escape maps printed on silk, compass buttons, and other odds and ends the details of which I've long forgotten, and my sheepskin-lined flying boots. My note pad, en route maps, and navigation calculator were strapped to my thigh. After the traditional superstitious pee on the tailwheel, I climbed into the cockpit. As usual the CO_2 inflation bottle of the survival dinghy in the seat cushion attached to my parachute managed to be exactly where it was most uncomfortable.

As I taxied to the takeoff end of the field, rarely could I see the other boundary through the fog and mist. I was in the cloud right after takeoff and would be there until I broke out at 29,000 feet, ten or twelve minutes later. There was a solid deck of cloud below me as far as I could see. Not until I neared the north

A very youthful Bill Carr receives his pilot's wings from Air Marshal W. A. Bishop VC, DSO, MC, DFC, ED in July 1943. *Via W. K. Carr*

coast of Spain did I see the surface. I cruised at 30,000 feet all the way, with an indicated airspeed of 195 to 200 mph. This gave me a true airspeed (ground speed) of 350 mph. My approved routing to Gibraltar required that I fly outside the territorial waters of Spain and Portugal and, when south of Cadiz, head for "Gib."

Having encountered no problems on my long over-water flight to the Spanish north coast, I decided to take a shortcut across Spain, intending to descend over the ocean just southwest of Cadiz. My thinking was that if I could avoid making vapour trails, it would be very unlikely that anyone would spot me at 30,000 feet as I flew south along the Spanish-Portuguese border. There was no air-defence system to worry about anyway—so far as I knew. The possibility of diplomatic problems because of my violation of neutral air space scarcely entered my head. And, while I didn't know for sure, I suspected that I wasn't the first to cut this corner.

On landing at Gib I was directed to the operations trailer, where I was required to explain who I was, where I had come from, and where I was going.

The serial number of PRU Spitfire Mk XI (RAF EN654), photographed over England, is only twenty earlier than the machine that the author "worked up" and delivered to Malta. *C. E. Brown/Imperial War Museum*

They had received no information from the U.K. about my flight. When I wrote my departure and arrival times in the Ops Log, the three hours and fifteen minutes it had taken to cover the 1,300 miles left me with the impression that they thought there was something fishy about the trip. I worried, belatedly, that my breaking of neutral air space rules might get me in some kind of trouble. However, I heard no more of it.

Next morning, before leaving for Fez, Morocco, on my way to Malta, a few aircrew who had nothing better to do came to look over my Blue Spit and to see me off. One of them, a classmate from my wings parade at Uplands (Ottawa) a year or so before, even joined me in the ritual good luck anointment of my Spit's tailwheel.

On arrival at Luqa Airfield, Malta, a day later, my aircraft was greeted with great enthusiasm by members of 683 PRU Squadron. I was ignored. I had sort of hoped, immodestly perhaps, to be personally welcomed and congratulated on having come so far so quickly, to deliver such a beautiful machine with not even a sign of desert dust on it.

Finally I was ushered into the presence of the fabled Wing Commander Adrian Warburton, DSO and Bar, DFC and two Bars, and USAAF DFC. He greeted me in the ground crew's revetment lean-to, where he often had his cuppa with the erks. He wore a white shirt, no rank badges, khaki pants, suede desert boots, and, of course, no medal ribbons. He looked me up and down and, after a question about who I was, said, in front of his buddies, "You can stay." I was pretty happy at this turn of events; I had heard that those he didn't want, for whatever reason, were sent to an aircrew pool somewhere near Cairo. "Warbie," referred to by Air Marshal Keith Park, the boss at Malta, as a one-man Air Force, had the power.

Here I was, in Malta a couple of months after I had been posted to 543 Squadron at RAF Station Benson from my OTU course at Dyce in Scotland. At Benson, the home of photographic reconnaissance activity in the RAF, I had done lots of "boring holes in the sky," experience building. But I had only completed two actual milk-run PR operations over the near coast of France.

Benson was commanded by Air Commodore John Boothman, later Air Chief Marshal Sir John, of Schneider Trophy fame. While he had made a tremendous contribution to the development of the PR Spitfire, it was the float-equipped Supermarine S-6B Schneider Trophy racer (which had set the

Bill Carr (right) and "Brockie" Brocklehurst, who would later be shot down and become a prisoner of war, with one of their Spitfire Mk XIs in a revetment at Luqa, Malta, in 1943. *W. K. Carr*

world speed record of 406 mph in 1931) stored in one of the hangars that really awed us young sprogs.

Ten days before I landed at Portreath, the Squadron Commanding Officer called me in and told me I was to sign out Spitfire EN674, just delivered, "work it up," and take it to 683 Squadron in Malta. That is the total briefing I was given. It was up to me to figure out how I was to do this once I had visited the Intelligence Section and been briefed. I knew I wasn't the first to fly this route; but how the others had fared was never passed on to me.

The officious non-flying-type Intelligence Officer, in his heady surroundings of classified material, told me to get some khaki battle dress from the supply section, leave my worldly goods there (I never saw them again), pick up some maps at the Nav Section, and head for Portreath. There they would give me everything else I might need. Despite this send-off I was excited to be going where the real action was. While I wasn't preoccupied with what the future might hold, like many others I suppose, I did wonder what might happen to me.

"Working up" Spitfire EN674 was a joy. Brand new, including the cameras, it was as good a performer as I had so far flown—rock steady at altitude and easily trimmed hands-off. It possessed a cool-running engine, a rare artificial horizon which didn't topple until one exceeded 45 degrees of bank, a directional gyro which precessed less than most, a slip-and-skid (turn-and-bank in our lingo) indicator which was quite sensitive without the built-in lag some had, and a fuel burn rate even better than shown in the Pilot's Notes. My logbook shows that I got to 43,000 feet once in this beauty—despite knowing the dangers of anoxia—without pressure breathing, which hadn't yet been invented. The medics at the OTU had told us that some of us might be able to fly higher than others. By watching the colour of our fingernails, we could tell when we were becoming anoxic—they began to turn blue. For me it worked 100 percent, and one day over Malta I managed to get to 49,000 feet indicated by clamping my mask to my face, turning the oxygen to emergency, and watching my fingernails. Foolish? Probably, but I'm still here.

EN674 was fitted with two 36-inch F52 cameras equipped with 500-exposure film magazines. From 30,000 feet, this split pair of cameras covered just over two miles laterally on the Earth's surface, so accuracy over the target was essential. A couple of miles laterally can result from a small error in normal

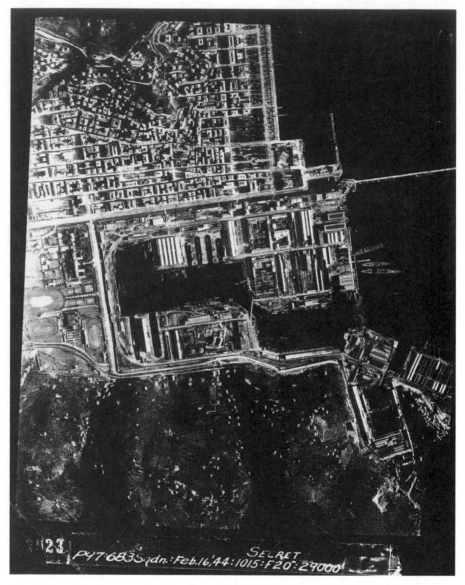

A typical aerial photograph taken from 29,000 feet over a northern Italian port by a photo-reconnaissance Spitfire Mk XI. Vehicles can be readily distinguished on the roads. *RCAF via W. K. Carr*

navigation at six miles up. The detail in the photographs from these cameras still surprises me. For example, I have one wartime vertical photo print where it is possible to see the power lines strung between towers even though the shot was taken at 29,000 feet.

The aircraft was also equipped to carry an oblique camera pointing through a small window out the left side of the fuselage, just behind the cockpit and depressed about ten degrees below the horizontal. This camera was fitted for use when low-level photography might be necessary because of weather or when the target detail wanted was only possible from a low angle rather than from above. To sight this camera the pilot lined up an "X" painted on the left side of the cockpit canopy at eye level with another "X" painted on the aileron. Not very sophisticated, but it worked.

One didn't fly a photo-recce Spitfire as much as one wore it. The cockpit literally fit around the pilot, yet it was totally functional. Once strapped in, the pilot became part of a man-machine system made up of a beautiful-looking and -flying aeroplane, sophisticated cameras and controls, and an outstanding all-round operational capability. No pilot could fail to be proud of his role in this remarkable combination.

Takeoff called for opening the throttle with the left hand while controlling direction and attitude with stick and rudder using the right hand and feet. Too much boost (manifold pressure) on takeoff would cause a swing to the left due to engine torque and, while easy to overcome directionally, the aircraft could be caused to skid sideways and, in fact, roll the tires off the wheel rims.

Once airborne, the pilot's left hand had to be moved to the stick so that the right could reach down to grasp the landing gear lever and move it to the up position. With experience, this became a smooth operation. One could judge a Spitfire pilot's time by watching the gyrations of the aircraft as he changed hands right after takeoff.

Climb power was set by reducing engine rpm and opening the throttle to its climb power setting. Unlike most aircraft, climb power was more than takeoff power simply because, once airborne, torque ceased to be a problem. In any case, even at the lower takeoff power, the run was so short that runway length was seldom a concern.

At operational altitude, say 30,000 feet, the long-range cruise-indicated airspeed would be set up at about 195 to 200 mph. To get this, the prop would be set at 2,000 rpm with the wide open throttle reading +1 psi, approximately, resulting in a true airspeed of 350 mph. Fuel consumption would be about 30 gallons per hour (better than our crew jeep!). The aircraft range at these settings was about 2,100 miles; enough to fly from Naples to London and back.

Our Mark XI Spitfires were very sensitive to elevator and rudder trim settings. There was no aileron trim. When a pilot reported a wing-heavy condition, the mechanic would take a rubber mallet and a short piece of two-by-four and gently hammer the trailing edge of the aileron against the wood block in the direction necessary to offset the heaviness. Guesswork perhaps, but it worked most of the time; though it was not unknown for it to make the problem worse because the erk had bent the aileron in the wrong direction.

At altitude, the Spitfire was superbly stable, but still extremely agile and responsive. For example, and again at altitude, trimming the aircraft hands-off, cracking the hood open a half-inch, and then sticking a finger out into the slipstream would cause the machine to enter a gentle turn. A finger out the other side, before the turn steepened, would restore it to straight and level flight. As well, leaning forward in the cockpit, when perfectly trimmed, would cause a gentle dive. On a long trip, this kind of entertainment was fun, so long as the pilot didn't fail to keep his eyes open for what could be unfriendly in the sky around him.

The aircraft's agility is best illustrated by its rate-of-roll, excellent for fighters of the day, at 14 degrees per second, progressing to 68 degrees in the later marks of Spitfire. Today's jet fighters are still in that ballpark, sixty years later! The rate-of-roll was so good that the navigation technique, to ensure that the aircraft was directly over the target to be photographed, was to do a quick roll in the few seconds between the reconnaissance photos. Upright, the earth below was blanked out of the pilot's vision by the wings and nose. Upside down, obviously, his line of sight to the target below was unrestricted.

My first operational sortie from Malta was to Naples. The mission was to photograph the harbour, rail yard, and two adjacent airfields. The trip took three hours and fifty minutes. Two days later I was sent to the same area and this time saw some very inaccurate flak way below my height. At debriefing the Intelligence Officer informed me that this was most likely 88-mm ack-ack. The tactic for avoiding this stuff was to watch your tail and, as the white puffs came closer along your track, alter course 30 degrees or so for a few minutes, and then resume the original heading. It was interesting to watch puffs creep up your track and continue along it after you had changed course. On picking up your altered course the guns would follow it. But there was always, supposedly, a delay, apparently due to the time it took to relay information from radar to the guns. This tactic didn't work, however, for the much-feared box barrage.

On one occasion, over Perugia, a rail and industrial centre, I was the target of a box barrage when ack-ack bursts appeared above, below, and all around me. Out of instinct I lowered my seat, as though the thin aluminum fuselage skin would give me more protection than the Perspex canopy top. A very loud bang from beneath my seat left me shaking. I was about to die, I was sure! But I still seemed to be in control of the aircraft—I might not be nearing the Pearly Gates after all. I reached under my seat and, when I saw a bit of blood on my flying glove, assumed the things hanging down were part of my anatomy. Happily they weren't. They were shreds of my parachute and the emergency seat-pack cushion. The blood later proved to have come from a small cut on my bottom.

However, the oil cooler, which sits on the bottom surface of the wing, had been smashed. When I finally noticed a complete loss of oil pressure and an oil temperature off the clock, I realized that the engine, by now, should have seized or quit. Since it hadn't and seemed to be running normally, I decided to head for our base at San Severo, about forty minutes away at low power, reduced airspeed, and in a gradual descent from the 29,000-foot height where I had been clobbered.

I couldn't risk a bailout because of my damaged parachute and, if I finally had to crash land on the way, at least I would be closer to friendly territory. While it was a long time ago, my logbook still seems to trigger this logic. Anyway, I babied the engine and made it safely back with that beautiful Rolls-Royce Merlin purring comfortably like nothing was wrong. Forty minutes without oil in the tank, even at low power, must have been some kind of a miracle. The box barrage was a scary and effective deterrent. I never again met one. Thank God.

After the invasion of Sicily, and when the Foggia Plains had fallen to the Allies, we moved from Malta and eventually settled at San Severo near the Adriatic coast of Italy. From there, our squadron was assigned the reconnaissance needs of both the British Eighth and American Fifth Armies as well as continuing to provide strategic coverage of the Balkans, southern Germany,

Bill Carr in the cockpit of his photo-reconnaissance Spitfire Mk XI at Luqa, Malta, in 1943. The absence of a bullet-proof windscreen identified photo-reconnaisance aircraft. *Via W. K. Carr*

Austria, southern France, and Czechoslovakia. Many sorties were for bomb-damage assessment of targets hit by heavy bombers from the U.K. and Middle East. The rest of our trips were to obtain mosaics of battle areas, defence lines, and targets like bridges, ports, and shipping and railway lines and yards. Over Bavaria, particularly, we met opposition in the form of flak and enemy fighters. Elsewhere the competition was perhaps less worrisome, but the concentration of friendly aircraft in our skies raised the twitch factor as much as did German fighters. Italian Air Force fighters weren't much of a threat and of course ceased to be any problem at all once Italy became an "Ally."

Our aircraft were unarmed mainly because the job of the photo-recce pilot was to gather information and bring it back. While the clean leading edge of the wing that resulted from the lack of guns gave room for much more fuel and also reduced drag, the real reason was not to present the recce pilot with the dilemma of having to subjugate his aspirations to become an ace to his main purpose of collecting intelligence.

To offset the lack of guns and to strengthen chances of survival in a hostile environment, OTU training had dwelt heavily on aircraft capability, instrument flying, accurate navigation, and the development of flying skills beyond the normal operational training level. The student was encouraged to fly his aeroplane to the very edge of its performance envelope and to try every stunt he could imagine. Even the heart-stopping tail-slide manoeuvre was practised. While a negative "G" push over was okay, a full bunt was a no-no.

It was the kind of training that built the pilot's confidence and made him aware that he could indeed out-fly and out-fox the other guy, whether enemy or friendly. And the "friendly" was often the more dangerous because the fighter jock's commendable motivation to shoot down the enemy didn't always guarantee he would positively identify his target before firing. From many angles a lone Spitfire could look like an Fw 190 or Bf 109. If the PR pilot saw the other guy first, he could likely escape. Most PR losses were to flak, oxygen, and mechanical problems, although many simply disappeared and the reason was never discovered. The great Warburton suffered this fate.

Navigation techniques consisted mainly of map reading and dead reckoning. No radar positioning, radio beacon, or outside aids existed, and the best one could hope for in bad weather at base or return was a VHF DF bearing followed by a by-guess-and-by-God approach. The DF bearing could not indicate whether the aircraft was to the left or the right or going away or approaching. If the pilot's transmission faded after some minutes then it was assumed the aircraft was going away from the station. He was then directed to do a 180 in the hope that his transmission strength would increase. As the aircraft neared the station, the airmen on the ground outside the radio trailer would listen for the engine sound, assess when it was closest, and inform the radio operator, who would relay "Engine west" or as appropriate, and suggest the pilot steer a heading that would avoid running into any hills or obstructions in the area. If the ocean was near, as on the east coast of the U.K., then the pilot would be directed out to sea for his letdown. The amazing fact is, no pilot I know of ever augered in on this very rudimentary bad-weather approach. PR pilots were good all-weather fliers too, and weather at the operating base was seldom a factor in operations.

Flight planning took care and calculation. The usual plotting of track and distance was supplemented by detailed plotting of photographic runs for mosaic coverage or for spot targets, on large-scale maps or air photos if available. The aircraft was sent on every flight with full gas tanks and oxygen bottles. This policy served two purposes. First, were it needed and you could be contacted, non-briefed targets could be added while you were en route. Second, and much more important to the pilot, the extra fuel and oxygen gave him the reserves he might need were he intercepted. Our escape tactic, in such instances, was a full-power climb. The full-power fuel flow, at four times

In San Severo, Bill Carr—with wet pants—is induced to climb from his Spitfire by photographers following a six-hour flight that included taking the first photographs of the Allied landing on the beach at Anzio, Italy. *Via W. K. Carr*

the normal long-range flow, meant the pilot needed all the reserve fuel he could carry.

I was intercepted by both sides, many times, but one particular instance sticks clearly in my mind. I had been assigned to photograph rail yards at Vienna, do a bomb-damage assessment run over Salzburg, and then cover the three airfields around Munich. As I started my first run over Munich at 31,000 feet, I sensed that there was someone else in the area. I looked to my left and spotted a totally unknown type of aircraft about 200 yards out. It didn't seem to have any propellers and it appeared to be looking me over rather than coming after me. I went to full bore and climbed, levelling out at about 40,000 feet. Hoping I had lost him, I searched the sky. He was still with me! I rolled into a vertical dive and pulled out on the deck as low as I could manage. Lo and behold, he was still with me! I headed for the Brenner Pass—on the deck. I have ever since contended that I was so low, he never could have gotten a shot at me—and the pass was a foot or two deeper after my passing!

I had never heard of a jet aircraft. If I reported this thing to the intelligence wallas, I wondered whether they would think I had gone 'round the bend. The aircraft, I later realized, was a Messerschmitt Me 262, still in test status, out of the research facility at Munich and probably unarmed. The Intelligence Officer showed little surprise when I finally decided to tell him about it. It seems our people knew about these things but felt we pilots shouldn't be told in case we were shot down and had to admit to the Germans that we knew what they knew!

The extra fuel helped me on another occasion when, en route back from the north, I was diverted to the Anzio Beaches to do a full recce of the Allied landings then in progress. We had not heard that this was to happen, and neither had the press. I did as I was told, dodging friendly flak as well as both enemy and Allied aeroplanes, and headed for San Severo. I had been airborne for nearly six hours and had to pee so badly I was bursting. Normally, when this happened at altitude, it was not unknown to wet one's pants. Because of the lack of air pressure, evaporation was almost instantaneous and no embarrassing traces remained on landing. In this case I held on as long as I could, but as I came down at San Severo, for some reason I could hold off no longer.

On landing I was greeted by numerous representatives from the press who had been told I would be bringing pictures of the invasion and would have seen

Bill Carr (right) meets King George VI at San Severo, Italy, in 1944.
Group Captain Millington has his back to the camera. *Via W. K. Carr*

the beachhead. I continued to answer questions about what I had seen; but I stayed in the cockpit. Finally one photographer insisted I get out so he could get a picture. I did as he asked, thinking that my khaki battle dress would probably camouflage my error, and I left my parachute in the cockpit. Unfortunately one of the erks climbed on the wing and slung my chute over his shoulder. He was showered. No ground crew mechanic had ever before offered to take my chute out of the aeroplane. So it served him right. Nobody said anything, but I was a very deflated hero.

War stories become more dramatic as they recede in time, and they sometimes inflate in importance in the mind of the individual telling them. However there are some impressions that still ring true and, on reflection, cause not just wonder but sadness and awe. The awe that an obviously brave pilot such as Warburton generated never wanes. And the sight of a first-class pilot misjudging his landing approach at Luqa and smashing into the vertical quarry wall just before the button of that runway never goes away. That pilot had survived the Malta "Blitz," flown over three hundred hours in enemy skies, been shot at, chased, and damaged. On his last flight to complete his tour and go home, he killed himself through a moment's inattention.

A similar last flight happened in front of several of us at our landing strip in central Italy. The pilot decided to beat up the flight line before landing. He roared across at a dangerously low height, just missing the parked Spits on the line, and jerked the aircraft into a vertical climb. He stalled while inverted and splattered himself over the dispersal.

One of the dangers of lone operation in the photo-recce role was boredom. Another was over confidence. These could lead to mistakes which, in the end, only the pilot involved knew about. There was no other witness as there would have been in a crewed machine or a single aircraft in a fighter sweep as part of a formation. This isolation could cause strange things to happen to people.

The whole PR business was not only impersonal but lonely. There was no real cohesion among PR pilots other than socially, because each operated on his own. Indeed it was so impersonal that the routine practice of sharing another pilot's things if he went missing was brought home sharply to me on one occasion out of Malta.

On my way back from a sortie to the Po Valley in northern Italy, my engine overheated and was running rough. Being over Sicily where our troops were still wrapping up the invasion, I decided to land at the strip at Syracuse rather than take a chance of having the engine quit over the water on my way to Malta. The airfield had a number of Spits parked on it, and the odds seemed reasonable that somebody could fix mine. They did eventually, and two days later I flew to Luqa.

When I got to our quarters I found that all of my stuff had gone from my bed space. I realized then that the message I had sent from Sicily had never arrived and it was assumed that I had gotten the chop. It took time to get my belongings back, and one fellow made me feel that I was almost a shit to insist. My "stuff" consisted of a camera worth about ten dollars, some Malta-tailored bush jackets and shirts, a pair of desert boots, and a few knick-knacks. That inventory was about as lavish as any of the other pilots owned.

My last operational sortie, my 142nd, was on 25 September 1944. My assignment included photo targets in the Budapest area, along the Danube, and then the Belgrade area. I met no opposition and the trip took four hours and thirty minutes. Once past Belgrade, there was little chance that any enemy aircraft or flak would bother me on my route back to central Italy.

I still had lots of gas and, though mindful of what had happened to some on their last op, I decided to low-fly all the way for the fun of it. On the deck past Sarajevo, I was barrelling down a straight country road, dodging the trees on the sides, when I came on a formation of soldiers ambling down the centre. When they heard my engine, they disappeared into the ditches on each side. However, I can still see the peasant lady with a bundle balanced on her head, striding proudly along the edge. She too must have heard me coming but ignored me. I rationalized later that it was her chance to show some defiance of the hated conquerors.

I returned home to Canada via ship to the U.K. and then to Halifax, just before Christmas 1944. Like most returnees, I was put on hold for the Far East. Luckily, that fight ended before I could be called.

I had survived partly out of luck and to a great extent because I was chosen to do photographic reconnaissance in an unmatched aircraft. Just over 50 percent of our cohorts did not make it home, and they have no known graves. They simply disappeared doing their duty. Thirty of us are still alive, not because we did it better, but because that is the way things are in war.

The final epitaph of the photographic-recce Spitfire was written when one set a never-to-be-equalled world speed record for propeller-driven aircraft of 690 mph (Mach 0.94) in a dive from 52,550 feet out of Hong Kong on 5 February 1952. Total Spitfire production of all marks was 22,729 and about 460 were Mk XI PRU versions.

The Spitfire was a dream to fly, and the opportunity to serve in such a superb example of man's superiority made one worry less about one's mortality. Obviously the Mk XI was the "Rolls-Royce" of the breed. Other aircraft types came close, but none equalled R. J. Mitchell's masterpiece.

The Meteor and I

Recollections of
Canada's First Jet Pilot

WILLIAM H. (BILL) MCKENZIE
FLIGHT LIEUTENANT RCAF (RET'D)

Bill McKenzie earned a place in the history of Canadian aviation when he became the first Canadian to fly a jet aircraft. Attached to an RAF unit—as were so many members of the RCAF—he was flying Spitfires with 616 Squadron, when, in July 1944, his unit was chosen as the first to re-equip with the RAF's revolutionary new twin-jet-powered fighter, the Gloster Meteor Mk I. Bill McKenzie was the first 616 pilot to be checked out—at the RAF's Farnborough Experimental Establishment—in one of these top-secret machines.

Bill enlisted in the RCAF in his hometown of Winnipeg. Where he did his elementary flying training is uncertain. His advanced training is thought to have been on Harvards at Trenton. Not mentioned in his account are the several months that he spent away from the squadron as one of the pilots selected for special training to fly Spitfires from the pitching deck of an aircraft carrier in the Mediterranean and deliver them to the hard-pressed RAF units defending the island of Malta where they were desperately needed.

Leaving the RCAF, Bill embarked on a career well suited to his ebullient personality. He became a very successful representative of a succession of breweries: Formosa Springs, Molson's, Dow, Labatt's, and finally Hudson's Bay Distillers. After leaving the RCAF, he continued to fly, on de Havilland Vampires with an RCAF Auxilliary Reserve Squadron at Downsview (Toronto). Squadron functions were never short of liquid refreshment. Bill McKenzie died in 1986.

Bill's wilderness experience on the shore of Flak Lake where he ditched his Meteor has not been forgotten. Not far from the present community of Elliot Lake, Flak Lake is now part of Mississagi Provincial Park. His campsite has become the starting point of the twenty-five-kilometre McKenzie Trail—a challenge for hikers. A rubber gas tank, a relic from Bill's Meteor, marks the site.

On 7 February 1941, the War Ministry put out a contract for a twin-engine "Gloster-Whittle aeroplane" to specification F 9/40, which eventually became the Meteor. In 1942 the original order for twelve was reduced to six production models, and then increased to eight. The prototype began taxi trials on 10 July 1942. With two 1,000-pound-thrust engines, it was so under-powered that it barely got off the ground. After that, it was used solely for taxiing trials. The first production machine, RAF EE210, was shipped to the United States early in 1944, as part of the Lend-Lease Agreement. It greatly assisted the Americans in starting their own jet aircraft industry. The first of six aircraft was delivered to 616 Squadron on 12 July 1944, to be put into service.

At that time, I was stationed at Exeter flying Spitfire VIIs, pressurized machines with two-staged blowers for high-altitude operation. In typical RAF fashion we were assigned to ground strafing and anti-shipping strikes, preparing for the Normandy invasion. Anyone who thinks they've ever experienced real heat needs to sit in a pressurized Spit, fifty feet off the deck, with the blower going constantly and the sun beating on the canopy. Some of the boys flew

The high-altitude Supermarine Spitfire Mk VIIs flown by Bill McKenzie with 616 Squadron RAF were a comparatively rare mark, identifiable by the extended wing tips. This example bears no squadron or aircraft designators. *Air Ministry*

without jackets and risked getting badly burned, should the aircraft catch fire for any reason. And yet, low flying was a lot of fun.

At Exeter, we flew with the Americans when they sent their Fortresses over Brest and St. Nazaire to attack the submarine pens—akin to dropping peas on a concrete sidewalk. But they kept at it. Escorting them in our Spitfires, we found it a hell of a long trip across water. Coming back, on the deck, heading for Land's End, the extreme southwestern tip of England, we kept edging just a little more to the right lest we miss our landfall and head out into the Atlantic. Instead we would all wind up in the middle of England, almost out of fuel.

All too often, Brest was covered in cloud and the bombs were dumped in the channel on the way back. Deciding that this was getting ridiculous, the brass decided to train a few pilots in meteorology, and I was one of those chosen. We went on a Met course, learning the CuNim business—how to identify clouds and other weather phenomena.

Our new job was to fly alone over the Brest area and write down a detailed weather report: what the weather was, what the cloud formations were, what our estimation was as to when it was going to blow over. After my first trip, I came back with a fine report. I was proud of myself—I had distinguished a CuNim from a Stratus! I was well prepared when an American officer asked, "Well, what's the weather?"

"There is ten-tenths Cirrus," I answered, "some CuNims and Nimbostratus."

"Man, what the hell are you talking about?"

"The weather!"

"Well," he said, "I don't want to hear all that BS! Is it good or is it bad?"

"It's bad!" So much for two weeks of training!

Half an hour later, the operations phone rang and down came the D-form: "There will be a Fortress raid on Brest." We did this for a month, and they never once aborted! In the American system, we learned, once the wheels started to turn, nobody in the organization could stop them.

With .50-calibre upper, lower, rear, and nose guns, and their Fortresses in tight box formations, the Americans felt, initially, that no fighter could get near them. We would take them in over the enemy coast, as far as our range permitted. Then we had to leave them. They would continue on in, and some of the penetrations would be quite deep into Germany. After about six months of our escorting them in and out from the coast, they decided that we weren't really needed. Shortly after this, they flew into Germany going in over Holland. Well along over the Dutch coast on the back, they began to relax.

The Germans chose that location to scramble about 150 Focke-Wulf 190s. They climbed into the middle of the formation and mauled the Fortresses badly. The next day we were back escorting them. We never saw much action, but we were enough to keep the Luftwaffe away.

One day, I think it was about D-Day plus 6, when the weather was too socked in for 11 Group and the Tactical Air Force, we got a call to patrol the Normandy beachhead. This we did with enthusiasm! We flew over on the deck and thrashed around, having a good look. When we returned we found that we had flown everywhere we shouldn't have—red zones and over battleships. But nobody had told us a thing. Luckily, we weren't shot down. Then, too late, we were briefed on where we should have gone.

If you had mentioned jet propulsion to any of our pilots on 616, they wouldn't have known what you were talking about. No one had ever heard of such a ridiculous thing as a jet aircraft. In April 1944, we were sitting in West Malling when the Old Man, our Commanding Officer, Squadron Leader Les Watts, was called up to London. On his return, he advised us that we would be moving up to Culmhead and would be re-equipped, but he wouldn't say what our new machines were to be. So, we moved, still doing low-level jobs with our Spits.

A clapped-out Oxford arrived at flight dispersal and the Old Man announced that this was to be our training aircraft—we were all going to become twin-engine pilots. This posed a problem—none of us had ever flown twins, except me. Fortunately, we had a Supernumerary Flight Lieutenant, G. Enderby, who had ten hours on Oxfords. Amazingly, he was appointed instructor for the squadron.

The next day the CO and I went up with our "instructor." I was in the right-hand seat while the Old Man stood behind me, watching—ready to get out fast if he had to. Enderby showed me how to taxi, then he took off, did a circuit, landed, and asked me to taxi the Oxford back.

I must now explain a premonition of mine that bears on my story—I knew that I was going to die in an Oxford. I would have nightmares about this, and hoped I would never ever see one. In my opinion, they embodied all the vices of

The unloved Airspeed Oxford. Spitfire pilot Bill McKenzie felt that if he was to be killed flying, it would be in an Oxford. *Airspeed Photo*

every multi-engine machine in the Allied air forces. I had lost a few friends on them during training, and they left me cold.

I sat at the end of the runway and I don't remember much, only that the sweat was running into the toes of my boots. I figured I had about three minutes to live. I opened the throttle, got off the ground, and did a vicious left turn, almost taking the control tower with me. But I survived, landed, and climbed out, letting the Old Man take over. I felt much better. I had more confidence in the aircraft, and I've never since had those nightmares. Eventually I came to enjoy flying the old Ox Box. The CO did a circuit much as I had, and we returned to our chores.

A week later I got another hour solo in the Oxford. A couple of days later the CO and I flew down to Farnborough to see our new aircraft. The next morning we were on our way over to what was known as "H" hangar, about to discover just what a weird place this experimental station was. Walking across the tarmac, we were startled when, without warning, there was a bang! Overhead was an aircraft just launched with the help of a rocket!

We entered the hangar, going through three checkpoints with Service police checking our ID cards and demanding signatures. I had my first look at the thing sitting there, looking like a monster with two big empty eyes. Wing

Commander "Willie" Wilson, a real character, was running the show. With his moustache, long cigarette holder, and white gloves, he was the RAF stereotype. But he wore an AFC with three bars. I was still just a bit skeptical—all the AFCs I had known of were earned on nonoperational flying. My opinion changed when I learned that he received all those AFCs for test flying.

"Good God," I said. "What the hell is that?"

"That," he explained, "is a jet."

"A jet? What's a jet?"

"It's an aircraft."

"Well, what exactly does it do?"

"It flies."

"There's no damn way in the world that thing can fly—it hasn't got any props!"

"Well, I guarantee it will fly. The air, you see, comes in here, heats up, and shoots out the back."

Finally, in spite of my misgivings, I had to agree: if he said it would fly, it would fly. He had it pushed out onto the tarmac and handed me two printed sheets, which I looked at: starting procedure, taxiing procedure, takeoff procedure, and landing procedure.

"Get your parachute," he told me. "Climb in and I'll run through this list with you." I climbed in, and the Old Man perched on the ladder while I sat reading the instructions. Right low-pressure cock on. I looked down and there was a lever marked LP, which I flicked "on" along with the left LP cock. Then I pulled the right HP cock. Finally I pressed Button B, then Button A, and all of a sudden this whining started.

"My God! What's happening? Is this right?" One engine was running and I was starting the other. It was unreal—so different, too much to accept. I couldn't fully absorb what was going on. All this is interesting, I thought to myself. We've had a good start—now let's go and have lunch. But Willie reached down, picked up my helmet, and handed it to me.

"Okay," he says, "you're on your own. Go take a trip."

"Good God!" I thought.

So I checked the instructions again, starting with the taxiing procedure. I read it, tried it, and found it very, very pleasant—it was the first tricycle gear I had ever operated—just like driving a car. And visibility was great. There was no fourteen feet of Merlin blocking my view, as in a Spitfire, forcing me to S-turn constantly in order to see. This was super. I could see ahead and drive straight down the taxi-strip. And, because I was up in front of the engines, it was very quiet. Reaching the end of the runway, I had a last look at the takeoff procedure—line up, hold brakes on, put on ten degrees of flap, full throttle, release brakes, and that was it.

I was launched! In the air! I raised the wheels and flaps. All I could do was sit there, glancing back at those holes where the props should be. "I see it, but I can't believe it! What's holding me up?" I was almost in shock! I flew about fifty miles before turning around. But it was gorgeous, so simple, one of the most enjoyable trips I've ever made.

Out with the instructions again—even on how to get into the circuit—flaps down, wheels down, the whole landing procedure. I landed. It was the simplest and most pleasant aircraft I'd ever flown. I taxied back and the Old Man went up—now that he knew the aeroplane would fly. We stayed at Farnborough flying the Meteor for about a week.

At that time the buzz-bombs were pretty active on the south coast, and Churchill assigned them as the number one priority target for the RAF's new jets. I don't think he expected us to shoot many down, but it was great propaganda. It was reassuring for the civilian population to know that we were countering the Horrible Hun's new weapon with a new one of our own.

There were two things that I wondered about and I brought them up with the design people. First, how did one bail out of these things? We had no ejection seats. "Just go over the side," I was told, "over the wing and under the tail-plane." Looking back at that beast of a high tail-plane, I said, "No way!" "Oh, you will go under it—no problem," I was assured. Then we took a look at the armament, four nose-cannon with ejection for the spent casings just in front of and above the leading edge of the wings. The Old Man and I both noted this. What a strange place to locate these things, we thought, when the bottom was clear and they could have been ejected straight down. "No," we were again assured, "the casings will go over the wing and under the tail." Just like a pilot bailing out!

We were ready to put a couple of Meteors into operation when, fortunately, someone decided to do a few armament tests. An Armament Officer did some air-to-ground gunnery with one of our machines, and that machine became the first jet write-off. There wasn't one spent shell casing that didn't hit the aircraft, be it wings, fuselage, or tail-plane. The gunnery man was lucky to get down alive. When word of this got to London there was action. They extended the chutes out the bottom, the obvious place for them.

We returned to the squadron—still flying Spits—to check the rest of the boys out. There were no medicals, courses, lectures, decompression chamber tests—all that stuff came in later. We put twenty-four pilots through and never scratched an aircraft—a pretty good record. Then we were transferred down to Manston. We had six Meteors at that time—Meteor Is with two Welland engines of 1,700-pound thrust. They weren't all that fast.

Like our Spits, they were designed for high-altitude flying. Fuel consumption on the deck was atrocious; but at high altitudes the aircraft came into its own, the speed increased, and the fuel consumption decreased. But there we were, back on the deck, chasing buzz-bombs.

It was an unusual situation. Mustangs off the French coast were the first to tackle the little, unmanned V-1s, followed by Typhoons and Tempests. Then, along the British coast, they faced five miles of solid flak. Spitfire XIVs took over next, followed by our Meteors. Finally—just a minute and a half away—

Meteor Mk Is of 616 Squadron refuelling at RAF Manston in 1944. Bill McKenzie was the first operational jet pilot and the first Canadian to be checked out on a jet. *RAF Photo*

there was the balloon barrage surrounding London. We were operating in a very confined space and had to be quick to get in a shot.

Buzz-bombs were ram-jet powered. Stabilized by a gyroscope, they were the first semi-guided missiles. The ram effect of launching them from a ramp started the small jet engine. Basically a 2,000-pound bomb, they carried only enough fuel for the time required to reach London. When their fuel ran out, the engine shut off and they came down. London, supposedly, was splattered with V-1s. But, surprisingly, a map showing where every bomb came down made it very plain that the south coast of England, Kent especially, was about four to one ahead of London.

Buzz-bombs came in at about 350 mph flying at 1,000 to 1,500 feet, and our Meteors performed best at 30,000. Low down, we had only a marginal edge in speed. With the time constraint I've mentioned, our work was cut out for us.

I remember shooting one down—the only one I got—and it dove into a farmer's field, neatly stooked with grain for harvesting. After the thing hit, that field was as bare as the floor! "My God," I thought, "the people in London may have taken a beating, but this poor guy had just lost his whole year's work!"

The first buzz-bomb to be brought down wasn't shot down. It was tipped over by "Dixie" Dean, a mad Englishman we had with us. As I've explained, Spit XIVs would pick up the buzz-bombs just inside the coastal flak. They might be in position, but would be losing ground. This pilot sat there, maybe two thousand yards back, blazing away. Obviously, our man couldn't get in between. So he had to slide up beside the V-1 and wait for the Spit to give up. Then maybe he could get in for a shot. But he had only had a minute and a half. Dixie was sitting there waiting to move in—the date was 4 August 1944—but the pursuing Spit wouldn't drop back until it was almost too late. Dixie didn't have time to get behind the bomb. So he edged over beside the bomb, slipped a wing tip under its stubby wing, and tipped it over. In it went, the first victory for an RAF jet.

The downside was never mentioned. The tipping had not been done gently, as with the airflow over the wing. The sharp contact, like two cars side-swiping at substantial speed, had damaged Dixie's Meteor (EE216). The wing was wrinkled, and the aircraft had to be crated and sent back to the factory. This left us with only five Meteors.

We had a little thing going with the manufacturers, Gloster Aircraft,

Rolls-Royce, and Lucas, the three major manufacturers of the component parts for the Meteor. They advised the Old Man that, when we shot down the first buzz-bomb, they would throw us a party. We finally qualified for our party, and went out foraging. For weeks, we bought booze. The Old Man had a couple of aircraft loads of Scotch flown down from Scotland. We hired a ballroom in Ramsgate, and even a band. We were in pretty deep financially; but we didn't worry because we had these great corporations behind us. Eventually we received a cheque accompanied by a letter inviting us to have a good party on them. The cheque was for five pounds!

Needless to say, we were shocked. I think I was in for ten pounds myself, and so was everybody else. We were informed that the Ministry of Aircraft Production had a wartime limit on such outlay—five pounds. But the three firms did find a way around this obstacle. They came through, and we had a bash that you wouldn't believe. I think everybody in Ramsgate was in on it.

We had a friend—a hell of a good guy—outside West Malling, just south of London, where we were stationed. He owned an estate there, with a super bar. Two of us decided to fly there one weekend in our old Oxford. The weather was right down, but we didn't want to miss his party. So we flew about ten feet off the deck, following the railway lines by Kenley and Biggin Hill. Every now and then I could see something flashing by through the fog. When we broke clear, just outside West Malling, we were in the midst of a balloon barrage. I had never seen so many of the damn things in my life! And we had just flown right through the heart of them—ten feet higher and we'd have been dead! We had flown under their cables, which still hung down over us. When we told the control tower where we had come from, they wouldn't believe us. Apparently the balloons, set at hundred-yard intervals, were staggered over a distance of ten or fifteen miles. Ignorance is certainly bliss.

The second Meteor we lost at Manston wasn't destroyed but badly damaged. One of our Sergeant Pilots was completing an air test, and had tucked his machine into the circuit behind four Mosquitoes from the night-fighter squadron that shared the field with us. Coming in to land, he suddenly heard gunfire. He looked back to see a Spitfire blazing away at him. It shot the hell out of him and the guy was lucky to get in before his controls fell apart.

The Spitfire landed and taxied over to the control tower. When the pilot tried to claim an Me 262 destroyed, our CO, Andrew McDowall, DFM with two

The Meteors that Bill McKenzie and Jack Ritch flew on the Continent were painted white for identification—in the forlorn hope that Allied anti-aircraft batteries would not fire at them. *RAF Museum*

bars, dealt with him rather harshly but appropriately. The Spit's pilot had just returned from France. Crossing the coast and still on the deck, he looked up to see our Meteor in the circuit with the Mosquitoes. Assuming it was a 262, he opened up on it.

Then the buzz-bombs stopped coming. Allied troops advancing across Normandy overran their launch sites, which, of necessity, were close to the coast. Prior to this, I might add, we went up to Debden and did some work with the Americans. On their raids into Germany they had been meeting occasional German Messerschmitt Me 262 jets and Me 163 rocket-powered interceptors. They didn't know how to defend against them. So four of us went up to Debden with a couple of Meteors and spent a week with them from 10 to 17 October. They were sufficiently concerned to lay on a formation of Fortresses with P-47 escorts. We went up and made runs at them.

In those days we had no dive brakes. From 30,000 feet, we had to be very careful coming down. We were running into something new—a high Mach number or compressibility—which we thought at first was a joke. Our Meteors had a limiting Mach number of .78, which is .78 of the speed of sound. Then we ran into what at that time we called the wall. What was happening, nobody really understood. When we hit the wall, the aircraft would vibrate. If we persisted, we lost control. The aircraft could even break up. So, we flew with Mach numbers, not airspeed. Coming down from altitude, we had to watch our Mach number. Unfortunately, with the Mark I Meteors, we couldn't throttle back more than half throttle or we would flame out.

We were up at 30,000 feet, trying to dive at half throttle, about 50 mph off our Mach number. Because our Meteors were very, very clean, with little drag, we could dive from 20,000 feet at 300 knots, go down about 10,000 feet, and then zoom back up to 20,000 feet, still at 300 knots. There was nothing to it. What did we do with the American B-17s and their P-47 Thunderbolt fighter escorts? Just what the Germans were doing. We would dive in for a pass at the Forts, and all the Thunderbolts would chase us down. Pulling gently back on the controls, we would zoom up and do slow rolls around the Fortresses while they struggled back. We tried to suggest more disciplined tactics, but Americans are hard people to persuade.

The 262 was not what it was cracked up to be. German jet engines ran at extremely high temperatures, requiring turbine blades of very high-grade metal. Since the Germans didn't have these high-grade nickel alloys, their engines had a life of maybe twenty-four hours flying time. Thus, for quick engine changes, the 262 was designed with two underslung units held on by only four mounting bolts. Disposable engines! Some of our pilots managed to fly a captured 262, not knowing whether it was in its fifteenth or twentieth hour. Fortunately, they didn't prang it.

After chasing buzz-bombs, I went to Colerne, where they were setting up a jet-conversion unit. They had taken me off ops as tour expired. With me was another Canadian from 616, Jack Ritch, who was also tour expired. The only jets in service belonged to 616 Squadron, my unit, and I was still flying with them, but stationed at Colerne. It was an unusual situation. One week later, Jack and I were detailed to visit our detachment in Brussels, where we had four aircraft. "Do a little flying and see what's going on," the Old Man advised. Plus a lot of partying, we thought.

Taking the week off, we flew over to Europe. Our problem there was certainly different. Whenever we took off out of Brussels in our Meteors, we had to file a flight plan with the Army, telling them exactly where we would be flying. But it made no difference. They still shot at us. They knew the Germans were operating 262s, and as soon as they saw a jet, they didn't hesitate. They didn't seem to know that we also had jets, so we had to be the enemy! We spent the rest of our flying time dodging Spitfires and every other type of Allied fighter. It was all rather hairy. We didn't do an awful lot of flying, just a little ground strafing of airports.

When we got to Colerne the squadron began re-equipping with Meteor IIIs. The Meteor I had a cockpit hood with hinges on one side. Since we had to clamp it down, this arrangement wasn't too satisfactory. The Meteor III was fitted with a sliding canopy. The early Meteors had 1,700-pounds-thrust Rolls-Royce Wellands, while the IIIs had Rolls-Royce Derwents with 2,000-pound-thrust—a real improvement. They also boasted dive brakes, which was absolutely super, one of the greatest improvements to the Meteor. At altitude, we could now dump our dive brakes and come straight down. We didn't need to worry about Mach numbers. The jet-pipes were also extended, and the nacelles enlarged. It was a faster, much-improved aircraft, and we enjoyed flying it.

At Colerne, where we started the Conversion Unit, the intention was to bring in complete operational Spitfire squadrons. I would take one flight, and Jack Ritch the other; between us, we would check them all out on the Meteor. A syllabus and lesson plans were drawn up, and Flight Lieutenant M. A. Graves, our CO, sent them to the Air Ministry to be okayed. They were returned with a single notation, "more lecture time." Eventually a couple of pilots from Training Command were sent to show us how to fly twin-engine machines on one engine, a good thing because engines sometimes do fail.

So we ran the squadron through in short order in the manner that had been used with us. We didn't scratch an aircraft, except for one that I'll never forget. We had a New Zealand Flight Lieutenant who came in from the Second Tactical Air Force in Europe and had been posted to be checked out on jets. He had no documents. These were coming—only held up by the war, he assured us. He was a great guy. We partied all the time and he earned the nickname "Social."

After two or three weeks he was still waiting to be checked out on jets. I felt

Left to right: "Shan" Baudoux, Bill McKenzie, and Jack Ritch with the Gloster Meteor Mk III that they flew at air shows on a Victory Bond Drive in September 1945. *PA132383*

sorry for him. "What the hell, Social," I said, "we might as well get on with this. You've been here long enough. I'll check you out tomorrow." So I checked him out on the Meteor. He took off and promptly came in with the damned wheels up! Then everybody wanted to know who he was, and all I could say was, "I don't know. He walked in here about three weeks ago." There was no paperwork on him; he could even have been a German spy. That Meteor was the only aircraft we wrote off.

Then the RCAF caught up with me and made me tour expired. I came back to Canada in August of 1945, after four and a half years overseas. Reading the *Maple Leaf*, our Canadian military newspaper, I had spotted an item reporting that the RAF had donated a Meteor to the RCAF. "Geez," I thought, "there's my chance to get home!" So I went up to London and introduced myself—they weren't aware of my existence—and proposed that Jack and I be posted back to Canada to fly that Meteor.

Jack Ritch, myself, and another officer, Shan Baudoux, a Squadron Leader who had come out of the Boscombe Downs test-pilot course, were posted up to Warrington, outside Manchester. The next day they had a roll call, and we weren't on it. So we gave the adjutant our names. For two weeks we attended roll call. Nothing happened—no passages and no postings. Then the Adjutant informed us that A-priority people were staying there and all the others were going to Torquay. He called out all the names. Ours weren't there.

"Who the hell are you?" we were asked.

"We're A-priority. We're going home to Canada to fly a Meteor."

"I've got nothing on you."

"Well, where did you get our names?"

"You gave them to me, three weeks ago."

So we phoned London, and they asked us where we were. When we answered that we were up at Dom Head their response was, "Good God. You were supposed to be in Canada a week ago!"

"Well, we're not there and they want us to go to Torquay."

"Your documents are in Torquay. You had better get down there!"

Two weeks later we finally boarded a ship for Canada. The Meteor had already been shipped to St. Hubert (in Montreal) by boat, and assembled. We flew it up to Rockcliffe, in Ottawa, where we put on demonstrations for foreign Air Attachés. The Russians would be there and we were to give them full co-operation. Jack Ritch put on a superb demonstration for them on 18 September, in the overcast weather and rain. They were the only really interested people, almost climbing through the nacelles! After the performance we received an invitation to a party at their embassy.

Squadron Leader Baudoux, our leader, was unable to attend, but gave us his blessing. Jack and I were Flight Lieutenants and, when we arrived at the Russian Embassy—my God!—those hats, blocks of them, all gold braid! "Flight Lieutenant McKenzie," announced the butler. There was no one there under the rank of Group Captain.

It was a good party, but it really shook me the way the senior officers seemed to go on about military matters and their plans. Possibly it was calculated. A little Russian Major, a pilot and a "Hero of Lenin," would join a group and sing out, "To Stalin!" All he did was float around, making everyone gulp their booze. The Russians were drinking ginger ale. The last I saw of the Hero of Lenin, he was in the bathroom retching into the toilet. He had done his job. That party certainly was an experience.

The federal government decided we should take part in a Savings Bond Drive in the fall. We were to hit Quebec City, Montreal, Ottawa, Belleville, Toronto, London, Windsor, and Niagara Falls, putting on an air show in each city. This was just six months after the Mosquito, *F for Freddie,* had been lost in Calgary on 10 May 1945. They had given a fabulous low-level demonstration before catching a wing tip on an airport building and crashing. So there was uneasiness about the nature of our demonstrations.

The Meteor that flew down Danforth Avenue in Toronto at a very low altitude during the bond drive? I wasn't the pilot. It was my buddy, Jack Ritch, whose family lived off the Danforth. Jack put on a special show for his mother—and she enjoyed it. I've never been on such an enjoyable trip. It was a lot of fun and we met a lot of nice people.

When it was over, we crated the Meteors for testing at the Winter

Gloster Meteor Mk III (EE311), with Jack Ritch at the controls, flies over southern Ontario farmland in September 1945. *PL38180*

Experimental Establishment (WEE) at Edmonton. With the Meteors' poor range there was no thought of flying them out.

We went with them as pilots. We had two Meteors, and Jack almost wrote the one off. "Jack didn't simply run into compressibility problems," Group Captain Baudoux later explained. "The Meteor III had (unknown till then) a design weakness in the elevator horn. In very exceptional circumstances, it would fail. In this instance, it bent about 60° but stayed together. Jack did a superb job of flying it back—the RAF were highly complimentary, since two or three mysterious crashes were explained and possible repetitions prevented." That Meteor was returned to the U.K. and Jack Ritch was awarded a Green Endorsement.

One of our pilots was at Churchill with a Halifax, sitting with the engines running, waiting to leave, when a group dressed in parkas came over. Their faces were covered except for slits for their eyes—the pilot had no idea who they were. They climbed aboard the aircraft. "Look," said our pilot to one of them, "if you don't want to wind up in Edmonton you'd better get the hell out of here, because I'm taking off." The man left, and our pilot revved up an inboard engine. He looked back to see the tubby little guy being bowled across the apron. He later learned that his party were all brass from Ottawa. The unfortunate one was the *Little Flower*, Fiorello La Guardia, mayor of New York City!

Colin Gibson, who was then Minister of National Defense for Air, lived in Paris, Ontario, and requested that, for Dominion Day, 1946, a Meteor should put on an air show at Hamilton. The people there had never seen a jet. I was chosen to make the flight. Since the Meteor had a limited range, we strapped on a 100-gallon ventral tank, a Rube Goldberg arrangement using air pressure to pump fuel from it. Tests over a two-week period led us to calculate a range of about 1,340 miles, in still air. Since jet fuel was not available en route, a Dakota dropped off drums of kerosene at Medicine Hat, Regina, Winnipeg, Armstrong, Pagwa, North Bay, and Toronto.

I took off, heading east. With prevailing tail winds, range was not a problem on the first few legs. The strapped-on tank was not a success. It had worked well in the hangar and around Edmonton. But at 30,000 feet, it would not function—instead of having 130 imperial gallons, I had 30.

With fuel almost gone, I made a rapid descent, having no idea where the hell I was. I couldn't call for help, the radio was another Rube Goldberg affair. There was no point in bailing out. There is more water in Northern Ontario than land, and I always felt that the Meteor, with its clean lines, would ditch beautifully. So I ditched, and it was simple!

I picked the only shallow lake in the area—about 35 feet deep while the others were 300. Coming in, doing a precautionary let down, I had maybe five gallons of fuel left. From 30,000 feet, I spotted a big lake. "Dammit," I thought, "if I end up in the middle I might drown trying to swim ashore." Next to it was a smaller lake. From the middle of that one, I wouldn't have too far to swim.

When I got down I realized that the surrounding hills were anywhere from 1,200 to 1,500 feet high. And I was about 1,000 feet up. So I did an overshoot and a real steep climb. In front of me was solid bush. The Meteor's single-engine safety speed was 110 knots, and I was under that, doing a turn right, when my outer engine quit! I should have been dead! I should have spun in! I brought the Meteor around and dropped it into the middle of the lake. We skidded to a stop—upright. Immediately there was a mighty hiss followed by a great cloud of steam. Water poured in through the nose.

I had dumped the canopy, so I scrambled out, grabbing my emergency kit—mukluks, a parka and everything for arctic survival—but no kapok for flotation. I swam toward shore pushing the kit ahead of me. I was almost there when it became waterlogged and sank. I almost drowned trying to reach it. I did have a piece of string and a bent nail to snag a fish should one happen by.

What did I live on? Mostly water—for twenty-three days. Up in the hills, there were ripe blueberries and raspberries. I lost forty-seven pounds. I waded into the lake to get washed, but the bloodsuckers came after me and I got the hell out. I stunk like a polecat, but it was preferable to getting eaten by those little monsters.

My stay in the bush would not have been so long had I known where I was. My lake was about twenty miles north of the present location of the town of Elliot Lake. In those days there was nothing there. Search aircraft did come over. Our emergency instructions were to stay by a downed aircraft, and keep a fire going. But how the hell was I to do this without an axe? I had to break up wood by hand, and it burned fast! The search people were looking for a huge bonfire and dismissed my little fire on a beach.

The ironical part was that I could see a fire tower about ten minutes away, as the crow flies. At the bottom of the tower was a fishing camp. But, for four consecutive weekends, it rained.

I was sitting there on the twenty-third day, burning a pile of moss. It was beautifully still and my lake was calm. I heard an aircraft, and God, just like I'd dreamed, a Dak came in at 500 feet. I threw more moss on my fire and the smoke went straight up, 2,000 feet into the air. The pilot altered course around it!

Soon, I knew why he hadn't stayed. Half an hour later, the sky fell in—with hailstones the size of marbles! My fire was doused. And I had no means of relighting it. If that guy hadn't seen me, then it was time I got moving. I started walking down to the other end of the lake, and eventually found the fishing camp.

When I went down, I disappeared from human ken, presumably dead. Twenty-six days later I came back to life.

What became of my Meteor? It was pulled from the lake by an RCAF recovery team. They had no trouble locating it. Because the lake was so shallow, the tail stuck out of the water. Had I landed in any of the deeper lakes nearby, the Meteor would still be there. It was taken to Toronto and displayed at the CNE.

Canadian Aviation Museums

Atlantic Canada Aviation Museum
Halifax, Nova Scotia
http://acam.ednet.ns.ca

Billy Bishop Heritage Museum
Owen Sound, Ontario
http://www.billybishop.org

British Columbia Aviation Museum
Sidney, British Columbia
http://www.bcam.net

**Commonwealth Air Training
Plan Museum**
Brandon, Manitoba
http://www.airmuseum.ca

Calgary Aero Space Museum
Calgary, Alberta
http://www.asmac.ab.ca

Canadian Aviation Museum
Ottawa, Ontario
http://www.aviation.technomuses.ca

Canada's Aviation Hall of Fame
Wetaskiwin, Alberta
http://www.cahf.ca

Canadian Bushplane Heritage Centre
Sault Ste. Marie, Ontario
http://www.bushplane.com

Canadian Harvard Aircraft Association
Tillsonburg, Ontario
http://www.chaa.ca

**Canadian Historical Aircraft
Association**
Windsor, Ontario
http://www.ch2a.ca

Canadian Warplane Heritage Museum
Mount Hope, Ontario
http://www.warplane.com

Comox Air Force Museum
Comox, British Columbia
http://www.comoxairforcemuseum.ca

Halifax Restoration Team
Willowdale, Ontario
http://www.halibag.com

Nanton Lancaster Society Air Museum
Nanton, Alberta
http://www.lancastermuseum.ca

Reynolds-Alberta Museum
Wetaskiwin, Alberta
http://www.cd.gov.ab.ca/enjoying_
alberta/museums_historic_sites/site_
listings/reynolds_alberta_museum/
index.asp

Shearwater Aviation Museum
Shearwater, Nova Scotia
http://www.shearwateraviation
museum.ns.ca

Toronto Aerospace Museum
Toronto, Ontario
http://www.torontoaerospacemuseum
.com

Western Canada Aviation Museum
Winnipeg, Manitoba
http://www.wcam.mb.ca

Glossary

109 See Messerschmitt Bf 109

190 See Focke-Wulf Fw 190

500-pounder Largest bomb carried by Spitfire or Kittyhawk for ground attack.

AA Ack-ack or anti-aircraft.

Adjutant Administrative assistant to a Commanding Officer.

Advanced Flying Units (AFUs) Flying schools set up in the U.K. to ease transition between Service Flight Training School and Operational Training Unit.

AFC Air Force Cross.

Ailerons Control surfaces on trailing edges of wings, operated by stick to control aircraft in rolling axis.

Air Attaché Officer on diplomatic mission responsible for aviation matters.

Airborne lifeboat Specially designed craft carried beneath fuselage of Hudson or Wellington aircraft for dropping to airmen forced down at sea.

Air Commodore (A/C) Rank above Group Captain and below Air Vice Marshal.

Air Marshal (A/M) Rank above Air Vice Marshal.

Air Vice Marshal (A/V/M) Rank above Group Captain and below Air Marshal.

Aldis lamp Hand-held light with movable shutters for signalling in Morse code.

Allison American V-12 liquid-cooled aircraft engine in 1,400 hp range, comparable with British Merlin.

Altimeter Instrument giving an aircraft's altitude based on air pressure or ground-reflected radio signals.

AMO Air Ministry Order.

Amphibian An aircraft designed to operate from land or water, usually a flying boat equipped with retractable wheels.

Anoxia (or hypoxia) Oxygen inadequacy resulting in unconsciousness.

Anson Avro Anson, most widely used RCAF/RAF twin-engine training aircraft.

Armed recce Information-gathering sortie by regular fighter aircraft.

Armourer Ground-crew member responsible for "bombing up" aircraft and reloading guns.

Artificial horizon Instrument important in blind flying, indicating aircraft's attitude in relation to surface of earth.

Astro dome Glazed hemisphere set into top of an aircraft for navigator to take star shots with his sextant.

Aural null Area directly above source of radio emissions for beam-approach flying, where they cannot be heard.

Auster British Taylorcraft single-engine high-wing light aircraft used for communications and artillery observation.

Auxiliary Reserve Squadron Unit

comprised of civilian pilots who fly service aircraft on weekends.

B-1, 2, 3, etc. Designations for temporary airfields with runways of steel mesh laid behind Allied lines over graded farm land.

B-17 Boeing B-17 Flying Fortress, or "Fort," American four-engine heavy bomber of prewar design widely used by the U.S. Air Force.

B-25 North American B-25 Mitchell, American twin-engine medium bomber.

B-29 Boeing B-29 Super Fortress, or "Super Fort," not used on European operations.

Bag Collapsible canvas hood erected over student pilot, eliminating outside reference and forcing him to rely on instruments.

Balloon barrage Non-rigid tethered balloons, spaced around targets such as cities, dangling cables to entangle hostile aircraft.

Baltimore American twin-engine light bomber built to RAF specifications and used by RAF in Middle East.

Bar (to decoration) Indicates award of a decoration for a second time.

BAT (Blind Approach Training) Instruction for blind landing of aircraft, utilizing radio transmissions.

Battle Order Daily operational assignments for aircrews.

BCATP British Commonwealth Air Training Plan, a massive scheme for training airmen in Canada for all trades.

Beam Approach System Blind landing technique taught on BAT course.

Beat up To fly low and attract attention.

Beaufighter/"Beau" Bristol twin-engine RAF heavy fighter developed from Blenheim.

Beech Expeditor Beech 18 (C-45/AT-11) American twin-engine light communications and training aircraft.

Belly tank Streamlined jettisonable fuel tank hung under an aircraft.

Black Widow Northrup P-61, American heavy twin-engine night fighter.

Blenheim See Bristol Blenheim

Blockbuster Originally a 4,000-pound bomb, later a generic term for very large bomb.

Blower See Supercharger

Blue Spit Spitfire aircraft used by photo-reconnaissance squadrons, painted an all-over medium blue.

Bofors 40-mm anti-aircraft gun with multiple barrels.

Bolingbroke Version of Blenheim built by Fairchild Canada for BCATP use.

Bomb-aimer Bomber crewman with ultimate responsibility for accurate delivery of bombs; also served as a gunner, observer, or navigator.

Bomb circuit Electrical wiring for arming and release of bombs.

Bomber belt Region in north of England, near the east coast, where bomber stations were concentrated.

Bombers' Moon Full moon above clouds.

Boost Intake manifold pressure for supercharged or blown (not necessarily supercharged) aircraft engines.

Bowser Tender for refueling aircraft.

Box (formation) Compact arrangement of aircraft for mutual protection and efficient flying.

Briefing Officer Officer responsible for instructing aircrews prior to an operation.

Bristol Blenheim RAF twin-engine light bomber of prewar design also used as a night fighter.

Buffalo de Havilland DHC-5, Canadian twin turboprop-powered short-field transport.

Bunt Abrupt lowering of an aircraft's nose into a steep dive or outside loop. Can cause pilot red-out (blood rushing to head).

Button (of runway) Beginning of landing strip.

Buzz-bomb German V-1 "secret weapon" ram-jet-powered robot flying bomb.

Cables Long wire ropes hanging from barrage balloons.

Caging the gyro Locking of gyroscopically stabilized instruments such as artificial horizon and compass to prevent upsetting or tumbling during violent manoeuvres.

Canadian Permanent Force Prewar RCAF complement of full-time airmen.

Canadian Vickers Montreal-based aircraft manufacturer.

Casings Expended shells remaining after a machine gun or cannon has been fired.

Catalina Consolidated PBY-5, large American twin-engine flying boat used by RAF and RCAF for coastal patrol.

Cessna Crane American light twin-engine trainer extensively used in BCATP.

CF-100 Avro Canada CF-100 twin-jet long-range interceptor.

Check out Familiarization flight acquainting a pilot with a new aircraft.

Cheetah British Armstrong Siddeley radial aircraft engine in 300 hp range.

Circuit Racetrack pattern flown by a pilot around an airfield prior to landing.

Cirrus Moth de Havilland D.H. 60 Cirrus Moth two-place open-cockpit biplane trainer.

Clapped out Worn out from much use.

CO Commanding Officer.

Coarse pitch See Pitch

Cock Valve.

Coding (squadron) Large uppercase letters on side of an RAF or RCAF aircraft. Squadron designated by paired letters and aircraft by single letter.

Compass button Special airman's tunic button which, when detached, functions as a rudimentary compass in an emergency.

Compressibility The aerodynamic effect on an aircraft as it approaches the speed of sound.

Cone of fire Convergence of fire from guns in the wings of a fighter to meet at a set distance ahead of the aircraft.

Confirmation Eyewitness support for a victory or "kill."

Control column Stick (joystick) or yoke, principal control with which a pilot flies an aircraft. A large aircraft might have a yoke for two-handed operation.

Conversion Unit School where crews

from one type of aircraft were introduced to a new type.

Corkscrewing Evasive manoeuvre used by pilots to make their aircraft a difficult target for a following hostile machine.

Cowling Panels covering an aircraft's engine.

Cross-feed (valve) Control for regulating fuel flow from one wing tank to the other.

Curtiss Major American manufacturer of military aircraft including famed Hawk and P-40 lines.

D+4 Fourth day after D-Day.

Dakota/"Dak" Military version of Douglas DC-3.

Dash 7 de Havilland DHC-7, Canadian four-turboprop-powered feeder-liner.

Dash 8 de Havilland DHC-8, popular Canadian twin turboprop-powered feeder-liner.

DC-3 Widely used American Douglas twin-engine airliner and transport developed in the thirties and still in service.

D-Day 6 June 1944, start of Allied invasion of Europe.

Dead reckoning Navigating a plotted course using only a map, compass, timepiece, and calculator.

Deck The earth's surface.

Decompression chamber Airtight compartment where pilots could experience simulated low pressure of high altitudes.

Degrees of bank Relative steepness of turn.

de Havilland Comet D.H. 106, world's first jet airliner. Two examples operated by RCAF.

Delta American Northrop all-metal, single-engine, high-performance transport, first such machine in RCAF.

Derwent Early Rolls-Royce jet engine of up to 3,600 pounds thrust used in later Meteors.

Desynchronize (engines) Twin engines on Allied aircraft were harmonized to fire in unison. If this harmony was disrupted they would sound like German aircraft.

DF (VHF) Very high frequency radio direction-finding.

DFC Distinguished Flying Cross.

D-form Posted mission assignment.

Dinghy Inflatable life raft carried in aircraft.

Directional gyro Stabilized compass capable of indicating a course when rough air would upset the normal magnetic instrument.

Dispersal/Dispersal area Locations, usually around perimeter of field, where aircraft were irregularly parked, sometimes separated by berms, to protect them from strafing.

Ditch To force-land in water.

Dive brake Panels, usually perforated, thrust into air stream to slow a diving aircraft.

Do Slang for operation or mission.

Dornier Do 217 German twin-engine light bomber and night fighter.

Douglas A-20 Boston American twin-engine light bomber and night fighter (as Havoc).

Downwind leg Portion of landing circuit with a following wind.

Drag in To make a very slow, nose-high landing approach.

'Drome Aerodrome, airfield.

Drop tank See Belly tank

Drop zone Location selected for paratroops-landing.

DSO Distinguished Service Order.

Dumping (dive brakes) Retracting.

Echelon Formation with aircraft uniformly stepped up behind and to right or left of leader.

Ejection seat Means by which a pilot can escape from a damaged jet fighter.

Elementary Flying Training School (EFTS) In BCATP, pilots' introduction to flying primary trainers such as the Tiger Moth.

Elevator horn Balancing weight to counteract forces on elevators.

Elevators Control surfaces on trailing edge of an aircraft's horizontal tailplane, operated by stick to change pitch attitude of aircraft.

Elsan Chemical toilet used in larger aircraft.

Endurance Time an aircraft can remain airborne, synonymous with range.

Erk Ground crew member, fitter.

Evaders Airmen who have parachuted or force-landed in occupied territory and attempt to reach Allied lines, usually with the help of the Underground.

Exhaust stub Short pipe carrying still-burning gases expelled from engine.

F52 Aerial camera used in Photo-reconnaissance Spitfires.

Fairchild (FC-2, FC-2W-2, 71) Widely used series of single-engine high-wing utility transports flown by prewar RCAF.

Farnborough See RAF Farnborough

Fawn Fleet 7 prewar biplane two-place open-cockpit trainer.

Feathering Rotating propeller blades so that their width parallels air flow to minimize drag after engine failure.

Fiesler Storch Very efficient German single-engine light high-wing liaison aircraft.

Fine pitch See Pitch

Finger-four Fighter formation devised by Germans and adopted by RAF with aircraft arranged like the fingertips of a hand held flat.

Fitter Mechanic, either engine or air frame; an erk.

Flak AA, anti-aircraft fire.

Flak helmet A leather-covered, high tensile steel shell worn over flying helmet by aircrew in hostile territory.

Flak suit Sleeveless coat lined with thin, flexible sheets of high-tensile steel.

Flame-out Loss of combustion in a jet engine.

Flaming onions Pyrotechnical type of anti-aircraft shell.

Flaps Surfaces that can be lowered into the air stream to slow an aircraft during landing, or to bring the nose down. They also enable an aircraft to fly slowly by preventing stalling.

Flat attitude Level aircraft.

Fleet (Fawn, II, or Finch) Popular series of two-place biplane elementary trainers built by Fleet Aircraft of Fort Erie, Ontario.

Flight Lieutenant (F/L) Rank above Flying Officer and below Squadron Leader.

Flimsy Mission instructions for aircraft captain, or map on very thin (edible) paper.

Flip Slang for flight.

Fluid fours, sixes, or twos Flexible formation based on units of two aircraft arranged variously.

Flutter Dangerous vibration in tailplane

Flying Officer (F/O) Rank above Pilot Officer or below Flight Lieutenant.

Flying Tigers American Volunteer Group (AVG) flying with Chinese against the Japanese.

Focke-Wulf Fw 190 German single-radial-engine-powered fighter, one of most successful aircraft of Second World War.

Fortress See B-17 Flying Fortress.

Fuel cocks Taps for controlling fuel supply.

Full bore Full throttle, wide open.

Fuselage The body of an aircraft.

Fusing switch Control for arming bombs.

Fw See Focke-Wulf Fw 190

Gen Information, data.

Gen Man Slang for Navigation School graduate.

Geodetics Strong and flexible basket-weave structure devised by Barnes Wallace and used in Wellington bombers.

Get the chop Euphemism for being killed; also "buying the farm."

GH Blind bombing device utilizing ground-originating transmissions.

Gipsy Moth Widely used de Havilland D.H. 60 open cockpit, two-place biplane elementary trainer.

Glider tug Aircraft used for towing gliders.

Globe Swift Post-war American low-wing single-engine light aircraft of very clean design.

Glycol Coolant used in liquid-cooled aircraft engines.

Gneisnau Heavy German warship.

Gosport tube Flexible speaking hose through which pilot and student in a tandem-seated trainer could communicate.

GR (course) General Reconnaissance training.

Gravity-flow (fuel tank) Fuel tank located above engine in older aircraft, negating need for pump.

Green Endorsement Official recognition of outstanding work, written in green ink in pilot's log.

Griffin Rolls-Royce liquid-cooled V-12 engine in 1,800 hp range.

Ground clutter Pattern appearing on airborne radar scope when aimed downward.

Ground loop Inadvertent abrupt turn while taking off or landing.

Group Captain (G/C) Rank above Wing Commander and below Air Commodore.

Grumman Goose (G-18) American twin-engine amphibian used by RCAF and RAF for communications.

Gyro compass Compass gyroscopically stabilized.

Gyro gun sight Aiming device relying upon gyroscopic effect for stability.

Gyroscope Rotating heavy-metal wheel

within a circular frame which retains its orientation when attitude of frame changes.

Gyro stabilized Remaining level because of built-in gyroscope.

Halifax RAF four-engine heavy bomber, partner of Lancaster on Bomber Command.

Hamilcar Largest of British gliders, built by General Aircraft, and capable of carrying light tanks.

Hangar Building designed to house aircraft.

Havoc Night fighter version of Douglas A-20 (DB-7) Boston.

Heavy stuff Large shells from fixed shore batteries.

Heinkel He 177 German four-engine heavy bomber with engines coupled in two nacelles.

Hercules Bristol radial air-cooled aircraft engine in 1,700 hp range.

Horsa British Airspeed large troop-carrying glider.

Hotspur British General Aircraft light training glider capable of carrying seven passengers.

Hudson American Lockheed medium bomber and trainer adapted from civil airliner.

Hun Euphemism for "the enemy."

Hurribomber Hawker Hurricane with bomb racks for ground attack.

Hurricane Hawker Hurricane, British single-engine fighter, partner of Spitfire in early war years.

Hydraulics Means of transmitting power to operate aircraft systems through oil-filled lines by means of pistons.

Identification Friend or Foe (IFF) Electronic means of distinguishing a hostile aircraft from a friendly one.

Identifying letters (coding) Markings on side of an RAF/RCAF aircraft. Paired uppercase letters indicated squadron and single letter the aircraft.

Initial Training School (ITS) First course, intensely technical, taken by trainee aircrew after Manning Pool, where aptitudes were assessed and streaming decided upon.

Intelligence Officer Air Force personnel assigned to interpreting latest infor-mation and using it against the enemy by briefing attacking crews.

Intruders Lone fighter aircraft, usually Mosquitoes, operating singly deep into occupied territory to harass the enemy by attacking airfields, transport, and targets of opportunity generally.

Invasion stripes Wide black-and-white bands applied to the wings and rear fuselage to identify Allied aircraft after D-Day.

Irving jacket Upper half of sheepskin-lined flying suit.

Jerry Euphemism for the enemy. A corruption of "German."

Ju 88/Junkers Ju 88 Versatile German twin-engine medium bomber, also used as night fighter.

Kammhuber, Josef "General of Night Fighters," the German officer in charge of defence against RAF/RCAF night bombers.

Kapok Cottonlike material found in milk-weed pods and used in life jackets.

Kite Euphemism for aircraft.

Kittyhawk Curtiss P-40E , principal single-engine American fighter of early war years, developed from P-40A Tomahawk.

Lancaster/"Lanc" Avro Lancaster, third of RAF's heavy bombers, after Stirling and Halifax, and possibly the most efficient of Second World War four-engine bombers.

Leading edge Front of an aircraft's wing.

Lightning/Lockheed P-38 Lightning American twin-engine long-range heavy fighter of distinctive twin-boom design.

Limey "Lime-juicer," a mildly deroga-tory nickname for an Englishman dating back to days of sail in Royal Navy.

Line overlap Marginal duplication of coverage for successive aerial photographic runs.

Linkage Mechanical connection.

Loftsman Keeper of the carrier pigeons on an RCAF coastal station.

Log An airman's personal record of his flying activities.

Loggy Sluggish and unresponsive feel of aircraft controls.

Lord Haw-Haw British defector and broadcaster of Nazi propaganda from Germany.

Lorenz Electronic system to aid aircraft landing.

Low time (pilots) Inexperienced pilots.

Luftwaffe German Air Force.

Macchi MC-202 Italian fighter equiva-lent of Bf 109 with similar engine.

Mach number Speed of an aircraft relative to the speed of sound.

"Mae West" Inflatable life jacket named in honour of busty American movie star.

Magnetos Devices producing ignition spark for internal combustion engines.

Mahoud Night-intruder mission relying upon radar to locate targets such as enemy night fighters.

Mainplane Wing of an aircraft.

Manning Pool/Depot Reception centre for new recruits where they were kitted out, received immunization shots, learned to march, and introduced to Service life generally, prior to attending an Initial Training School (ITS).

Marauder Martin B-26, American twin-engine high-wing medium bomber.

Marks (of aircraft) RAF-system of iden-tifying successive aircraft variants.

Master British Miles two-place, single-engine advanced trainer comparable to Harvard.

McKee Trans-Canada Trophy Prestigious annual award to individual who has made important contribution to Canadian aviation.

Merlin Rolls-Royce liquid-cooled V-12 aircraft engine in 1,400 hp range.

Messerschmitt Bf 109 Principal German single-engine fighter at start of war until joined by Fw 190.

Messerschmitt Me 110 German twin-engine heavy fighter, unsuccessful in day role but effective as a night fighter.

Messerschmitt Me 163 German rocket-propelled aircraft designed for bomber interception.

Messerschmitt Me 262 Revolutionary German twin-engine jet fighter.

Messerschmitt Me 410 Much improved version of Me 110, a very effective night fighter.

Meteor British Gloster, twin-engine fighter using revolutionary new jet engines. RAF's first jet aircraft.

Militia Reserve of civilian soldiers who can be called up in an emergency.

Milk run Safe trip with little danger, "a piece of cake."

Mitchell North American B-25, American medium bomber extensively used by RAF and later RCAF.

Mitchell, R. J. Designer of the Spitfire.

Mod Modification.

Monoplane Aircraft with single wing (as opposed to biplane).

Mosaic Pattern created by piecing together aerial photographs.

Mosquito/"Mossie" British de Havilland D.H. 98 twin-engine light bomber/fighter bomber/night fighter/photo-reconnaissance aircraft of wooden construction.

Mushing Flying nose high, on the verge of stalling.

Mustang North American P-51, very successful single-engine American fighter built to RAF order and specifications.

Nacelle Engine housing.

Navigator Crew member responsible for setting a bomber's course and keeping track of its position.

Nav Section Department responsible for plotting missions.

Needle-and-ball Instrument indicating attitude of aircraft relative to horizon.

Negative "G" Cancelling out of gravity, usually by means of centrifugal force.

Nissen hut Building of semicircular section, constructed of corrugated metal. Similar to American Quonset construction.

Noball V-1 (buzz-bomb) launching site.

Norden Standard bomb sight used by Allies at start of war.

Norseman Canadian-designed and -built Noorduyn single-engine high-wing utility transport used by RCAF and USAAF.

Nose trim Nose up or down attitude of aircraft, controlled by small tabs on trailing edge of elevators.

Number Two/Three/Four Identification of members of a section and a flight.

Oblique (aerial photography) Aircraft cameras mounted facing sideways and angled downward.

Observer Earlier name for Navigator, prior to elimination of gunnery and bomb-aiming responsibilities.

Old Man Familiar euphemism for Commanding Officer.

Oleos Shock absorbers utilizing oil compression.

Operation, Op A mission or sortie.

Operational (aircraft) Machines capable of being flown in action.

Operational (aircrew) In action against the enemy.

Operational Training Unit (OTU) School where aircrew were introduced to combat flying practices.

Operations trailer Mobile location for briefing and debriefing aircrews.

Overshoot Land too far along a runway, leaving insufficient room to stop.

Oxford/"Ox Box" British Airspeed twin-engine trainer extensively used in BCATP and for communications.

P-47 See Thunderbolt

Panzer German armoured vehicle, usually a tank.

PBY-5 American Consolidated Catalina (PBY-5)/Canso (PBY-5A), long-range flying boat/amphibian used for maritime patrol.

Pegasus British Bristol air-cooled radial engine in 1,000-plus hp range.

Permanent Force Full-time Air Force personnel in peacetime.

Perspex Plexiglass.

Pesco pump Means of transferring fuel from tank to tank in Mosquito, powered by port engine.

Photo-recce/Photo-reconnaissance Obtaining pictorial documentation with camera-equipped aircraft.

Pitch (fine or coarse) Angle at which aircraft propeller "bites" into air.

Pitot static head Tubular device fitted to leading edge of wing providing either air pressure or vacuum to operate cockpit instruments.

Plus one (+ 1psi)/Plus six boost See Boost

Port Left.

Prang A crash or to crash.

Pratt & Whitney Canada PT6 Widely used Canadian-designed and -built turboprop aircraft engine.

Precautionary let down Cautious landing approach in bad weather.

Production (aircraft) Aeroplanes approved for building in quantity.

Provisional Pilot Officer (PPO) Temporary rank awarded prewar RCAF flight cadets during training.

Pump-handling Violent movement of an aircraft's control column.

Pumping (wheels down or up) Emergency lowering of under-carriage.

Push over Lowering the nose of an aircraft into diving attitude.

Queen's Flight Aircraft assigned to transport of Royal Family.

RAF Farnborough Experimental Testing Establishment where new aircraft were evaluated by Service pilots.

Rambler Canadian-designed and -built Curtiss-Reed two-place open-cock-pit biplane trainer of prewar years.

Ramjet Small jet engine with no moving parts. Fuel burns in air compressed by the forward movement of air-craft. Power for V-1 buzz-bombs.

RCAF Personnel Reception Centre Facility at Bournemouth, England, where newly arrived BCATP gradu-ates were billeted until they could be placed with an OTU or sent on a course.

Recce Reconnaissance sortie.

Reservist Member of nonpermanent auxiliary force.

Revetment Open enclosure with sandbag walls to protect aircraft on ground from strafing or bomb blasts.

Rigger Ground-crew member responsible for either engine or airframe maintenance.

Ropey Much used, well worn

(equipment) or badly executed (manoeuvre).

Roundels Circular markings used on Commonwealth aircraft.

Route Planning Operations Room Where routes for missions ("trips") were decided.

R/T Radio telegraph.

Rube Goldberg (device) An improvisation suggestive of the whimsical drawings of a popular American cartoonist.

Rudder A control surface, the movable after-portion of the vertical tail.

Rudder trim See Trim

Run up Warming of engine for peak efficiency prior to takeoff.

Scharnhorst German heavy warship.

Schneider Trophy Prestigious award for winner of international seaplane race held annually until won outright by Britain in 1931.

Scramble Rapid response (takeoff) by fighter pilots.

Seafire Navalized development of Spitfire for carrier operation.

Section Two aircraft, half of a flight of four fighters, or four aircraft with medium bombers.

Self-sealing fuel tanks Fuel storage lined with compound that flows into and plugs bullet or shrapnel holes.

Sergeant Pilot Non-commissioned (NCO) rank below Pilot Officer.

Service Flying Training School (SFTS) Phase of BCATP where pilots obtained their wings and were introduced to aircraft (Harvards and Ansons) approaching perform-

ance of operational types.

Sideslip/Slipping Means of losing altitude rapidly on landing approach, in an aircraft without flaps.

Smith & Wesson America-made (revolver) sidearm.

Smoke pot Device for marking a runway.

Sortie Trip or mission.

Spam Brand of canned meat.

Spitfire Outstanding Supermarine single-engine RAF fighter powered with V-12 liquid-cooled Merlin or Griffin engine.

Sprog Green or tyro airman.

Squadron Leader (S/L) Rank above Flight Lieutenant and below Wing Commander.

Squadron scramble Offensive action with all of a unit's aircraft taking to the air.

Stall sequence Nose high, slow flight preceding stall.

Standard Beam Approach System (SBA) Means of guiding an aircraft flying blind to base via radio transmissions.

Starboard Right.

Star-wheel Circular aircraft control with protruding points around the rim.

Steel mesh/matting Means of quickly providing firm surface on emergency landing strip carved from farmland.

Stick Joystick or control column, principal means by which the pilot operates the control surfaces of an aircraft.

Stick (of bombs) Bomb load.

Stirling Short Stirling, first of the RAF's

four-engine heavy bombers to enter squadron service.

Strafe/Strafing Attacking ground targets with an aircraft using cannon or machine-gun fire.

Stranny/Stranraer British large Supermarine twin-engine biplane flying boat of prewar design used by RAF and RCAF. Also built in Canada by Canadian Vickers.

Stratus Low-lying flat grey cloud formation.

Streaming (air crew) Dividing of RCAF recruits into the various "trades," supposedly by aptitude.

Submarine pens Massively built covered berths for U-boats.

Supercharger Device for supplying additional air to aircraft engine at higher altitudes.

Supermarine S6B Single-engine racing twin-float aircraft in which a speed record for seaplanes of 406 mph was set in 1931.

Supernumary (officer) An officer not part of a unit's complement.

Sweep Low-level offensive action with aircraft flying abreast.

Sweet Caps Popular North American brand of cigarettes.

Tactical Air Force Squadrons assigned to attacking targets for short-term tactical purposes as opposed to strategic targets.

Tail slide A dangerous manoeuvre in which an aircraft climbing vertically comes to a stop and then slips directly backwards.

Target Illumination (TI) The lighting of the target for a night raid by means of flare concentrations.

Taxiing Moving an aircraft on the ground under its own power.

Tempest British Hawker single-engine fighter, improved development of Typhoon.

The Rock Gibraltar.

Thunderbolt Republic P-47, heavy American single-seat, radial-engine fighter flown by USAAF.

Tiger Moth British de Havilland D.H. 89, RAF/RCAF two-place enclosed-cockpit biplane elementary trainer also built in Canada.

Tomahawk American Curtiss single-seat single-engine fighter, lower-powered predecessor of Kittyhawk.

Torque Twisting moment created by turning propeller, exaggerated in more-powerful aircraft.

Tour Specific number of operational missions flown by a fighter pilot or bomber crew before stepping down for leave and a new posting.

TR-9 Aircraft radio with limited range.

Tracers Slugs containing phosphorous that burns to illuminate trajectory.

Transponder Radio or radar transceiver that automatically sends a signal when it receives a predetermined signal.

Tricycle (undercarriage) Third wheel at nose of aircraft rather than tail, resulting in level attitude on ground and improved visibility.

Trimmed hands-off Trim tabs adjusted so that aircraft will fly straight and level with no pilot input.

Trim/Trim setting Small movable tab on trailing edge of rudder, elevators, and ailerons to control aircraft's attitude in horizontal, vertical, or rolling planes.

Trip Part of a tour, mission, sortie.

True airspeed Speed of an aircraft with air movement factored in.

Turbo-Beaver Canadian de Havilland DHC-2 Mk III, turboprop conversion of Beaver.

Twin Otter Canadian de Havilland DHC-6, twin turboprop-powered commuter liner.

Twitch factor Scare potential.

Typhoon British Hawker heavy single-engine fighter with H-24 liquid-cooled engine, successor to Hurricane.

Up-float Tendency of ailerons to be forced up in high speed dive.

USAAF United States Army Air Force, successor to U.S. Army Air Corps.

V-1 See Buzz-bomb

Vampire British single-engine jet fighter with distinctive twin tail booms. Second RAF jet to enter service. Also flown by RCAF.

Vapour lock Obstruction in fuel flow caused by trapping of vapour bubble formed by fuel evaporation.

VC Victoria Cross, Britain's highest award for bravery.

V cigarettes Cheap wartime brand of cigarettes.

Vedette Small Canadian Vickers single-engine flying boat operated by prewar RCAF.

Ventura Lockheed twin-engine patrol bomber developed from civil airliner, used by RAF and RCAF.

Very light Pistol-fired flare.

VHF Very high frequency radio.

Vic V formation, usually of three aircraft.

V^{ne} Velocity not to be exceeded.

WAAF Womens' Auxiliary Air Force.

Wall, the The sound barrier (speed of sound).

Wapiti Westland two-seat, single-engine biplane light bomber used by prewar RCAF.

Wash, the Body of water off the northeast coast of England.

Weavers Aircraft in an old-style line-astern formation specifically assigned to watch for attackers.

Wehrmacht German Army.

Welland Early Rolls-Royce jet engine in 1,700-pound thrust range.

Wellington/"Wimpy" Widely used British twin-engine Vickers medium (originally heavy) bomber with geodetic construction conceived by Barnes Wallace.

Whitley British Armstrong Whitworth twin-engine heavy bomber, contemporary with but not as successful as the Wellington, used mainly on OTUs.

Winco See Wing Commander

Windmilling Freewheeling of propeller in air stream after engine has been shut down. Feathering prevents windmilling.

Windsock Cloth tube held open by circular frame, free to rotate, indicating wind direction.

Wind vector Direction and strength of moving air.

Wing (unit) A unit of several squadrons.

Wing Commander (W/C) Rank above

Squadron Leader and below Group Captain, usually in charge of a squadron.

Wing de-icing Means of removing ice from leading edge of wing using heat, vibration, or fluid.

Wingman Number Two pilot/aircraft in a section of two.

Wing roots Part of an aircraft's mainplane where it meets the fuselage.

Wing spar The principal member extending the span of a wing, providing its strength.

Wing tank Fuel cell located in wing of aircraft.

Wings parade Presentation of pilot's wings to successful SFTS graduates in formal ceremony.

Wire cutters Device attached to leading edge of wing of larger aircraft designed to sever cables hanging from barrage balloons.

Wireless Air Gunner (WAG) Bomber crewman combining duties of gunner and radio operator.

Wobble-pumping Using small one-handed pump operated with back-and-forth motion.

Works-and-bricks people Crews of civilians repairing or improving runways.

Wright Cyclone American radial aircraft engine in 1,200 to 1,700 hp range.

Yale North American NA-64, two-place advance trainer, lower-powered predecessor of Harvard with fixed undercarriage.

Zoom Steep climb utilizing momentum built up in a dive.

Index

OTHER FIFTH HOUSE BOOKS ABOUT TRANSPORTATION PIONEERS AND ADVENTURES

FLYING UNDER FIRE:
CANADIAN FLIERS RECALL
THE SECOND WORLD WAR,
selected and edited by William
J. Wheeler, 256 pages, $21.95
paperback, ISBN: 1-894004-79-5

FROM SUMMIT TO SEA: AN
ILLUSTRATED HISTORY OF
RAILROADS IN BRITISH
COLUMBIA AND ALBERTA,
George H. Buck, 208 pages, $24.95
paperback, ISBN: 1-894004-93-2

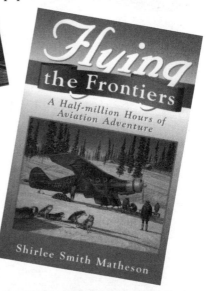

FLYING THE FRONTIERS:
A HALF-MILLION HOURS OF
AVIATION ADVENTURE,
Shirlee Smith Matheson,
226 pages, $16.95 paperback,
ISBN: 1-895618-51-7

PILOTS OF THE PURPLE
TWILIGHT: THE STORY OF
CANADA'S EARLY BUSH
FLYERS, Philip H. Godsell,
240 pages, $22.95 paperback,
ISBN: 1-894004-98-1

TALES OF THE CPR,
David Laurence Jones,
208 pages, $27.95 paperback,
ISBN: 1-894856-05-8;
$39.95 hardcover gift edition,
ISBN: 1-894856-10-4

SKIPPERS OF THE SKY:
THE EARLY YEARS OF BUSH
FLYING, selected and edited
by William J. Wheeler,
$29.95 hardcover,
ISBN: 1-894004-45-0

Prices subject to change